# Chinese Economists on Economic Reform – Collected Works of Li Jiange

This book is part of a series which makes available to English-speaking audiences the work of the individual Chinese economists who were the architects of China's economic reform. The series provides an inside view of China's economic reform, revealing the thinking of the reformers themselves, unlike many other books on China's economic reform which are written by outside observers.

**Li Jiange** (1949–) is one of the most notable and powerful economists holding office in China at present. He is currently the Vice-Chairman of the Central Huijin Investment Company, one of the most influential financial institutions in China. He is also a member of the National Committee of the Chinese People's Political Consultative Conference, and a Professor at the Chinese Academy of Social Sciences and other academic institutions. He has held many important positions in the state Research Office and the Department of Policies, Laws, and Regulations, and has been Director of the China Securities Regulatory Commission. His work has included major contributions to debates about maintaining financial stability, about achieving equitable income distribution, and about China's overall economic development.

The book is published in association with **China Development Research Foundation**, one of the leading economic and social think tanks in China, where many of the theoretical foundations and policy details of economic reform were formulated.

# Routledge Studies on the Chinese Economy

## Series Editor
Peter Nolan
*Director, Centre of Development Studies;*
*Chong Hua Professor in Chinese Development; and*
*Director of the Chinese Executive Leadership Programme (CELP),*
*University of Cambridge*

## Founding Series Editors
Peter Nolan, *University of Cambridge* and
Dong Fureng, *Beijing University*

The aim of this series is to publish original, high-quality, research-level work by both new and established scholars in the West and the East, on all aspects of the Chinese economy, including studies of business and economic history.

# Routledge Studies on the Chinese Economy – Chinese Economists on Economic Reform

Li Jiange

# Chinese Economists on Economic Reform – Collected Works of Li Jiange

**Li Jiange**

**Edited by China Development Research Foundation**

LONDON AND NEW YORK

中国发展研究基金会
China Development Research Foundation

First edition of *A Collection of Li Jiange's Works on Economic Reform*, written by Li Jiange, ISBN: 978-7-80234-208-8 published 2008 by China Development Press.

This edition published 2017
by Routledge
2 Park Square, Milton Park, Abingdon, Oxon OX14 4RN

and by Routledge
711 Third Avenue, New York, NY 10017

First issued in paperback 2017

*Routledge is an imprint of the Taylor & Francis Group, an informa business*

*British Library Cataloguing in Publication Data*
A catalogue record for this book is available from the British Library

*Library of Congress Cataloging in Publication Data*
Names: Li, Jiange, author.
Title: Chinese economists on economic reform. Collected works of
    Li Jiange / Li Jiange; edited by China Development Research
    Foundation.
Description: Abingdon, Oxon; New York, NY: Routledge, 2017. |
    Series: Routledge studies on the Chinese economy; 10 | Includes
    bibliographical references and index.
Identifiers: LCCN 2016011586| ISBN 9781138671263 (hardback) |
    ISBN 9781315617114 (ebook)
Subjects: LCSH: Economic development–China. | China–Economic
    conditions–2000- | China–Economic policy–2000-
Classification: LCC HC427.95 .L5348 2017 | DDC 330.951–dc23
    LC record available at https://lccn.loc.gov/2016011586

ISBN 13: 978-1-138-48196-1 (pbk)
ISBN 13: 978-1-138-67126-3 (hbk)

Typeset in Times New Roman
by Sunrise Setting Ltd, Brixham, UK

# Contents

# Brief biography of Li Jiange

Li Jiange is a native of Nantong, Jiangsu Province. He holds a Bachelor of Science from the School of Mathematics, Nanjing Normal University, and a Master of Economics from the Graduate School of the Chinese Academy of Social Science.

Mr. Li is currently the Vice-Chairman of the Board of the Central Huijin Investment Company, Ltd. (Central Huijin). He held the position of Chairman of Shenyin & Wanguo Securities in 2013 after leaving China International Capital Corporation, Ltd. (CICC) as the Chairman of the Board. Prior to joining CICC, Mr. Li held the following positions: in the State Planning Commission, he was Deputy Director of the Research Office and Deputy Director of the Department of Policies, Laws, and Regulations; in the State Economic and Trade Commission, he was Deputy Director and then Director of the Department of Policies, Laws, and Regulations Department; in the Securities Commission of the State Council, he was Director of the Office; in the China Securities Regulatory Commission, he was Vice Chairman and Executive Vice Chairman; in the State Council, he was Deputy Director of the Economic Reform Office, and Deputy Director of the Development Research Center.

Mr. Li also currently serves as a member of the 11th National Committee of the Chinese People's Political Consultative Conference (CPPCC). He is a professor and PhD supervisor at the Graduate School of the Chinese Academy of Social Sciences, the Graduate School of the People's Bank of China, and the School of Finance at Renmin University of China. He is also a professor at the Institute of Taiwan Studies at Tsinghua University. He has been awarded the Sun Yefang Economics Award three times, in 1991, 1997, and 2001. Since 2002, he has served on the Awards Committee for the Sun Yefang Economic Sciences Foundation.

# Foreword

This series of books is authored by economists who were witnesses to and direct participants in China's "reform and opening up" over the past three decades. Nearly three generations of Chinese economists are represented, for they include both older and younger economists. Articles that were selected display the characteristics of the period in which they were written. Most exerted a direct impact on China's economic-reform policies, whether they were policy recommendations, theoretical works, or research reports. Most of these works are being published for the first time.

The China Development Research Foundation organized and published this series in Chinese in 2008, to commemorate the 30th anniversary of the start of China's "reform and opening up" and to further promote this historic social transformation. Authors and their descendants responded enthusiastically to the proposal. All the articles were edited and finalized by the authors themselves, except for those of the late Xue Muqiao and Ma Hong, which were edited and finalized by members of their families.

This series has been broadly welcomed in China. I am confident that this English edition will be helpful in giving foreign readers a better understanding of China's economic-reform policies.

I gratefully acknowledge the contribution of the World Bank, Ford Foundation, and Cairncross Foundation, who supported the translation and publication of this series in English. I would like to thank Justin Yifu Lin, Pieter Bottelier, Peter Geithner, David Dollar, and other experts for their valuable support and candid comments. My gratitude also goes to Martha Avery for her excellent translating and editing.

Wang Mengkui
*Chairman*
*China Development Research Foundation*

# Preface by the author

It has been a full 30 years since this great ship of China, carrying the largest population of any country on Earth, began to navigate its way through the difficulties of "reform and opening up." Looking back, nobody can fail to be astonished at the economic progress China has made, and at the improvement in people's lives. This holds for observers both inside and outside China, but it has particular significance for those of us who experienced the "three years of hardship" and the Cultural Revolution. Reform and opening up has turned around and transfigured our world.

People who are now entering middle age may therefore be inclined to regard changes in China's political, social, and cultural arenas over the past 30 years as even more important than changes in the country's economy, despite all the achievements. The "liberation" of our very way of thinking has enabled tremendous improvement in productive forces over these years. Beyond that, however, it has also profoundly changed the rational as well as emotional mentality of Chinese people. This awareness has been foremost in my mind as I assembled various articles for this compendium. I have recognized the evolution in thinking in my own writings. It has been apparent in the scope of ideas that I discussed, the logic with which I presented arguments, and in my very style and presentation.

In an article commemorating Xue Muqiao, I gave tribute to this towering figure who had just celebrated his 100th birthday. I applauded his outstanding contributions in the field of economics. Economists gathered together in Beijing to commemorate him as well, which garnered extensive media coverage. Younger people were soon asking questions about him, however, which cropped up on the Internet. Who was this person? What kinds of contributions had he made? It made me realize that those who did not experience the times that Xue Muqiao went through could not adequately appreciate the nature of his contributions. They could not understand the influence that his contributions had on our lives, the way they changed our very social fabric.

Change in China over these years has been too fast, our economic progress has been too fast, for younger people to grasp what came before. Those who were brought up in a market economy simply cannot comprehend what was behind the writings of Xue Muqiao. They cannot understand how hard it was to criticize a planned economy and to espouse a market economy using a vocabulary that was still steeped in an earlier age. They cannot understand how hard it was to argue for change while still operating within a "traditional" conceptual structure. They cannot comprehend the painstaking effort that was required, nor the mental courage and the extent of political risk.

Today, we read about things like "the market," or "property rights," and think nothing about it. It can be said, however, that if such concepts were put into an article 50 years ago, the author would be declared a "capitalist and a rightist element" and a "right-leaning opportunist" whose political life would summarily be over. If the article were written 40 years ago, the author would be declared a "reactionary" who was arguing for revisionist ideas and who aimed for the resurrection of capitalism. He could be punished for the crime of speaking out. If the article were written 30 years ago, the author would be severely attacked for being a counter-revolutionary capitalist roader. If it were written even just 20 years ago, the author would be subjected to "political criticism" due to "spiritual pollution" and for espousing "bourgeois liberalization in the economic sphere."

Given this, it is not hard to understand why Chinese economists have used oblique and circuitous writing styles over this period in which "reform" came to be better understood. Indeed, it was impossible for them not to do so. It was impossible not to make reference to the "classics" (Marxist classics), nor to hide arguments for reform in the midst of long-winded covering statements, nor to employ ideas that appeared to be what they were not, as well as being illogical and unscientific. Naturally, this all had to do with the education and training that Chinese economists received in those years. At the same time, however, such writing styles were also a kind of strategy. They were an attempt to ensure the success of the great endeavor of reform, while also being an attempt at self-preservation. They were the product of many years of experiencing the trauma and damage inflicted by political movements.

My general feeling, therefore, is that economic articles over these past 30 years do not amount to a great deal in terms of purely technical or "scholarly" aspects. Most of them look at the process of Chinese economic development and reform from a limited perspective, and have just a modicum of reference value for economic history. In technical terms, they simply present or reiterate the fundamentals of economics and stem from the already existing beliefs and intuitive knowledge of the author.

Naturally, just because articles over the past 30 years deal with basic economics does not mean that people could accept their ideas at the outset of China's reform. Humanity took a very tortured and circuitous path in the twentieth century. Chinese people were able to cast off the mental shackles that had bound them in the past as they attempted to survive utter disaster and revive the country, but at the same time they encased themselves in new constraints. Only after the country embarked on the track of reform and opening up were people able to view "reality" in any kind of rational way. Only then were they able to start addressing the practical questions the country faces with new eyes.

People tend to believe that an immutable truth resides in traditional systems. They place their hopes on a kind of "single key that unlocks all doors." With disregard for the ever-changing realities of actual experience, they cling to what no longer serves the present. Over time, this creates a rigid mentality. I often think of Chinese medicine in this regard. It has served our people over many generations and there is little doubt that it works in many situations. Acupuncture and herbal remedies can have marvelous results and have a certain standing in the scientific community within China. Why is it, therefore, that this recognition does not extend to scientists outside of China? Why is Chinese medicine not universally recognized and respected among the intellectual community? One important reason is that the education and traditions underlying Chinese medicine rely on classics that date back as many as 1,000 years. One cannot deny that those classics have some distilled wisdom. Given the current knowledge of mankind, however, it is quite apparent that they also contain a large number of fallacies. People might pose the same question of economics and social studies. If there is indeed any "science" in these, how can all of "truth" be said to reside in ideas that were posed 100 years ago? How can we rely exclusively on the classics to resolve all of today's practical issues?

By now, it is rare to find anyone who thinks that economic affairs should be conducted strictly according to traditional (Marxist) theories. Nevertheless, the influence of this approach still exists among certain circles. Indeed, I am baffled by many strange things that have appeared in China in recent years. Certain economists, particularly among those who supported reform in the early years, now say that reform and opening up is devoid of any merit. They cite phrases from the classics in support of this, and various "standards" set forth in the old textbooks. They ignore the economic development of the country and the apparent fact of improved living standards. Most of these people had no vested interest in the political movements of the past, or in the planned economy. Indeed, they often were those who were the targets of criticism in "movements," and who experienced hunger during the period of "hardship," so it is unfathomable why they should paint the past as a kind of pastoral paradise. Before, people had little to wear and nothing to eat, while voices were kept silent—all had to speak as one. Today, people's energies are released and they have ample food and clothing, yet certain economists seem to find the situation unacceptable.

The first thing they find fault with is income distribution policies. It should be recognized that traditional theory is innately incompatible with the fundamental principles of market economics. At the same time, many feel in their hearts that traditional theory has a higher moral standing. China has an old saying about how people prefer to have less all around than to endure a situation where one has more than others. This egalitarian approach is deeply rooted in the very soil of China's more backward areas, with their tradition of small-scale agricultural production. Government officials, sociologists, and economists alike are fully aware that income distribution is a highly sensitive topic that can arouse people's emotions. Whoever takes up income distribution as a rallying cry is able, quite naturally, to occupy the high ground in terms of a moral advantage. When the subject is stirred up, the resulting controversy turns into a competition for scholars and government officials alike. This intensifies social problems and puts any attempt at solutions in a defensive position.

To measure whether or not reform is successful, we must first determine whether or not there has been an absolute improvement in the standard of living for the majority of members of our society, including low-income people. If there is such improvement, then such reform is successful and the income distribution policies of such reform are sound in overall terms. In the initial period of reform, Deng Xiaoping took aim at the traditional system by which everyone enjoyed "universal poverty" when he espoused the idea of "letting some people get rich first." This sparked an enormous response. It opened up the wellsprings of social wealth and enabled China to become the fastest developing nation on earth. It also provided the necessary material foundation for resolving income distribution issues and for taking care of vulnerable groups within the population.

The fundamental purpose of reform is to release productive forces. From time immemorial, "development" has been what really counts. The ancients had sayings that can be paraphrased as "Wealth is the nation's lifeline and basis of all its affairs, determining all success or failure," and "Every member of society has a role to play in creating wealth, and wealth collected from across the entire society is intended to be used for all." Developing the economy and creating wealth are the lifeline of the nation and the root of all things. Even though egalitarianism is deeply rooted in Chinese culture, people believe even more strongly in the plain truth that "hard work is the basis of a better life, and, so long as they work hard, people will have enough."

Chinese economists should now focus on practical economic research that looks at the kind of economic structure and the kind of development strategy that will enable our national economy to move ahead. They should look at what kinds of income distribution policies will increase the size of the economic pie.

Common sense in economics tells us that a distribution system will always depend on the underlying economic structure. A distribution system cannot exist on its own, independent of the fundamental system. Our system of distribution will necessarily depend on whether we have a planned-economy system, or a market-economy system, that is, whether we have one that concentrates on "the bigger the better and the more public the better" or on having a variety of economic sectors (public and private) that coexist together. China's current system of distribution is determined by the basic attributes of a socialist market economy.

Reforms that were initiated 30 years ago were oriented in the direction of the market from the start. In the early period, most Chinese economists felt that resource allocation or "distribution" was determined by the interactions of three interrelated components. These were the structure of decisions (D), of information (I), and of motivations (M). Economists designed market-oriented reform using DIM analytical methodology. All economists generally believed that the key issues related to setting up a pricing system and a system of property rights. Opinions diverged, however, when it came to the question of whether to reform the pricing system first, or that of the system of property rights. They debated endlessly about the choice of the proper "breakthrough" for reform, and set forth two different reform agendas that were actually very similar in the essentials although they differed in details. These formed two different "paths" to reform that, in the end, led to the same goal.

Looking back on the process now, these two approaches were like the two sides of a coin. It is impossible for a coin to have only one side. With similar logic, we could only achieve the initial formation of a market economy if we achieved decisive progress in both of these aspects of reform. Over the past 30 years, our breakthroughs in reforming the pricing system and the property rights system have come in alternating stages. As a result, we have set up the beginnings of a market-economy system with obviously improved efficiency. It is by now impossible for anyone to disregard the role that China plays in the fiercely competitive global economy.

At the same time, we observe with some concern that reform is not always plain sailing. In the actual conduct of economic activity, we recognize the appearance of backward movement, of the stopping of reform. We see ideological relapses, reconsiderations. As a result, we are still far from enabling the market to play its fundamental role in allocating resources. Right now, government departments are ever more inclined to carry out direct interference in the economy. As a result, market prices are increasingly inflexible and particularly those of factors (product inputs). Monopoly enterprises are stifling the vitality of the private sector. The abuse of power is leading to ever greater corruption. As reform begins to impinge upon interests that were previously untouched, or were only moderately affected, government officials are very clearly less inclined to support it.

Since "marketization" reform has been proceeding for 30 years now, the public at large has become accustomed to the idea that there will indeed be income differentials in the course of market competition. Differences in innate ability and degree of effort must necessarily create differences in results, and the public has accepted this to a large extent. What the public has not accepted is differences in income that are traced to corruption and to monopoly privilege. Generally speaking, these two things are not the result of income distribution policies. Corruption grows out of the abuse of power and is enabled by a lack of constraints. It can only be rooted out through strict adherence to laws and through tough crackdowns. Meanwhile, monopolies kill competition and allow excessive income. They can only be changed through setting up effective corporate governance systems, and sound pricing and taxation systems. In a fundamental sense, problems relating to these two things can only be resolved through reform—and they will be resolved through reform. Right now, some people equate income differentials with "unfair distribution." They say that the public is unhappy with reform, since they misinterpret the public's opposition to corruption. Not only is this not helpful in resolving distribution problems, but it manipulates the overall mood of the people. It can have the effect of creating a sudden deterioration in social attitudes.

At different stages in the process, reform has a material impact on different levels of interests. Because of this, it is impossible for the process not to arouse resentment and opposition from certain members of society. In the end, however, reform represents the overall interests of society. For 30 years now, the public in general has therefore supported it. Not only have they expressed approval, but they continue to have high hopes for the success of reform moving into the future.

The people of China waited a very long time for this tremendous social change and they paid a high price as they waited. Reform has not only rewritten Chinese history, but it has rewritten the destiny of an entire people. Chinese economists, meanwhile, are worthy of this era. They have contributed what was necessary over this period as they mobilized everyone's efforts, carved out the proper path, formulated the proper policies, and sought to put them into effect.

I personally feel that we have been very fortunate to be born at this time and participate in this process. As we commemorate the 30th anniversary of reform and opening up, we should sum up what has happened but also look towards our plans for the future. We should define the direction of reform with greater clarity. We should be more specific about the pathway and its policies, and more incisive in how we analyze the costs that reform will and must entail. We should describe the future in realistic terms, including how reform will affect economic development and people's lives. We must aim for broadly based solid support for reform from our entire society, including consensus on what reform involves and enthusiasm for what it can achieve. If our celebration of the 30th anniversary of reform achieves these goals, then we can say it has been meaningful and constructive.

Quite a few publishing houses, newspapers, and journals are compiling commemorative editions to celebrate this anniversary. I have received a number of requests to participate in these. I have not written much in the way of articles, however. Of what I have written, even fewer are worthy of putting in a compendium. I am therefore only accepting the invitation of the China Development Press, which is affiliated with the Development Research Center of the State Council, where I work. I take this opportunity to convey my sincere apologies to other publishing houses and magazines for being unable to submit articles to them, or to respond to their requests.

Li Jiange
June 2008

# 1 A debate on the relationship between planning and the market[1]

## (1991)

The relationship between planning and the market is an issue that has long been debated in the field of economics. It has been controversial since the very birth of socialist economics. The ebb and flow of the issues can be charted in China's theoretical circles even prior to the start of reform in 1978. The discussions back then developed from an exploration of the ideas of commodity production and the law of value under a socialist system. We can discern four main periods of debate on the issue.

The first occurred in the year 1953 and revolved primarily around the views put forth in a book by Stalin called, *Issues on the Socialist Economy of the Soviet Union*. The debate in China attempted to integrate those views with the realities of China, and to evaluate the role of the law of value in a socialist economy. The second was in 1956 and 1957, when the debate focused on the relationship between the law of value and a planned economy. The third was in 1958 and 1959, when the focus was on the role of the law of value given the formation of people's communes in the countryside. The fourth was between 1961 and 1964, when the focus was on the relationship between the law of value and the management of a socialist economy (including the basis for price formation).

These debates were not merely academic and of little consequence. They were brought on by and carried out in the context of major economic events. They also were not a matter of polite quibbling among scholars. Some of our most courageous elders, such as Sun Yefang, paid a heavy price for their steadfast adherence to the truth. At the time, economists may not have been able to use plain-spoken language to describe their correct views, but they nevertheless were tenacious in pursuing and exposing the truth. In doing so, they were able to create an example for the generations of economists who have followed, and it is an example that cannot be erased.

After the Third Plenary Session of the 11th Central Committee of the Communist Party of China, an approach that called for "seeking truth from the facts" received official policy support, which broke through mental bonds that had held back people's thoughts and energies. In the sphere of economics, a great debate began about the theories that would support reform of the overall economic system. The key subject of this debate was presented as the relationship between planning and the market.

This debate was to rise to a high pitch several times over the next ten years. At the outset, around 1978, the topics centered on whether or not commodity production and commodity exchange could or should be carried out under a socialist system. Around 1982, the topics focused on which was to be "primary" and which "secondary," or "supplemental," as the relationship between planning and the market evolved. The third high point of debate came in 1984, when the subject was defined as "whether or not a socialist economy is a commodity economy with a plan." The fourth high point came in 1987, when the subject was whether or not "a commodity economy with a plan" could in general be described as one in which "the government regulates the market while the market guides enterprises."

It is not hard to see the tracks of how the debate proceeded among economists over this past decade or so. One can read the progress in the topics discussed. Colleagues from other socialist countries felt that China's theoretical explorations in this period were pioneering in terms of the reform of socialist economic systems. The real accomplishments of China's economic-system reform during this period have been apparent to all. Naturally, there has been an enormous and unanticipated gap between understanding theoretical models and putting them into practical reform proposals. After achieving consensus on theoretical models, we frequently found there were different views on how to implement reform. On the heels of each initial debate on theory, therefore, came the debate among economists about implementation. The most disputed aspects related mainly to the question of whether reform should start with price reform or with enterprise reform. The two sides of this question became defined as those espousing "price reform first," and those espousing "enterprise reform first." Debate on this issue began in 1986, after which it proceeded through several periods of moderate intensity.

More recently, the debate within China's economic circles on "how to integrate a planned economy with regulation by the market" can be seen as a continuation of the four main periods of debate as described above. It marks a fifth chapter. Many, however, feel that this time the debate is going around in circles, without making the kind of progress that the four previous periods of debate were able to make. Many of the articles this time seem to repeat what was said over and over again in recent years. Naturally, correct points of view often do need to be reiterated and expounded upon. The problem is that many concepts and ways of stating things are now being set forth as indisputable and proper, while in fact they deserve reexamination and new understanding. I feel that the term "industrial policy" is one of these. This term began to be used extensively in China in 1987, together with an associated concept that was regarded by some as self evident: "[the prices of] upstream products should be controlled by planning, while the prices of downstream products can be released." This assumption has become one way to try to integrate planning with the market. I feel that in fact it deserves close examination and further research.

In early 1986, under the guiding spirit of the *Recommendations of the Central Committee of the Communist Party of China on the 7th Five-Year Plan*, relevant government departments in China gathered their forces to come up with a reform proposal. Centered on price reform, this included sets of complementing reforms in taxation and public finance. At this point, however, some comrades put forth the idea that reform should start with enterprise reform as opposed to price reform. Price reform should be postponed until new enterprise mechanisms were ready and able to handle it.

Given this opinion, which was in opposition to price reform, and given the over-heated economy at the time, the situation was not conducive to price reform. The complementing sets of reforms were therefore also put on the shelf. At the end of 1986, a kind of enterprise reform was gradually instituted nationwide that focused primarily on what was called the "*cheng-bao*" or contract system for enterprises.

People very quickly discovered, however, that mobilizing this kind of partial reform could not resolve problems of inefficient allocation of resources. Merely stimulating greater production among enterprises, and encouraging their profit seeking, created greater problems so long as it did not also allow for the formation of a real market. Relationships among industries in modern China are quite complex. While reform proceeded to "marketize" and "monetize" some parts of the economy, other parts retained very considerable administrative interference. They retained "administrative special privilege," and a system of "administrative control." A "two-track system" was applied to all market parameters, including prices, interest rates, and exchange rates. As a result, the system itself distorted the market and the distortions were amplified by the profit incentive that the system provided to enterprises. The result was an intensification of "rent-seeking" activity which served to corrupt society in profound ways. Due to an improper sequence in reform measures, chaotic and corrupt behavior characterized economic activity. The result aroused dismay and anxiety among people working in the area of economic theory, as well as people heading up the process of reform.

Various alternative ideas then began to arise to meet the needs of the time. These sought to realize an improvement in resource allocation while still retaining the two-track system and still skirting around the idea of complete price reform.

Three proposals were among the more influential at this time: (1) The first was to set up a "system of decision-making prices." This substituted artificially calculated prices for prices as determined by the market. It evaluated the economic performance of each enterprise by the use of accounting methods and determined the percentage of profits that should go to the State and the percentage that should be kept by the enterprise. Based on the resulting "pricing system," State economic management departments would formulate macroeconomic policies that rationally allocated resources. (2) The second was to have governmental administrative departments rate industries in accordance with their importance. Then, using a set of "industrial policies" that included such considerations as public finance, tax revenues, interest rates, and licensing procedures ("review and approval procedures" undertaken by administrative departments), the government would "optimize industrial structure." It would restrict the growth of certain industries and promote the development of others. (3) The third was to abolish the two-track system that allowed for two prices for the same commodity, but to retain the price-formation mechanisms that allowed for two different prices for different kinds of commodities. That is, for upstream commodities, only the planned price would be applied. For down-stream commodities, the market price would be employed. This would allow the formation of a socialist-economy model that integrated both the plan and the market.

At the time, China's relevant leaders gave support to each of the above three recommendations and ways of thinking to varying degrees. People recommending the first proposal, however, did not buttress it with a clear-cut set of ways to implement it or do the accounting. Moreover, many Chinese as well as foreign scholars felt that this was an "illusion" that had long since been regarded as a kind of "computer-generated Utopia," so it quickly disappeared. The other two proposals soon became popular among theoretical circles as well as relevant departments, due to the strong support of government leaders. A minority of economists raised objections, but the majority went along with these views without very serious reflection. Among these were economists of various theoretical backgrounds. These two views have therefore become entrenched in recent years, and are among the few that have not caused any notable debate.

I personally feel that these two ideas have serious shortcomings. It is not accidental that they appeared in the spring of 1987. Their appearance is linked quite profoundly to systemic and theoretical causes. The systemic causes relate to the fact that the "*cheng-bao*" or contract system for enterprises appeared as a "solo reform" without any reform of resource-allocation mechanisms that should have accompanied it. The theoretical causes relate yet again to the issue of the relationship between planning and the market. Naturally, there may well be other reasons this issue continues to this day to provoke a "counter-reaction in people's understanding." Discussing such things is not within the scope of this particular article, however.

In what follows, I present my own views on the two concepts as sketched out above.

"Industrial policy" is a concept that China's economists imported from Japan in the early 1980s. It must be said that this approach did make positive contributions to the high-speed growth of the Japanese economy, as many people in the international community have said. However, one thing has been remarkably overlooked—there is a great disparity between the conditions for implementing industrial policies in Japan and in China. This is true even as China is inclined to have a vastly exaggerated opinion of the role of industrial policy.

Quite a few Japanese economists persist in emphasizing the role of industrial policy in Japan, particularly those who work with government organizations,[2] but this is by no means the consensus of all economists in the country. Many Japanese economists have consistently had doubts about the role of industrial policy, and even rejected it altogether.[3] As representative of this school of economists, Professor Ryutaro Komiya of Tokyo University feels that the fact of Japan's rapid economic growth is not sufficient to prove that Japan's industrial policy made the difference. Japan's economy would have grown even without broadly based intervention. Of course, despite shortcomings, post-war industrial policies did serve the purpose of collecting, exchanging, and disseminating industrial information. They were effective in this, but Professor Komiya has repeatedly pointed out that they had an impact mainly on areas in which the market had ceased to be effective.

In evaluating the role of industrial policies in Japan, I feel that at the very least we should take the following points into consideration.

First, Japan's industrial policy is not all-inclusive in the sense that it does not include everything within its scope. Japan's government encourages private enterprises to invest in industries that it feels are important through the use of direct funding, tax policies, and subsidies. In no way does it limit or restrict private enterprises from investing in industries that it feels are not "key" industries. Moreover, Japan's supportive policies are targeted at entire industries. Because of this, competition among specific enterprises in any given industry is intense. Industrial policy in Japan does not stifle the vitality of the market economy.

Second, industrial policy, like the economic plans of the Japanese government, is the product of coordinated opinions and cooperative actions among government officials, the financial community, the trade unions, and insightful economists. Despite such coordination, neither the national economic plan nor the government's industrial policy has any binding force. Nobody in Japan feels that he must comply with numbers put forth in the government's plan, or that he is responsible for the figures.

Third, Japan's industrial policy has brought on considerable negative side effects in the past. For example, industries that are protected and supported are frequently those that are already well established, not those that are young and in need of help. This has had the effect of creating excessive demand for labor in an economy that is already fully employed. The result has been to damage all industries across the board. This uses preferential policies to develop a particular industry, while forcing other industries, and indeed the entire society, to pay an excessive price.

One cannot overlook the case of the Republic of Korea when talking about the positive and negative side effects of industrial policy. Many scholars are loud in their praise of that country's industrial policy when they evaluate its high-speed growth, but such an evaluation is not sufficiently thorough in its analysis. Starting in the 1960s, the Republic of Korea gave preference to developing heavy industries and the chemical industry. In addition to various internal and external conditions, this contributed to 20 years of high-speed economic growth. By the late 1970s, however, severe inflation and a heavy external debt forced the country into a profound economic and social crisis. After some bitter struggles, the country transitioned from being "an economy dominated by the State," to being "an economy dominated by the market." This enabled it to get through a very difficult period and establish its economy on a stable and more coordinated basis. It began to enjoy more efficient growth. Among other measures, the Republic of Korea resolutely gave up a discriminatory policy that leaned in the direction of certain industries. In a more equal approach, it encouraged investment in all industries, and this is regarded as one of the more significant measures leading to its economic success.

When we discuss the role that industrial policy might play in the economic growth of China, as compared to Japan, we should first look at the differences between the underlying systems of each country—that is, the context within which industrial policy must operate. This is more important than looking simply at the benefits and drawbacks of industrial policy in China alone.

In Japan, the basic principle behind industrial policy is that it "operates through the market to enable the initiative of private enterprises. It respects the autonomous standing of private enterprises."[4] Therefore, when people are loud in their praise of the success of Japan's economic planning and of its industrial policies, they should not forget that "the core of Japan's economic system is free market enterprise." "All government measures are carried out under the premise of protecting a free market system. Any interference by the government in the economy is temporary, supplementary, and indirect."[5]

In China, however, there has been a profound misunderstanding of Japan's experience ever since we began to import ideas of industrial policy from Japan. Some comrades feel that all we need to do is master some of the specific methods by which industrial policy is applied, and we too can then optimize our industrial structure and achieve high-speed growth. They go even further in believing that the government can now reassert itself in managing economic affairs. China took the initial steps in releasing authority to lower levels of decision-making, they say. Now, in order to address certain shortcomings in the process, such as the "blind" nature of distorted industrial structure, the government can again step in with greater intervention. I regard this kind of thinking as overly simplistic.

First, China's market is still highly immature. The ability of its market mechanisms to allocate resources is weak. What's more, the two-track system has created a chaotic situation, in that the market operates with one set of rules, "releasing prices," while the planned sector operates by another set of rules, controlling prices. The scientific value of any kind of industrial policy that is formulated on the basis of such a situation is suspect. Any such industrial policies are based on distorted information about social and economic behavior.

Second, administrative interference still constrains enterprise behavior in China. This is so even though the country's enterprises, and in particular its State-Owned Enterprises, now enjoy decision-making autonomy that would have been hard to imagine prior to reform. Such interference weakens the control that any enterprise might have over its own budget. This is especially true given that administrative interference is coupled with the ongoing existence of "State paternalism." Enterprises are therefore unable and also unwilling to react in a timely manner to changes in the market in ways that serve their own interests or even those of the State. This makes the State unable to use the market as an intermediary in implementing policy. The market is unable to serve the role of "guiding" or "enticing" enterprise behavior. So-called industrial policy therefore becomes nothing less than direct administrative interference in the micro-affairs of individual enterprises.

If industrial policy is understood to mean that the government adopts support-ive policies toward certain key industries while placing restrictions on others, or even forbidding the development of others, we should all recognize that this kind of thing is nothing new. Slogans of China's past reveal an "industrial policy" that leans in the direction of developing certain industries: "Take agriculture as the base; put industry first"; "Agriculture, light industry, heavy industry"; "Take steel as the key link"; "Take grain as the key link." When the idea of industrial policy became so "hot" in 1987, some comrades made quite pointed comments about how this was something China had practiced long ago. Trying to use this kind of thing now to rebalance the country's entire economic structure was nothing more than a delusion. It was out of touch with reality.

There is another aspect to this problem. China's industrial structure is highly uneven and its pricing system is simply chaotic. If one hopes to use a set of poli-cies to address this, such policies have to be all-encompassing. They have to cover absolutely everything. The industrial policies that we are seeing, therefore, are highly complex. They try to handle a limitless number of "things to develop" and "things to limit," from the big to the small. Any problems are naturally not due to the incompetence of those formulating policy, but rather to the extent of China's economic scope today, the number of categories, the complexity of interrelation-ships, the depth of existing contradictions. These cannot compare with the way things were in the past. Since we were unable to handle the scale of things in the past, we are even less able to handle them today.

Some comrades are attributing the meager results of industrial policy to date to the existence of "blockaded-off feudal economies" in China, and the heedless pursuit of individual advantage among interest groups. If one takes the question further, however, one has to ask why each "principality" wants to carve off and protect its markets. Why can't each interest group come together to form a system that is in the interests of the public at large? There are many legitimate reasons, such as the system of local public finance that promotes an isolationist approach, or the enterprise contract system with all its many defects. Nevertheless, the most important reason, I feel, is that China lacks a sound market. Local governments and various interest groups will always respect and follow the commands of price. (Since price is currently distorted, they follow the wrong commands.) They will respect and follow these commands even over the direction of State industrial policy.

From this, it is evident that industrial policy cannot achieve its desired results because the law of value is outside the reach of human control. Humans are pow-erless to go against its force. Any effort to rebalance industrial structure, in the context of distorted markets, is akin to tilting at windmills. Right now, we see a very unfortunate trend developing. That is, the authority of departmental "lines" is constantly being strengthened, under the guise of implementing industrial policy. I believe that this deviates from the proper orientation of reform. In the early 1980s, the majority of economists in China came to a common understanding. The reason we were not able to get out from under the "vicious cycle" of alternat-ing periods of "releasing to the point of chaos" and then "controlling to the point of killing the economy" is that we were going round and round in adjusting power among "lines and patches." That is, we were simply adjusting authorities among (vertical) lines of departmental control and (horizontal) patches of geographic authority. We had not set our sights on resurrecting enterprises or on setting up a market. Even today, the common understanding that we developed back then is correct and quite incisive.

I should clarify that pointing out the defects of the currently popular industrial policy is not the same as rejecting industrial policy out of hand or saying it has no role to play. It is quite clear that correct policies can indeed be positive for economic growth, given that our economy is so backward, our territory so vast, our population so large, and our development so uneven. Such policies must be carried out on the basis of an effectively operating system, however, and the problem is in creating such a system. The two most important parts of this are rectifying the market and revitalizing enterprises. Right now, as we are discussing the relationship between planning and the market, we need to undertake a radical overhaul of our industrial policy. We cannot treat it as a kind of slogan, a tag we stick on policies, a concept that is adopted wholesale without discrimination.

In 1987, "industrial policy" was strongly promoted within the government, together with the idea of an "integrated model of planning and the market" that "reinforced control over upstream products" while "releasing controls over downstream products."

These things were consistent in terms of the orientation of an overall system, but in terms of practical implementation, they contradicted one another. The very industries that the former statement intended to develop were suppressed by the industries being released by the second statement.

Recently, some of our economic colleagues have expressed the notion of "integrating" these two statements in terms of a "horizontal" integration of the market. They again encompass both in the idea of a model that controls upstream products, meaning basic commodities, and that releases downstream products, meaning value-added or processed products. (The comparable analogy in vertical integration states that, "the plan controls the macro-economy, while the market controls the micro-economy.") They feel that this mode of integrating planning and market is determined by what they call the "fundamental nature" of a socialist-economic system, and they believe that it is necessary for the current stage of history and for a long time to come.

One has to ask, however, what inevitable link there is between a socialist-economic system and a model that "controls upstream products while releasing downstream products." In implementing a planned economy, why is it necessary for the State to impose controls on just some goods, particularly just certain means of production? Is the optimum allocation of resources in fact helped by controlling one kind of price while releasing another? This is a rather fundamental question, but nobody seems to have taken the time to address it. Some propositions are not what they seem, yet people quote them widely and also incorrectly.

In arguing that the prices of some goods must be controlled, some of our colleagues cite the way in which western countries also intervene in the pricing of some goods and services. They use this to prove that price controls are reasonable. Indeed, it is correct that the government is responsible for supplying certain goods and services under market-economy systems, and that the government intervenes in the pricing of these goods. It also intervenes in the pricing of agricultural goods and services deemed to be monopolies for various reasons. The reasons the State intervenes in pricing are generally as follows: first, the goods or services constitute a natural monopoly; second, they are in sectors that provide public services; and third, they pertain to specific policy objectives. Such countries intervene in prices through a decision by Congress, or a decision or permit by the government, or a negotiated agreement by a public utility in a given locality.

Judging purely by the appearance of things, interference in pricing is indispensable even in market economies and this does not seem any different from price interference in our own country. If one examines things more closely, however, the differences are absolutely apparent. For example, the Japanese government applies strict controls over the wholesale pricing of rice. Japan does not, however, use grain coupons to ration the supply of grain to its people. Virtually all market-economy countries intervene in the pricing of railroads, electric power, and telecommunications, but one never hears about a black market in railroad tickets in these countries, or "electricity barons" who control the electricity supply, or the practice of giving gifts (bribes) in order to get a telephone installed. From a purely economic perspective, what this means is that the prices being controlled in other countries generally approach what prices would be under supply and demand (some prices are determined by domestic supply and demand in markets that are protected by the State). Such prices create neither excessive demand nor supply shortages. On the contrary, they maintain stable supply and excellent service.

It is incorrect to compare the price intervention of other countries to ours by looking only at the surface of the matter. We must apply more in-depth research to price intervention and price decisions. Only if we use a scientific approach will we be able to escape from a disastrous situation in which the more we control prices, the more we have scarcities, shoddy goods and services, poor performance, and a stagnant economy.

A glance at the actual situation in China tells the story quite clearly: the price controls that the country currently applies to basic commodities and basic infrastructure has led to a situation that allows for no escape. The country's problems with respect to the fuel industry are particularly pronounced. The petroleum sector used to be a major provider of tax revenues. It began to show a loss, industry-wide, in 1988. In that year the loss came to RMB 1.4 billion. By 1989, the loss was RMB 4.2 billion, and by 1990 it had gone over RMB 7 billion. If prices are not adjusted, the losses will be ever greater in the period of the 8th Five-Year Plan. Due to operating losses in production, there is now inadequate funding for exploration and development. Proven oil reserves are increasingly being "eaten away" by current production as shown by the situation in the 7th Five-Year Plan period in which total oil production exceeded the increase in proven reserves.

Losses being generated by centrally-controlled coal mining are also increasingly severe on a nationwide basis. The practice of "*cheng-bao*" or contracted coal mining was begun in 1985. The Ministry of Finance determined that the loss that it would accommodate every year, the "deficit," should be RMB 300 million. The actual loss in 1985 came to RMB 1.2 billion. By 1986, it was RMB 2.56 billion. In 1987, it was RMB 3.12 billion, in 1988, it was RMB 9.03 billion, and in 1990, it was over RMB 10 billion. Meanwhile, due to the need for ongoing cash flow, any funds for investment in greater production are being cut. The amount of coal produced during the 7th Five-Year Plan period turned out to be 80 million tons, which was 100 million tons less than in the original Plan. Capacity increased by 120 million tons, but this was 47 million tons less than in the Plan. During the 8th Five-Year Plan period, investment funds were provided to finish production of 95.88 million tons of coal. This was 54.12 million tons less than in the Plan, even if the "coal investment quota" transferred over from the end of the 7th Five-Year Plan period was included.

Our fuel industry is being seriously undermined, in that we are losing sustainable production capacity and replacement reserves. Taking in the profits today and not re-investing adequate funds means that we are pushing problems off into the future. What's more, our railroads and other forms of infrastructure are also falling into a situation that is irremediable—in this case, overly low prices mean that problems are mounting up.

On the one hand, we have adopted discriminatory pricing policies with respect to basic infrastructure, both goods and services. The result is that these sectors are generating massive losses. On the other hand, since the national economy requires the effective operation of these sectors, we have no alternative but to pour financial support into them and subsidize them using huge investment that will never be repaid. Not only are these sectors unable to develop properly, to the extent that they are actually shrinking, but our entire society is paying a price that is not by any means low. According to knowledgeable estimates, the public has subsidized the coal industry to the extent of over RMB 80 per ton in these past few years, if one includes all the subsidies, supplemental fees, and "gratis" investments. Given that China has a wealth of coal resources, and very low labor costs, the public is paying a price that is exorbitant.

Overlooking the proper role of prices and lavishly dispensing money in the form of subsidies lowers the efficiency by which resources are allocated. It does enormous damage to any positive initiative on the part of producers. It leads to seriously poor management in sectors handling China's basic infrastructure. At the same time, some producers adopt a kind of negative approach that seeks to take the greatest advantage of the State. They devise all ways to turn a small loss into a greater loss, realizing that for them it is better not to earn money, but rather to lose the maximum amount. The means by which they achieve such losses could be called "Five variations on a theme."

The first device involves fabricating costs, setting the price of inputs at levels far higher than is reasonable, knowing full well that the government will not grant permission for such figures and will be discounting the amount requested in the end. This could well be called "eating off the public." Rather than earning profits through one's own efforts, this makes money purely off the public through the use of high input prices. The second device could be called "eating off public finance." When the State does not allow a producer to raise prices as it might wish, the producer then reports a loss and requests a public subsidy. Knowing that the subsidy it requests will be cut down, the producer artificially inflates the amount requested at the outset. The third device could be called "eating off banks." Even though a producer may have received a subsidy, this does not satisfy the full appetite for funds. As a result, the producer takes out bank loans (from State-owned banks), and then neglects to pay them back. The fourth device could well be called "eating off oneself" in that an entity eats up its own capital reserves at the expense of the future. This involves playing with the accounting for costs. It includes some expenses that should not be included as "costs," while deliberately excluding some costs that should be included. On the one hand, costs are artificially exaggerated, while on the other, cost structures are manipulated. Depreciation is lowered accordingly or not included at all. The fifth device could be called "eating off the customers." This uses crooked means to increase income and grant more bonuses. Through the deception of short-changing people, it extracts money from customers.

Due to these variations on a theme, the public has already paid far more than it would have had to pay if price controls had simply been released. Where, then, is the rationale for continuing to control prices?

Some comrades insist on believing that price controls and ongoing subsidies in certain sectors are the practice in many countries of the world. They cite coal as an example, in Germany, Japan, and Poland before its upheavals. I'm afraid that this too requires further analysis. Subsidies may be the result of two different goals, and they also may result in two different outcomes. Take the first two of the countries listed above. Germany and Japan are both developed and industrialized nations with very high labor costs. If there were no subsidies for coal in these countries, the coal industry would decline to the point of disappearing, given the rules of comparative advantage. From a strategic perspective, however, the governments of these countries recognize the need to maintain capacity in energy production. They therefore provide subsidies to the industry. Once the industry receives subsidies, it is free to sell its products on the open market at competitive prices (such prices may even be lower than cost, but they are in any event prices that are set by the market).

Poland is different. The price of coal in Poland is established by the government, and the actual commodity is distributed to people by quota allocations according to the Plan. The resulting price is divorced from market supply and demand, and is very substantially lower than the international market price. The result is that Poland pays an inordinate amount in subsidies that are both unchecked and inefficient. One consequence has been the eruption of grave economic, social, and political crises. The country has been left with a bitter regret at what it might have done differently.

Given the above analysis, we may perhaps be able to arrive at the following understanding.

First, there will always be a cost to pay when we implement price controls and allocate goods through planned quotas. Weighing up the pros and cons of this, we should try to limit the products we impose controls on to a scope that is reasonable and as small as possible.

Second, for the small number of goods and services on which we must impose price controls, our State-mandated pricing should still respect the law of value and the laws of market supply and demand. The underlying principle should be that our pricing should not lead to shortages in either supply or demand. In particular, it should not lead to shortages in supply. Neither should it lead to the growth of a black market in quota allocations.

Third, we should not regard it as necessary for the State to implement controls on every price for every basic commodity or form of basic infrastructure. If a sector can be made to conserve resources through the use of competition, then we should allow the market to regulate that sector. The so-called "importance" of a given sector must not be the sole reason for implementing management by the Plan.

Fourth, providing subsidies for certain products, in fact, has the effect of shifting the cost burden on those products to the public at large. In most circumstances, such a distribution of costs is not reasonable. Wanton use of subsidies can only lead to low efficiency in production, the waste of resources, and the "eating up" or erosion of public funds.

I want to emphasize one point here, which is that releasing prices on a given commodity or service is a necessary step in enabling competition, but it is still not sufficient. China's current situation is such that industries involved in basic infrastructure enjoy a high degree of monopoly power. Simply relaxing price controls will not, in and of itself, create balanced supply and demand and stable prices. In some of our basic industries, one or a small number of enterprises make up the entire market, or a large share of the market. Some of these entities cannot really be considered "enterprises." They are administrative departments masquerading under the name of enterprises. In order to release prices, stimulate competition, and create a real market, therefore, we must first dismantle and reorganize these "enterprise organizations" that have a high degree of monopoly authority. In any given market, we must ensure that there are adequately competitive alternatives if we intend to develop the vitality of the entire industry.

Naturally, industrial sectors that are classified as natural monopolies should, by and large, be regulated by the State. Two points are worth considering in this regard. The first is that not all of them need to have operations that are handled directly by the State. On the contrary, operations should be handed over to legal-person enterprises as much as possible. The second is that a "natural monopoly" needs to be defined in a very rigorous way. Some sectors that once were regarded as such can now be turned into competitive industries, given changes in economic, scientific, and technological considerations. Japan's railroads can serve as an example. These were originally regarded as natural monopolies. The construction of expressways and the dramatic increase in privately owned cars has changed that, together with the increase in alternative forms of transport such as shipping via air and ocean freight. All these have meant that transport via railroads is facing tremendous competitive pressure. At the same time, competition has developed between railway lines, and even between railway companies operating on the same line, given the tremendous improvements in computer technology, financial accounting methods, and so on. The result is that the Japanese government decided to privatize a "National Railway" that was increasingly inefficient. It did this to promote competition and raise levels of efficiency.

I raise two main issues in this article and would like to say that the above discussion and analysis of these is far from being incisive or remotely adequate. My intent has been to raise issues and draw the attention of people to these issues, including economists and colleagues actually engaged in various sectors. I would like to open out the discussion on a broader basis, in order to achieve a renewed understanding of the relationship between "planning" and "the market."

At present, we in China have a rather muddled way of describing the "target model" for our economic structural reform. We are not aiming for a command economy with a totally centralized and unified planned system, nor are we aiming for a pure market economy. We say that we are aiming for a system that "integrates a planned economy with regulation by the market." Exactly what kind of system is this? If we are talking about a system that plays the dual role of enabling both "planning" and "the market," then this description encompasses virtually every economy on Earth. Take the former Soviet Union as an example of one end of the spectrum, prior to its implementation of reform. This was a classic planned economy, yet the retail sales of some goods, the repair shops and so on, all had market components. Hong Kong can serve as the other end of the spectrum. It has been described as the "final bastion of free market economics" by western economists. The Hong Kong authorities themselves say that they implement "actively non-intervention" policies. At the same time, the Hong Kong government is not without its ways and means when it comes to economic activity. Its permits for land use and investment in certain public projects exert a very considerable influence on the Hong Kong economy. In a certain sense, no country exists that operates under a purely planned or a purely market economy.

When it comes to the "target model" for China's economic reform, we should come up with a more explicit and precise formulation. I believe that our understanding of what we are aiming for will become clearer if we approach the discussion in an atmosphere that permits sound thinking, and with a spirit that conscientiously seeks to derive truth from the facts.

## Notes

1  This article was originally published in the magazine *Reform,* Issue 1, 1991.
2  Morris Bornstein: *Economic Planning, East and West*, Commercial Press (China), 1980, 263.
3  Ibid, 267.
4  *A Dictionary of Modern Japanese Economy*, China Social Sciences Press, Japan Soken Press Corporation (Beijing), 1982, 193.
5  Ibid, 144, 146.

# 2 "Futures" in China

## Theory, policy, and systems[1]
## (February 20, 1994)

Until several years ago, the term "the futures market" was utterly foreign to the absolute majority of people in China, and even to the majority of people working in the field of economics. In the past two years, however, a "futures frenzy" has swept over the country. The tide has swept along those who intentionally promote it as well as those who are blindly following in its direction. As for what the futures market can really do for us, or what problems it is already presenting to us, there is little consensus in the midst of many contending voices.

Our era is one in which "any opinion backed by deep pockets prevails." Those who make money are those who write the script, and those who make the most money speak with the loudest voice. A plethora of articles, books, and advertisements promoting this thing called a futures market is making the subject even harder to simplify and get clear. At present, futures markets set up by various local governments and departments have begun to cover the landscape. All kinds of legal as well as illegal brokerage firms dealing in futures are parading from north to south, competing with one another in what amounts to an unregulated war.

The futures market has undeniably become a hot topic in economic life. Some people are profoundly worried about this, knowing that money will always win over reason and knowledge, particularly in an imperfect legal environment. Rational behavior will succumb to provocation. It may well be that people have to endure a period of calamity before they come to their senses and enjoy some kind of rebirth. Some younger economists among our ranks are not so pessimistic, however. They feel a particular sense of responsibility. They are not willing to watch the futures market come to a premature end in China. They have therefore written the book that I am reviewing in this article. They aim to treat the subject in an objective way by looking at the futures market as it was originally intended to be.

Almost all confusion about the futures market derives from a misunderstanding about what it actually is. Inaccurate understanding of the subject persists despite the universal availability of written materials. Some comrades think that a futures market is the same as a wholesale market for forward delivery. In fact, a futures market is a market that trades in the contracts for forward delivery of both material commodities and financial instruments. What is being traded is forward delivery contracts, commonly referred to as futures. The contracts are standardized. Those

dealing with commodities include standardized units of weight, product specifications, the designated place or warehouse where the transaction is to take place, the
date at which the transaction (or delivery) is to take place, the amount of guarantee money (or margin), the time of the trade itself, the unit of the price quotation,
the method by which the trade takes place, the limits on trading volatility allowed
each day, and so on. The futures market associated with any given commodity
generally is linked to the organization that operates the trading in that commodity.
This commodity trading exchange supplies a market that is stable and ongoing,
that ensures sustainable buying and selling of the futures. A futures market is not
simply an extension of a spot market. The two operate with different methods,
rules, and substance and indeed are considerably different from one another.

In a mature market economy, a futures market generally complements and
coexists alongside a spot market. The basic function of a futures market is to protect commodity producers and dealers against adverse price changes and resulting
losses between the time of production and the time of actual sale. This function
of "risk mitigation" is achieved through hedging. That is, the producer or dealer
takes a position in the futures market that is opposite to his position in the spot
market. Exactly how a person handles the trade depends on his evaluation of
future price moves and on his own judgment. He handles the business in order to
protect or preserve the value of his underlying product.

How do hedging operations disperse and shift risk? The answer relates to the
fact that there are two parties involved in every trade. One party aims to preserve
the value of his underlying product and so hedges to cover his risk. The other
is a speculator who aims to make money off the trade. The first party shifts the
price risk in order to conserve value. The second accepts the risk, in the pursuit of
profit. Professional investors or "venture investors" have generally been regarded
as people who "speculate" or who buy and sell without owning the underlying
product. From the perspective of taking on the risk of price movements, however, they deal specifically in the market of expectations. Relying on information
and analysis, their professional knowledge enables them to be investors who seek
profits from risk taking. In modern market economies, "risk capital," or venture
capital, is an important component of commercial capital and financial capital.

In the futures market, the probability of winning or losing for a speculator is
one to one. (In the securities market, both sides can profit from a given transaction, while in the futures market this is not possible.) Because of this, the futures
market is said to be a zero sum game. For those who engage in it, the stakes are
"I win you lose" or "You win I lose." The entire activity does not generate actual
wealth for society, but it does in fact have a very positive aspect. Speculators normally buy or sell futures contracts at a value that is many times the value of the
physical settlement of the underlying commodity. This highly speculative activity
enables the person hedging his risk to carry out that hedging smoothly and easily,
and to shift risk with great ease. Trading activity on the futures market, by the very
nature of its frequency and turnover, allows for prices to smooth out by preventing excessive volatility. Speculators are indeed the recipients of profits from risk
taking, but they are also the ones who shoulder the burden of that risk. Without

them, the futures market could not function. Only with a thorough understanding of these things can we realize the true significance of a futures market.

Is a futures market absolutely necessary when a market economy is just being set up? In setting one up, moreover, must the process take its own course and be unrestricted? How should we evaluate the role and standing of a futures market in a market economy with any degree of accuracy? Many misunderstandings are embodied in these very questions.

Some comrades believe that a market must generate its own dynamics as it is initiated and develops—it must be left on its own to grow. They feel that any market, under any conditions, will come to equilibrium. So long as equilibrium is reached, the optimum allocation of resources can be achieved. In the initial stages of market development, there is no need to impose any laws or regulations on the process, for any such restrictions will only hinder growth. Whether or not conditions are ripe for a futures market, therefore, and whether or not that market is highly irregular, the very existence of such a market will be beneficial to the setting up of a market economy system. (This sentiment is applied to both equities or real estate.)

This point of view is rather lopsided. In the past 20 years, developments in economics tell us that when markets are incomplete, and when financial markets also exist (including equities markets, and futures markets), then the equilibrium of the market is uncertain (or indeterminate). Because of this, external conditions must be imposed on the market from outside. Such "conditions" generally refer to government intervention. Without such additional conditions, the market will not find equilibrium and optimum resource allocation will not be realized.

The earliest period of futures markets was not completely unrestrained, even though the markets were basically a spontaneous process. The self-discipline of the wholesale dealers' association, as well as the quasi-legal authority endowed upon the association by the government, meant that the association was fairly effective in preventing cheating and reneging on contracts. By modern times, regulation of the futures markets has been more stringent and laws are far tighter. Some countries have taken a more lax approach to the establishment and conduct of their futures markets and have paid a huge price for this.

Looking at the underlying trends of futures markets, there has been a shift from commodities to financial futures in recent years. The market for commodity futures began to contract in the 1970s, while that for financial futures gradually rose to take its place as the dominant form of futures trading.

The market in financial futures can roughly be divided into three types: interest-rate futures, exchange-rate futures, and stock index futures. The rise of financial futures reflected increased risk in real economic activities; this created the need to have new mechanisms to counter this risk. In the early 1970s, after the collapse of the Bretton Woods Regime, fixed exchange rates were replaced by a system of floating exchange rates. Western economies then faced more extreme inflation and interest-rate volatility in financial markets intensified as a result. All of this brought enormous interest-rate and exchange-rate risk to various countries, as people attempted to handle investment activities and financial management as well as domestic and international trade. Banks, corporations, and other important participants in financial markets were constantly now facing the threat of unpredictable changes in interest rates and exchanges rates. It was against this backdrop that financial futures were developed and then grew with great speed.

It should also be noted, however, that as financial futures began to depart from the underlying material basis of economics, as they came to be a kind of purely monetary activity, the futures markets themselves changed in nature. In fact, one of the reasons for the appearance of financial futures, in addition to the objective causes noted above, was the promotion of this market by speculators. This group of professionals constantly put out new categories of financial futures. These took the place of a shrinking market in the older futures, so the professionals dubbed themselves "pioneers" in this field, carving out new territory for their own existence and for their ability to generate wealth.

Because of this, a new group of financial futures appeared that were not linked to any kind of underlying goods at all, including any underlying physical commodities but also financial instruments. These included, for example, a futures market in stock-market indexes. A stock index is generally composed of stocks that have been selected as representative of the overall market. Chosen stocks are generally called constituent shares. A price index is generated through calculating the closing price of all these shares each day on the market. The futures market in the price index itself has no corresponding material object, and there is no "delivery" or consummation of a trade in any physical object. There is only the delivery or "settlement" in cash. Trade in this particular kind of futures has increasingly become the target of speculators. The function of this kind of futures market has increasingly become divorced from the need to hedge in order to preserve value.

In China, for the time being, there is no need to develop this kind of purely speculative activity.

In general terms, there is no reason to oppose speculation in the course of conducting a market economy. On the contrary, we should recognize the legality and usefulness of certain kinds of speculative activity, while not promoting and championing speculation in its own right. We certainly do not want to disparage the honest work that goes into the physical production of goods and that is indispensable to our daily lives. Speculation that aims solely at garnering a profit involves behavior that is highly spontaneous. Every country has explicit laws governing this behavior, as well as codes of ethics and social constraints. These serve to limit the damage that speculative behavior can do to a society.

Gambling is also speculation. Some countries allow gambling under the rigorous constraints of laws and regulations. In China, however, gambling does not in any way add to the material wealth of society and does not enjoy proper standing, whether that is by the codes of traditional Chinese culture or whether it is in light of the modern commercial culture that is now being established.

In order to derive the benefits of a futures market, therefore, while avoiding the pitfalls, China should satisfy the following conditions as established by international practice:

1   It should formulate trading rules that apply in a uniform way nationwide. It should not allow each exchange to set up its own rules.
2   It should set up a regulatory agency that governs futures trading and that is directly under the authority of the State Council, as well as a self-policing organization for people engaged in the business of futures trading.
3   It must set up a nationwide consolidated market for each kind of futures commodity. If one given commodity or type of futures is traded on more than one exchange, then these exchanges must have an interconnected system for exchanging price quotations.
4   It should undertake all trading in futures on the basis of competitive market prices.
5   It should set up thorough and reasonable regulations that pertain to trading, as well as accounting standards and a system for settlement.
6   It should set up a spot market that is effective and sufficient for the purpose and that has the appropriate corresponding financial structure.
7   There must be an organization that conducts the market (a futures exchange), brokers, and a sufficient number of dealers (entities that "make a market," or provide both supply and demand of the futures), as well as speculators (who seek economic profit and can also assume economic risk).
8   There must be a well-trained cadre of people who can conduct trading and also provide research on futures markets.
9   There must be a smoothly operating communications system, a highly efficient price quotation service system, and adequate transport and warehouse systems.
10  The country's futures market should be designed with China's current resource situation in mind (including commodity resources and financial resources). The commodities must be able to be defined in standardized terms.

China's existing legal system and its current economic structure do not allow for the necessary conditions as listed above. Generally speaking, some of the elements above can be created in the course of establishing a futures market. Others must be prepared in advance. In such a high-risk industry, operations should not be carried out if there is any doubt about a healthy system. Otherwise, the potential consequences may be disastrous while the potential benefits may be slim.

China's futures markets are already setting forth in the midst of highly unstandardized conditions, however. They are already what could be called a premature baby with congenital defects. In order to prevent their early demise, the important thing for us to do now is to make the correct diagnosis and treat the problems rather than hide the sickness for fear of the treatment.

One prerequisite is that a proper evaluation of the role of a futures market in China must be carried out. When that is done, we must evaluate the institutional requirements that will be needed by a futures market that functions properly. We must keep in mind that the context for this market is an economy that is transitioning from a planned to a market economy.

I believe that, at the very least, we must create the following institutional underpinning for a futures market that functions properly: (1) We must have price-formation mechanisms that operate freely and that are based on a spot market that functions in a sound manner. (2) We must have an adequate number of market participants, who have clearly defined property rights. (3) We must have a financial system that corresponds to the futures market, together with a foreign-exchange administration system and foreign trade administration system. (4) The establishment of the futures market must be under the unified planning and leadership of a national futures trading regulatory and supervisory body. The establishment should move forward in a staged and gradual way.

We must also formulate laws and regulations, among which the following two are most fundamental. The first is national legislation for trading domestic futures. The second is legislation for Chinese enterprises that are engaged in trading overseas futures. In terms of our own legislation, it will not hurt to "transplant" and make use of the laws and regulations of other countries.

One of the most important lessons we have learned from the success of China's economic reform is that we must hold fast to "emancipating" our way of thinking. We must adhere to a path of seeking the truth from facts. We must encourage exploration and allow for experimentation. Instead of sticking with dogma, we must proceed in all cases from reality. This has been vital to our ability to cast off the constraints of the old system, to break out of the "cage" of a rigid way of thinking, and it has been vital to mobilizing economic reform when things were at their worst.

At the same time, reform is an extremely complex form of systems engineering. We should approach it with a very cautious and scientific attitude. We should not think that we can accomplish everything, no matter what, and therefore disregard all potential conditions, not take account of the right timing. We should not think that we can accomplish anything we imagine. That way of thinking, based purely on willpower, may lead us into serious mistakes and problems in reform. We must recognize that the great majority of us involved in reform were steeped in the theory and practice of a planned economy. This includes those among us who were engaged in economic research. We all have a very long, hard road ahead of us as we learn the fundamentals of a market economy from the start. After beginning to doubt a planned economy and then to lose hope in it altogether, some among us warmly embraced and supported the idea of a market economy as our objective for reform. However, some of these have not gone on to make a thorough study of market economics. Instead, they simply mouth the slogans of a market-economy system. This is very much like the muddled way of thinking that regards macroeconomic regulation as somehow being in opposition to a market economy. Or it is like the thinking that allows for deceitful business practices as a part of "normal competition." Such things will unavoidably lead to major trouble.

As a result, I would like to reiterate the statement in the Decision as put forth by the Third Plenary Session of the 14th Central Committee of the Communist Party of China ("*The Decision on several issues to do with establishing a socialist market-economy system*"). That decision noted that we must "focus on learning the basic knowledge that underlies a socialist market economy." We must foster an environment that tolerates speaking the truth and that respects a scientific approach. We must avoid the wrongful practice of ignoring people who suggest that it is wise to take precautions against potential dangers.

This book was written by a group of several young economists, on my recommendation. In the course of their writing it, my only contribution was to suggest an opinion regarding the overall framework and the underlying principles. Once the final manuscript was ready, I gave it only a cursory review. As a result, this book is the result of their efforts. Naturally, since I was its chief editor, I take responsibility for any inadequacies and mistakes.

## Note

1 This article is the preface of the book *Futures in China—Theory, Policy and System* by Xing Zhang and Linan Zhu, published by The Commercial Press in 1994. It has been abridged to avoid repetition of contents covered in later chapters.

# 3 On making China's system of circulation more market-oriented, and on creating institutions to handle the market[1]

## (1995)

Now that China's reform has gone on for more than a dozen years, and has been extended to cover such things as enterprises, public finance, taxation, the financial industry, foreign exchange, foreign trade, social security, and so on, people generally assume that price reform is pretty much accomplished. Price reform represents both the basis for the market reform of all the above, and a prerequisite for their reform. Even if we have not completed the task, people think, at the very least, we can declare the completion of a major chapter in the process.

In fact, the situation is not what it seems. In the course of proceeding with reform, we now begin to realize that we are far from having market-determined prices and a functioning market-oriented system. Not only does this present an urgent task for our immediate economic reform, but it should be recognized as a task that will be with us for a very long time.

### A market economy requires market-determined circulation of goods

By the late 1980s, China had already accepted the idea that prices must be "released" or liberalized, and that the circulation of goods must be done via a market, if China was to set up a market economy. This economic proposition was no longer up for debate since the conclusion was apparent, whether it was derived from economics textbooks, Chinese and foreign, or from economic systems operating in the real world. People's understanding of this was pretty much in accord. This consensus was reached particularly after the Third Plenary Session of the 14th National Congress of the Communist Party of China set forth the Decision ("*The Decision on several issues to do with establishing a socialist market-economy system*") stating that the goal of China's intended reform was to establish a socialist market economy. In actual practice, however, in the conduct of economic activity, things were less clear-cut than they were in this theoretical understanding.

A brief review of the history of economic thought may serve to clarify our thinking on these things. First, it must be said that traditional Marxist political economy did indeed regard socialism as being incompatible with "the market." The reason was that traditional theory saw the very origins of capitalism arising from the most rudimentary practice of exchanging "commodities" (goods that are purchased for money). This seemed true in both logical terms and in historical terms. The very substance of capitalism, and its "relations of production," was therefore tied to goods exchange on a market. (We detoured around this issue, in fact, when we set up the theoretical basis for establishing a socialist market economy in China.)

As economic theory developed, a long debate ensued about precisely how socialism would allocate resources, using a "plan," once there was no longer a market. In the early twentieth century, Enrico Barone (1859–1924) suggested using a system of simultaneous equations to carry out the accounting and allocate resources in a rational way. This was rejected by such people as Ludwig von Mises (1920) and Friedrich Hayek (1935). The rejection itself was then opposed by other economists, including Oskar Lange (1936–7), and Abba Lerner (1934–7). Lange took the use of simultaneous equations further by suggesting that a "trial-and-error" method could help resolve the equations. He felt that the State's planning departments could simulate the market through the use of calculations. They could balance supply and demand by specifying prices, wages, and interest rates in this manner.

Debate between the two sides proceeded for roughly half a century. The actual substance of the debate revolved around how to allocate resources: should this rely on a plan (including one that simulated the market), or should it rely on a real live market? After the Russian Revolution in 1917, the idea of relying on a plan to allocate resources took hold. As a replacement for markets, the use of a "plan" then became a real-life experiment that was conducted on millions of people. What's more, in quite a few countries, it became the conceptual basis and system by which people were ruled in all aspects of life.

What had not been resolved by theoretical debates was in fact resolved in actual practice. Actual practice was to prove decisively that a planned economy, originally held to be an expression of the high rationality of humankind, was in fact unadulterated "bureaucratism" and "adventurism." It resulted in rampant waste and low efficiency. Starting in the 1950s, some countries that were practicing a planned economy began to have doubts about the system, and gradually began to implement reforms.

At the start of China's reform, an enlightening debate about the overall system focused on certain issues. Should the plan be abandoned as a method for allocating resources, or should it not? Was price reform absolutely necessary and should the orientation of reform be in the direction of releasing market prices? Should farmers and enterprises be allowed the right to sell their own goods, or should they not? As it happened, the actual process of reform did not wait for clear answers to such questions before getting started. In the early 1980s, government policies began to allow farmers to sell goods that they had produced that were above and beyond what the State purchased. Policies allowed enterprises to sell "excess" production that exceeded what was required by the Plan. Policies also released prices on these "extra" quantities. This then formed a pricing system that was unique to China's reform, called the "two-track system." Excess production was sold at (higher) market prices; planned production, required by the State, was sold at (lower) State-mandated prices. By roughly 1985, the great majority of economists as well as practitioners were united in recognizing the absolute and urgent necessity of price reform. (A minority still insisted that a rash approach to price reform would lead to the failure of China's overall reform.)

The process of releasing price-control systems was only gradual, however. It happened in ways that were referred to as "incremental." These required whittling away the jurisdiction or authority of the plan in different areas. Many people had reason to think that the process could have gone more quickly, but this incremental style of reform in fact produced much better results than "shock therapy" would have done.

By 1993, controls on the prices of the great majority of goods and services had been released, with the exception of such things as cotton, petroleum, some coal, and so on. The elimination of coupons for food was an epoch-defining event in China. The rationing of grain had been the practice for decades in a country beset by food shortages. In writing about the success of China's agricultural reforms, most economists focus on the aspects that "divided up fields and allocated land to specific households," and that gave operating responsibility for production to households in a *cheng-bao* or contractual system. Their analysis of other aspects has been less prominent, particularly the setting up of markets for agricultural byproducts, the ability to set prices independently, and the ability to distribute (or "circulate") goods freely. In fact, China's agricultural reform would never have achieved its massive success if the second part of the story had not also occurred. If land had been distributed to farmers, who then carried out their own farming and kept for themselves all but what was required as a tax to the State, and if they had then sold the portion that they did not consume themselves—but at prices mandated by the State—agricultural reform would have been quite different. Reform of industrial enterprises was the same. The most fundamental right granted to enterprises was the right to set prices on their own products. A dozen or more years of the actual experience of reform indicates that the supply of a given product becomes plentiful when price controls on it are released. Only when the great majority of goods are "price released" does a market begin to flourish.

Given the above, this should have ended the debate. In the past one or two years, however, a rather peculiar allegation has begun to stir up muddy waters. The reports of State delegations who make "investigation tours" overseas have noted that quite a few prices of goods and services are in fact controlled in the majority of market economies in the world. This can be seen particularly in the more developed economies. Indeed, not a single market-economy government fails to intervene in the way enterprises set some prices.

People reading these reports are therefore now posing a whole new set of questions: why did the initial investigations not discover this fundamental "fact?" What, in fact, does a "market economy" really mean? If such an economy does not really have prices that are set freely by supply and demand, is there in fact a market? Has our reform over these years been off course, as we reformed prices and distributed goods via markets? Have we gone too far?

Textbooks on economics give various definitions for the term "market," but fundamentally all carry the same general meaning. As one textbook notes, "The term 'market' is a simplified way to describe a process. In this process, decisions are regulated by the rise and fall of prices, whether those decisions relate to a household deciding on consumer goods or an enterprise deciding on what and how much to produce, who to hire, and so on."[2] Yes, it is true that no government in today's world refrains from intervening in its economy. What exactly does that "intervention" mean, however? How is it carried out? The answers hold the key difference between a market-economy system and a planned-economy system.

Government departments in market-economy countries primarily carry out macroeconomic measures to make adjustments in their economies. The target of this kind of management is at the aggregate level of the economy, that is, aggregate demand and aggregate supply, the overall price level, and the general "rules" of the market. If there were no distinction between this kind of management and a micro approach, with the government even setting prices on goods that companies produce, how would this be any different from the traditional planned economy? Why should we go to all the trouble of reform, trying to set up a market economy? The problem is that, over these past few years, no term has been more misunderstood and abused by our economists than the term "macroeconomic regulation."

These days, any department that wants to stick its finger into economic affairs does so under the excuse of engaging in "macroeconomic regulation." The original sense of the term relates to regulation of the overall national economy. Any individual sector or part of the economy is not, by definition, part of the "macroeconomy."[3] Right now, though, what we have is departments, local governments, even enterprises, all wanting to engage in "macroeconomic regulation." This represents a gross misunderstanding. It is quite apparent, however, that straightening out this misunderstanding is going to require much more than a simple definition of terms.

In point of fact, the number of things that our economic management departments would like to "manage" is already excessive. One could also point out that the things such departments should in fact handle are not handled well, or not at all, while there is far too much interference in things they should not handle. The outstanding example is the macro-economy. Over these years of reform, the planning departments of the government seem to have overlooked that aspect of things, while still managing to deal with extremely specific details. Indeed, the trend is in the direction of increasing authority over and interference in the "micro."

The most fundamental principle of market economies is that of "self responsibility." In a market economy, an individual, a term that includes a legal person, is fully responsible for his own gains and losses in the market so long as he complies with rules and regulations. It is not up to others or to the State to get involved. Even if the desire "to help" stems from the best intentions, therefore, when government departments take responsibility for things that should be the sole responsibility of individuals and enterprises, this does nothing but hurt the sound development of a market-economy system.

Let us take the securities and futures market as an example, that is, the most classic representation of a market economy. In these markets, the most fundamental responsibility of the government is to preserve and protect market order. It is to ensure that the market operates in a way that is open, just, and equitable. The government should not and cannot be responsible for prices on these markets, or for the profits and losses of any given market participant. The actual situation right now is quite different, however. The regulatory bodies governing these two markets are overstepping their authority, which is one of the most obvious indications that the markets are immature. Such behavior is reflected in the actual work of the regulatory bodies, but is also demonstrated by the way most market participants misunderstand the role of these bodies.

A certain number of China's investors in futures markets are not adequately informed about the risks involved, plus they have a highly speculative mentality. They are unprepared to face losses in both psychological and financial terms. When they do face losses, they immediately take their case to government officials. Using the pretext of supporting the central government's right to undertake "macroeconomic policy measures," they make exaggerated claims about price differentials between spot and futures markets or all sorts of other specious arguments in order to require "the government's administrative intervention." Their aim is simply to get protection for their own private interests, either to minimize a loss or even to turn it into a profit.

Looking at the actual circumstances of past cases through the means of later investigations, we know that many of the plaintiffs were in fact speculators who either misrepresented the facts by presenting only one side of the matter or who falsified facts altogether. By merely bringing forward a case, however, all such plaintiffs gained positive results, some more than others. The people bringing their cases forward were very astute in reading the psychological weakness of government officials. When market participants made money, they felt the situation was only right and proper. When they lost money, however, the story was different. Market participants now declared that the government owed it to them to set things right.

Regulatory bodies had trouble with this, but at the same time they generally bowed to the pressure of interest groups. They took measures to influence market prices, consciously or unconsciously bailing them out under the pretext of "saving the market." In the short run, such measures might relieve problems. In the long run, they distort the market and also habituate individuals and enterprises to the idea that they will be bailed out. In the end, this only incubates much greater problems.

Under market-economy conditions, the government's role in determining specific prices is extremely limited. Nevertheless, when prices of a given item rise precipitously, the natural and intuitive response is to clamp on price controls. That replaces market exchange with administrative allocation of the product. In fact, however, this is somewhat like trying to hold down a pot of porridge that is boiling over by clamping a lid on it. If one decides to control the price of a certain commodity, then all the prices that go into the production of that commodity must also be addressed if one is not to hurt the interests of the producer. Prices of all the inputs and also the outputs must be rearranged. As the scope of the situation widens out, it inevitably damages market mechanisms. The immediate consequence is that there is little incentive to produce. The more far-reaching consequences relate to economic structure, in that such controls make restructuring more difficult. Obviously, this is not an enlightened approach.

The supply and demand of agricultural products is a case in point. Every three or four years, the government's agricultural policy should indeed iron out cyclical fluctuations but every attempt should be made not to overreact. Excessive intervention will only have the effect of amplifying the degree of volatility. At the end of 1993, prices of agricultural goods rose dramatically. Their increase did indeed go beyond what could be addressed through compensatory structural adjustments. Nevertheless, the law of value tells us that excessively high prices will fall back to reasonable levels over time. From the end of 1994 to early 1995, an extreme shortage of pork turned into hugely overstocked inventories. Prices gradually fell back, just as they had done with both grain and food byproducts, serving as evidence of the rule.

In recent years, as prices of grain rose too quickly, some parts of China resumed the practice of issuing grain coupons. This was to ensure a basic standard of living for low-income people. Meanwhile, in order to "rectify" (or put in order) circulation issues, the State increased controls over the prices of petroleum and refined oil products, as well as the way in which these are distributed or circulated. With respect to the circulation system governing cotton, the government reiterated its policy decision not to "open up" the market.

Nevertheless, reform is still intended to be "market-oriented," as a colleague in the State Council said when he was talking about cotton and how to reform its method of being distributed. This policy guidance is absolutely correct. My own feeling is that this term "market-oriented" should apply not only to reform of the cotton circulation system, but to reform of the circulation systems that govern all agricultural and industrial products.

The excuse one generally encounters among those who oppose or want to delay market-oriented reform is that, "We face material shortages." This is a carryover from war days, when it became an ingrained form of habitual thinking. Planned and rationed allocation became an even more deeply rooted concept during the "three years of hardship." It became standard government behavior that was simply the correct way to handle things, apparent in its own right. It became a system that we could not imagine departing from for an instant.

In fact, this approach was appropriate during wartime. There was absolutely no elasticity of supply, and not remotely enough of anything to satisfy demand. The command economy, price controls, and planned allocation were necessary and also somewhat effective. In normal times, however, supply and demand do indeed have some elasticity. They are regulated by the rise and fall of prices and therefore trend in the direction of equilibrium. Both theory and practice have proven this over and over again: controlling prices and stopping up circulation can only exacerbate shortages, provide incentives for speculation, and create rampant black markets. Releasing prices and allowing for the flow of goods enrich markets and prevent price explosions and chaotic circulation.

In addition to the above, we have another problem. Planned-economy methods that may have been effective in the past are no longer possible because we now lack the socio-political foundation by which to carry them out. We no longer have the necessary means to achieve "administrative allocation." By now, both the State-owned commerce and supply-and-marketing cooperatives carry out their own independent accounting. They employ corporate operating methods, with each entity enjoying economic profits for itself as is only appropriate. Without State subsidies to cover the costs, it is irrational to require entities to cover social benefits with disregard for their own profits, and to ask them to serve as the major conduit for stabilizing commodity prices without any regard for their own interests. That is like asking a horse to work hard without allowing it to eat hay.

In similar fashion, it is unrealistic to require local governments to obey the dictates of central authorities, unconditionally, with respect to unified prices and allocation plans. Local governments already have their own interests at heart. Administrative allocation depends on two key things. The first is obedience. The second is subsidies. Obedience that could once be maintained by adherence to the idea of "class struggle" no longer exists. No longer is there a disregard for economic interest. At the same time, large subsidies from public finance coffers are a thing of the past.

China began a new system of taxation in 1994 that divided tax revenues between central and local governments. Given that division of revenues, China would be dragged down by the burden in short order if the central government still had to try to feed the entire country. Prior to reform, we all fought against "the market" for more than two decades. In the end, what we got for this was an impoverished nation in addition to not winning any kind of victory over the market. Finally, our only option, the only possible way out of our predicament, was market-oriented reform.

Since 1993, all parties have strengthened management controls over agricultural products and their markets. The intent as expressed has been to protect the interests of farmers, while also taking the interests of urban residents into consideration. As departments and local governments implement these measures, however, we find very few market-oriented approaches and quite a few administrative commands. We find numerous mandatory restrictions, and the results of all of these things are therefore rather meager. Urban residents get no actual benefits while farmers themselves are loud in protests and opposition.

In most cases, the State uses the two different methods of "firm orders" and "negotiated price orders" with regard to how it handles the circulation of grain. Through these, it controls around 80 percent of the supply of all "commodity-type grain." Despite this, however, random-sample surveys indicate that the majority of grain is not in fact purchased by people at "grain distribution stations." Instead, some 80 percent is purchased from markets. This is true for residents of large cities as well as government institutions, and the figure is undoubtedly higher for people in smaller cities and towns who rely on local markets.

Is it not possible to say that these two 80 percent figures express the possibility that the great majority of the State's subsidies in this area are going to feed the system itself? That is, that subsidies nurture the system of State purchase, State storage, and State circulation of grain?

The subsidies do not in fact achieve their purpose of smoothing out and holding down prices and protecting the welfare of the people. In the past two years, farmers have been somewhat more motivated to grow grain. This naturally is related to the decision by the government to increase its mandated purchasing prices considerably. It is even more connected, however, to the fact that market prices have gone up even more quickly. Yet again, this goes to show how the "marginal price" regulates supply and demand in the market.

Agricultural issues in China are of great interest to Chinese and foreign economists alike. In 1994, a report issued by the World Bank on China's current economic situation pointed out that, "It is not necessary for the State to control 70% to 80% of all wholesale grain trade in order to ensure adequate domestic supplies or to stabilize domestic grain prices. Bringing the percentage down to, for example, some 10% to 20% would help improve efficiencies in both the storage and trading of grain. It would improve the ability of [all involved] to react to changes in consumer demand and would enable farmers to receive more favorable prices." This report went on to say, "There is plenty of room in this area for a reduction in State controls."

In 1995, a US-based research institute called World Watch made the comment that China may well be "starving out" the rest of the world in the coming century (by eating all the food). For a while, this provoked a lively response from the public. Some concurred with the conclusion and others refuted it. Such an approach might be thought of as alarmist, but nevertheless, it should be noted that the majority of articles being written by economists are grim in their forecasts for Chinese agriculture. The only way out, they say, is reform. On this, at least, everyone speaks with one voice.

We feel that China's market distribution (or circulation) system is indeed now facing the need for a major episode of reform. The circulation system that applies to a certain number of products still has to be addressed. Some of these products were never really touched upon by reform at all. Some have been reformed to a superficial degree. Reform of the rest has been attempted but efforts were then pulled back to the point that nothing was accomplished in the end. One particular issue is that some of these product categories are in short supply on a temporary basis while resources also appear to be inadequate over the long term. Opposition to reforming this kind of product is particularly strong. The obstructive forces of traditional ways of thinking are one reason. Highly entrenched vested interests are another. Both mean that carrying out reform of the circulation systems is going to come up against very stubborn resistance.

The fact is, however, that there is no alternative to moving forward with market-oriented reforms. If we do not reform, we will bankrupt our system of public finance as well as our banks. (The bulk of the "suspended" bad debts carried by our banks relates to policy-type losses as well as non-policy-type losses in this area.) We will also be forced to postpone the transformation of our corporate operating mechanisms, to the point that enterprise reform stops altogether. Not carrying out reform will also have a negative effect on relieving bottleneck constraints in resources.

The question of whether or not the circulation system of a given commodity should be opened up to market forces does not hinge on whether or not that thing is in short supply. Rather, it depends on whether or not competition can be applied to its supply and demand, and whether or not such competition can have the effect of lowering costs. Only industries that are by their nature natural monopolies are inappropriate for competition. The prices of such areas should be set by negotiated arrangements arrived at between the government and the public. So-called "natural monopolies" generally refer to those industries in which average costs decrease progressively. That is, efficiency is at its highest when products are manufactured by a single entity, while it declines if production is carried out by too many competing entities. In such cases, monopoly production can be used to realize economies of scale and technological efficiencies.

We must avoid having monopoly industries limit production purely in order raise profits and earn higher profits at the expense of the consumer. The classic cases of natural monopolies include the supply of running water, natural gas, electricity, and sewage treatment. Strict controls must be maintained over the prices of these industries. It should be pointed out that industries classified as natural monopolies can change with the development of new technologies. Examples are railroads and telecommunications. These were regarded as natural monopolies in the past but the governments of some countries are now using various means to force these industries to accept greater competition.

The Third Plenary Session of the 14th Central Committee of the Communist Party of China set a clear goal for reform: liberalize the prices of competitive goods and services. China currently has some goods with "circulation systems" that are entirely controlled by artificially devised administrative-type monopolies. These must now be subjected to reform. Indeed, the conditions exist for them to be reformed immediately.

Reform of the circulation system that governs grain should take the following direction. Grain distribution should proceed through one major channel supplemented by a variety of other channels and both of these should be given equal weight. Policy-type grain reserves and commercial reserves should likewise be given equal weight. We should hold firm to the primary channel while releasing controls over other channels. Policy-type grain reserves should be aimed primarily at ensuring adequate supplies in time of war and in time of famine. Commercial reserves should be used mainly to respond to market supply and demand. Grain subsidies to low-income people in urban areas should be made in kind or in cash and should replace the grain coupons issued universally in the past.

The grain circulation system should be operated by a group of grain wholesalers that are truly commercial in nature (not quasi-government) and that we support as viable competitors. These should include professional entities in the countryside that deal in grain distribution and processing. We should take a hands-off attitude to these, allowing them to expand in size and scope of business, and we should allow them to compete on a healthy basis with State-owned grain companies. The State-owned system should be separated out from this commercial system.

With respect to cotton, reform should enable producers and sellers to meet and do business directly, while we eliminate the State-plan form of allocation. In past years, we have been concerned about how to handle cotton production, harvesting, and circulation. We assumed that if prices and circulation were not firmly controlled, factories would close down production, workers would be out of jobs, and consumers would not be able to buy cotton garments. In point of fact, so long as the government continues to undertake planned circulation, the textile sector will not concern itself at all with reducing costs or improving competitiveness. So long as the government mandates the price at which cotton is to be bought, and there is a major difference between that price and the market price, local protectionism will not disappear. The tiny cotton-garment factories in towns and villages will continue to keep their doors open.

In the 1993 cotton season, we tried hard to figure out how to purchase more cotton in order to have adequate raw material supplies for the large- and medium-sized textile enterprises. In fact, however, these enterprises got along fine in 1994. They quickly absorbed and processed the cotton they had bought at high prices, and cotton that farmers had been reluctant to part with earlier began to flow into the market. Naturally, the price of cotton textiles also rose quickly, but this coincided with a change in the market. Pure cotton was no longer looked upon as a cheap item—global trends now treated it as more of a luxury item. People began to change their ideas about cotton and more and more began to use substitutes. Meanwhile, given excessive price hikes in the cotton market, local protectionism began to fail as tiny factories that should have closed earlier now began to shut down. The market therefore achieved what we had wanted to do by planning for years, but had been unable to accomplish.

Reform of the petroleum industry, and refined products, should first undertake to break up industry monopolies. Given this prerequisite, the orientation should be to release prices and foster competition. Experience has proven that carrying out policy-type support for certain industries by providing them with affordable raw materials is not a successful approach. For example, in the past we used affordable diesel oil as an incentive to farmers to produce and sell more agricultural products. The amount of diesel that actually reached the hands of farmers was minimal, however, once it had gone through layers upon layers of "discounts" by people in power. From now on, therefore, this kind of policy-type "support" should be changed. Better methods should be used. These include releasing prices on the goods and services that are produced by the industry in question, and using actual cash subsidies from public finance that go directly to the recipient. Not only will these things raise efficiency, but they will greatly reduce the opportunities for corruption.

As for reform of other kinds of commodities or materials, such as chemical fertilizers and other agricultural inputs, the prices of these were originally controlled as a way to keep prices of agricultural commodities down while also trying to reduce the cost burden on farmers. Once the circulation system for agricultural commodities is resolved, issues relating to reform of these other materials can be dealt with quite easily.

A market that is "institutionalized" is the end result of our efforts to turn the circulation system in a market-oriented direction.

For years, economists in China have been grappling with the question of how to sequence reforms. Should we first grow the market, or first attempt to regulate and standardize it? Do these two things stand in opposition to each other? That is, if we focus on regulating the market, will that not constrain its progress? Does the growth of a market have definite laws unto itself, or can it be fostered in an incremental way, according to a certain sequence?

I would like for a moment to review the debates among Chinese economists about setting up a futures market, since I feel that might be helpful in our understanding of how to "institutionalize" the market. Back then, a prevailing view was that the market had to be developed and made "deeper" on a constant basis. It had to be "upgraded" constantly and, in particular, this meant developing a futures market. As for "regularizing" or standardizing the market, that was something that could be worried about after the market itself had achieved major growth. Another point of view took a different position, however. This view felt that a futures market was something that only appeared in the more advanced stages of a market economy. Only after a spot market was quite well developed could one even think about a futures market, for only then did it have a chance of developing in a healthy manner. If, instead, we implemented reform by "going down the stairs backwards," we would have a very high price to pay.

Unfortunately, it is difficult for a level-headed scientific approach to reform to counter the seductive appeal of profits and the desire for material wealth. China's futures market was indeed begun at a time when people, including those in the business, were not yet equipped with the most rudimentary knowledge. It was launched to great fanfare when the government had not put in place any legislation or regulatory supervision. Tragic losses were the result, and people learned some acute lessons.

Until recently, the very term "futures market" has remained opaque to the great majority of Chinese people, and even to the majority of people engaged in the field of economics. Not long ago, however, a "futures fever" swept across the country. It wreaked havoc with people's way of thinking and also with their daily economic lives. Essentially all of the misunderstandings and resulting chaos stemmed from having only the vaguest notion of what a futures market really is. The subject is rarely addressed in the standard works on economic theory. In more specialized works, moreover, it is dealt with in highly abstruse and prejudiced ways, and in terms that are motivated by self interest. Works on the subject are ubiquitous by now, but the number of people actually reading these works is quite small.

Some comrades tend to mix up a futures market with a kind of wholesale spot market that incorporates forward delivery. In fact, a futures market does buy and sell forward contracts of various physical commodities as well as financial instruments, but what is traded is the forward contract itself, generally called a "futures contract." This is a contract whose various terms comply with standard-ized descriptions. These include standardized units of weight, the specifications of a representative sample, the place at which delivery is to take place as well as the date, the amount of payment due up front as a guarantee (or margin payment), the time of the transaction itself and unit in which the price is being quoted, the method of exchange, the allowed range of daily volatility in trading, and so on. The futures market in any given commodity generally refers to the organization governing trade in that commodity. This organization provides a sustainable and stable market that enables futures trades to take place and in which market par-ticipants have sufficient faith that they are willing to participate. A futures market is not simply an extension of a physical or "actual" market. The two are consider-ably different in terms of operating methods, rules, and substance.

In a mature market economy, a futures market generally coexists with and supplements a physical market. The basic role of a futures market is to provide producers of commodities and those who deal in commodities with a method whereby they can mitigate risk, during the period between production of the prod-uct and when it is eventually used or sold. It allows them to limit the losses that may arise from adverse price changes during that period. This function of limiting risk is achieved through hedging. That is, one risk is limited by taking a position in the futures market that is opposite to the position one holds in the physical mar-ket. Precisely how a trader carries out the "preservation of value" through hedging depends on his own predictions regarding the market and on his own judgments.

How exactly can hedging disperse and shift risk? The answer lies in the fact that there are two types of participants in the market. One is interested in "hedg-ing" or preserving value. The other is a speculator. The former shifts price risk in order to preserve value whereas the latter takes on price risk in the pursuit of profit. Professional venture ("risk") investors were previously always regarded as opportunists. From a different perspective, however, they are simply profes-sionals engaged in the business of market forecasting—people who rely on the analysis of information and specialized professional knowledge who take price risks in order to gain risk profits.

In modern market economies, "venture capital" (or "risk" capital) has become a significant component of commercial capital and financial capital. In the futures market, the probability of winning or losing for a speculator is one to one. (In the securities market, both sides can profit from a given transaction, while in the futures market this is not possible.) Because of this, the futures market is said to be a zero sum game. For those who engage in it, the stakes are "I win you lose" or "You win I lose." The entire activity does not generate any actual wealth for society, but it does in fact have a very positive aspect. Speculators normally buy or sell futures contracts at a value that is many times the value of the physical set-tlement of the underlying commodity. This highly speculative activity enables the person hedging his risk to carry out that hedging smoothly and easily, and to shift risk with great ease. Trading activity on the futures market, by the very nature of its frequency and turnover, allows for prices to smooth out by preventing exces-sive volatility. Speculators are indeed the recipients of profits from risk taking, but they are also the ones who shoulder the burden of that risk. Without them, the futures market could not function. When we have a thorough understanding of these things, we can begin to realize the true significance of a futures market.

As a constituent part of market economies, therefore, futures markets do indeed have a positive role to play. In this regard, the following issues should be examined. First, is a futures market absolutely necessary in the initial period of setting up a market economy? In setting one up, moreover, must the process be laissez-faire and unrestricted? How are we to assess with any accuracy the role and standing of a futures market in a market economy? Why don't all developed market economies in the world have well developed futures markets? On the contrary, why do some developed market economies actually adopt policies to prevent the development of futures markets?

Second, what are the institutional requirements for setting up a futures market? Under what kind of conditions can price discovery mechanisms and hedging functions play their proper role? Is the price-discovery function of a futures market irreplaceable, or can something else substitute for it? What role does a futures market play in both price discovery and also price distortion?

Third, within a publicly-owned economic system, is it right and proper to promote speculative activity that does not in fact add to society's material wealth? Without the constraints of any underlying assets, what kind of aberrant behavior is fostered by futures trading? Are the consequences or results of futures trading different when the trading is undertaken in a publicly-owned system and in a privately-owned system?

Fourth, given a situation in which the RMB is not fully convertible, and restrictions still apply on foreign trade, what are the possibilities of developing futures outside the borders of China ("offshore trading")? Is it really necessary for us to pay the price of some hundreds of millions or even billions of US dollars just to engage in offshore futures trading that has enormous drawbacks associated with it and very little in the way of benefits?

Some comrades believe that a market must generate its own dynamics as it is initiated and develops—it must be left on its own to grow. They feel that any market, under any conditions, will come to equilibrium. So long as equilibrium is reached, the optimum allocation of resources can be achieved. In the initial stages of market development, there is no need to impose any laws or regulations on the process, for any such restrictions will only hinder growth. Whether or not conditions are ripe for a futures market, therefore, and whether or not the market is highly irregular, the very existence of such a market will be beneficial to the establishment of a market economy system. (This kind of thinking also applies to equities and real estate markets.)

I feel, however, that this point of view is rather lopsided. In the past 20 years, achievements in economics tell us that when markets are incomplete, and when financial markets also exist (including securities markets and futures markets), then the equilibrium of the market is uncertain (or indeterminate). Because of this, external conditions must be imposed on the market from outside. Such "conditions" generally refer to government intervention. Without such additional conditions, the market will not find equilibrium and optimum resource allocation will not be realized. "Pareto Optimality" will not be achieved. As Keynes has said, "Investment may well proceed in a blind fashion when the growth of a country's capital is the mere byproduct of casino operations."[4]

In fact, the start of futures markets in the world was not a completely laissez-faire process, even though it was basically a spontaneous development. The self-discipline of the wholesale dealers' association, as well as the quasi-legal authority endowed upon the association by the government, meant that the association was fairly effective in preventing cheating and reneging on contracts. By modern times, regulation of the futures market has been more stringent and laws are far tighter. Some countries have taken a more lax approach to the establishment and conduct of their futures markets and have paid a huge price for it.

In this regard, certain countries and regions of Southeast Asia can provide some valuable lessons that are worth our attention. China's Taiwan Province went through a period when the trading in futures was flourishing, but at a time when no relevant laws or regulations had been passed to deal with the situation. Highly irregular behavior was the result. Some illicit futures brokers took advantage of customers who lacked any basic knowledge of the subject yet participated in international futures trading. Some customers were unable to receive any real market information at all, while their orders did not in fact enter any legitimate market but were settled under private arrangements. Some illicit brokers absconded with the guarantee funds (margin funds) of customers. All such activity brought grievous loss to the customers.

In Hong Kong, the process was different. Hong Kong first passed legislation and then set up a futures market. When some people strongly recommended setting up a futures market in the early 1970s, Hong Kong authorities determined that this should not happen and they would not permit it until the proper laws and regulations were in place. On August 1, 1973, the government therefore issued an order forbidding the establishment of any futures trading exchange. Not until after September 1976, when the Legislative Council formally passed proposals to set one up, did Hong Kong finally establish its first futures trading exchange. Despite the caution of Hong Kong authorities, however, Hong Kong's futures market was not able to escape the calamitous impact of the global stock market crash in the 1980s.

Let us take a look now at the role that a futures market plays in a modern market economy. The principal role relates to price discovery and risk avoidance but one cannot conclude from this that, without a futures market, one cannot determine prices or avoid risk. One cannot draw the conclusion that setting up a market-economy system cannot be done without a futures market. The fact is that futures markets encompass no more than a few dozen commodities. Meanwhile, the market itself does an excellent job of price determination and risk avoidance by allocating items for which pricing is more indeterminate, items like manufactured goods. Market-economy countries that do restrict futures markets have not found that their economic growth or market development has suffered as a result. Over-inflating the importance of a futures market is similar to over-inflating the importance of a stock market or a real estate market. It must in the end lead to skewed policy decisions that have negative consequences in the real world.

Looking at the underlying trends of futures markets, there has been a shift from commodities to financial futures in recent years. The market for commodity futures began to contract in the 1970s, while that for financial futures gradually rose to take its place as the dominant form of futures trading. The market in financial futures can roughly be divided into three types: interest-rate futures, exchange-rate futures, and stock index futures. The rise of financial futures reflected increased risk in real economic activities; this created the need to have new mechanisms to counter this risk. In the early 1970s, after the collapse of the Bretton Woods Regime, a system of floating exchange rates replaced the old system of fixed exchange rates. Western economies faced more extreme inflation. Interest-rate volatility in financial markets intensified as a result. All of this brought enormous interest-rate and exchange-rate risk to various countries, as people attempted to handle investment activities and financial management as well as domestic and international trade. Banks, corporations, and other important participants in financial markets were constantly now facing the threat of abnormal changes in interest rates and exchanges rates. The use of financial futures developed in this context, and then grew with remarkable speed.

It should be noted, however, that as financial futures began to depart from their underlying material basis, as they came to be a kind of purely monetary activity, the futures markets themselves also changed in nature. In fact, one of the reasons for the appearance of financial futures, in addition to the objective causes noted above, was the promotion of this market by speculators. This group of professionals constantly put out new categories of financial futures. These took the place of a declining market in the older kinds of futures, so the professionals dubbed themselves "pioneers" in this field, carving out new territory for their own existence and for their ability to generate wealth.

China too has its traders. They are sometimes called *chao-jia* in Chinese, people who "stir" things up in order to gain a profit. Not only do they speculate on futures, but they are able to stir things to their advantage. In recent years, the focus of their speculation has included the plant called "clivia," and postage stamps. These could be called notable "achievements" in the physical sphere of their activities. Anything is possible as a target for speculation if its price is highly indeterminate and able to be manipulated.

Because of this, a new group of financial futures has appeared that are not linked to any kind of underlying goods at all (including physical commodities but also financial instruments). These include, for example, a futures market in stock-market indexes. A stock index is generally composed of stocks that have been selected as representative of the overall market (chosen stocks are generally called constituent shares). A price index is generated through calculating the closing price of all these shares each day on the market. The futures market in the price index itself is has no corresponding material thing, and there is no "delivery" or consummation of a trade in any physical thing. There is only the delivery or "settlement" in cash. Trade in this particular kind of futures has increasingly become the target of speculators. The function of this kind of futures market has increasingly become divorced from the need to hedge in order to preserve value.

In the past few years, all kinds of financial as well as physical goods have been packaged into products that are then traded on the market as what are known as financial derivatives. They are loosely "derived" from the underlying goods. They are traded in forms that include futures but also "options" and "swaps." Financial speculation in these derived products has become extremely popular but they have greatly increased the complexities of the market and therefore added to the demands on institutions that handle the market.

It can be said that there will always be speculation so long as there is a market. Speculation is not necessarily unique to futures markets. Nevertheless, the futures market changes both commercial and financial speculation into something that is far more sophisticated, emotionally charged, and self-justifying. One cannot oppose speculation in the process of creating a market economy. On the contrary, one should recognize the lawful right of certain kinds of speculative activity to exist. At the same time, there is no great need to foster and encourage speculative activity, or certainly to deprecate the kind of honest work that goes into the production of real goods that we cannot do without for a single day.

Speculation is a kind of behavior that is highly self-initiated (spontaneous), and nations with a strong tradition of business are particularly susceptible to its attractions. Every country has explicit laws governing this behavior, as well as codes of ethics and social constraints. These serve to limit the damage that speculative behavior can do to a society. Gambling is also speculation. Some countries allow gambling under the constraints of strict laws and regulations. In China, however, gambling that does not in any way add to the material wealth of society does not enjoy proper standing, whether that is by the codes of traditional Chinese culture or whether it is in light of the modern commercial culture that is now being established.

It is clear from the above considerations that the correct approach to negative aspects of a market economy is not to evade them, or try to suppress them, but rather to use institutional means to deal with them. Institutionalized procedures should enable the market itself to allocate resources effectively and to draw forth the benefits of a market while avoiding its drawbacks. A market economy that does not have such institutionalized procedures may well be even worse than a planned economy. In line with well-developed international experience, we should therefore ensure that the following conditions are met if we intend to have a futures market that fulfills its price-discovery and risk-avoidance roles and is not just manipulated by gamblers for private benefit:

1 China should formulate trading rules that apply in a uniform way nationwide. It should not allow each exchange to set up its own rules.
2 China should set up a regulatory agency that governs futures trading and that is directly under the authority of the State Council, as well as a self-policing organization for people engaged in the business of futures trading.

3 China must set up a nationwide consolidated market for each kind of futures commodity. If one given commodity or type of futures is traded on more than one exchange, then these exchanges must have an interconnected system for exchanging price quotations.

4 China should undertake all trading in futures on the basis of competitive market prices.

5 China should set up thorough and reasonable regulations that pertain to trading, as well as accounting standards and a system for settlement.

6 China should set up a spot market that is effective and sufficient for the purpose and that has the appropriate corresponding financial structure.

7 There must be an organization that conducts the market (a futures exchange), brokers, and a sufficient number of dealers (market-making entities that provide both supply and demand of the futures), as well as speculators (who seek economic profit and can also assume economic risk).

8 There must be a well-trained cadre of people who can conduct trading and also provide research on futures markets.

9 There must be a smoothly operating communications system, a highly efficient price quotation service system, and adequate transport and warehouse systems.

10 The country's futures market should be designed with China's current resource situation in mind, including material resources and financial resources. The material commodities must be able to be defined in standardized terms.

China is currently in the midst of switching from one "track," one form of economic system, to another. Its existing economic and legal structures are not adequately prepared for conducting a futures market. It is for that reason that I note that our existing futures market is somewhat like a premature baby with congenital defects. In order to prevent its early demise or constant illness, we must consider the proper course of action. Some of the requirements for a properly functioning futures market can be set up as we go along. Some must be instituted in advance. When it is highly likely to malfunction, the negative consequences of having this very high-risk business go forward are considerable.

China is already not a blank piece of paper in this regard, however. Future markets are already sweeping across the country, and the fortunes of quite a few interest groups and individuals engaged in the business are already tied to their fate. All we can do at this point is face reality. We must adopt proactive policies that combine elements of "blocking" with elements of "channeling," in order to rectify and clean up the situation. Given that a futures market is indeed part of a market economy, and given that ours is already born into the world, all we can do is try to ensure that the child grows up in ways that are healthy and safe.

When futures markets first appeared in China, the thing that was most problematic and damaging was the practice of offshore futures trading. Illicit speculators, outside China's borders, used the ignorance of people inside the country to cheat them of very large sums of money. They did this through the means of "private settlement," (*chi dian*), fabricating market information, and even just absconding with people's money. Media reports outside China noted that, "The mainland has seen little benefit from futures, while hundreds of millions of U.S. dollars have already flowed outside the country."

Inside China, relevant documents have already ordered that any domestic trading on foreign exchanges be stopped immediately, on a nationwide basis. This move was well received by people in China, and earned a positive media response from abroad as well.

Naturally, the situation is not ideal within China's domestic markets either, where the key issue relates to inadequate laws and regulations. If we all make a concerted effort to put an end to problems, however, we should be able to get on the right track within a few years. Relatively speaking, the situation inside China is not as bad as it was outside. Although disputes within China are having a certain negative effect on the national economy, we can resolve these through administrative intervention as well as legal ways and means. The situation is not as out of control as it was in overseas trading, which caused the State an enormous loss.

One worrying thing about all this is that a futures market surged into existence before people had any idea about what it really was, while now the proper official market may well fade away to nothing before the fog clears and people know what happened. We feel that it may be politically and economically unwise to let the official futures market die altogether, whether that is from natural causes or whether the government puts a stop to it. It should be recognized that the State Council approved the establishment of 15 separate "pilot project" futures exchanges. Quite apart from these, illicit markets are springing up everywhere, under the guise of every kind of camouflage. Underground markets that trade on overseas futures exchanges are also being resurrected as they reignite from the embers that had not been put out altogether. The heedless impulse to trade on futures markets is also infiltrating every local government and department, including certain State-owned entities.

I fear that our manpower as well as our material capacity to deal with this may be insufficient. Our regulatory powers are inadequate, as well as our ability to simply prohibit these things that are raging outside the proper bounds of the system. Instead, as shown by international experience, a more effective way to handle things is to bring these (illicit) energies into the sphere of a properly organized system. It will thereby be easier to emphasize the positive aspects while dealing with the negative.

Therefore, we should candidly recognize the problems with the pilot projects approved already by the State Council, and take stricter measures in dealing with these. As with the pilot projects for other aspects of reform, we should be disciplined and constantly seek to improve, while also having a degree of patience and allowing for a process of improvement. We believe that China's futures markets will indeed enjoy a sound development as all sides put effort into the process, as the institutional context improves, and as people's mentality matures.

## Several issues to do with building an institutional context for the market

In 1993, the Nobel Prize for economics was awarded to Douglass C. North, whose theories relate to the institutional context for markets. He pointed out that the underlying conditions and context for market exchange in the real world rely to a large extent on political systems, while the very existence of and subsequent changes in a political system reflect the beliefs and inclinations of its people. Meanwhile, technological advances can have the effect of readjusting and revamping entire economic systems—they do not merely change the costs of production and costs associated with transactions.

As we attempt to "institutionalize" our market economy, therefore, I feel that we must address and come to terms with the following theoretical understandings.

The first issue relates to what the market can and cannot do. As the saying goes, "Not everything is possible with the market, but without the market, nothing is possible." The most important function of the market is that it is able to allocate resources in an efficient manner. Prices as determined by a market are a form of information that is highly acute and rich in content. Countless numbers of disparate producers and consumers rely on this information as they constantly adjust their own behavior. The market also stimulates competition, and serves in a very effective way to heighten people's attention and intelligence. The market enables different countries, regions, and individuals to use their competitive advantage in trading with one another despite enormous differences in levels of technology, national power and status, and resource endowment.

There are also many things a market cannot do, however. If one is not realistic about this, it becomes very easy to ask a market to perform functions that are beyond its power.

One of the basic functions of a futures market is price discovery. The market is not able, however, to *stabilize* commodity prices. A futures market can discover, reflect, and forecast future price inflation but it cannot create and either push forward or restrain future price inflation. Because of this, international scholars generally agree that a futures market is not the initiator of inflation, but rather a device that measures and forecasts the speed of inflation.

Trading on a futures exchange is carried out through price bids, with customers going either "long" or "short" depending on their own evaluation of price trends in the future. Since a great number of factors influence price changes, there is generally a differential between the price of an actual commodity and its futures price over time. As the date for settlement approaches, that differential tends to be reduced but it fluctuates until then. It is normal, therefore, for a futures price to be slightly higher or lower than the price of the underlying commodity until the settlement date.

Our experience over this past year has indicated that the price at time of settlement of the actual commodity is essentially the same as the spot price on that date. Even if trading of a particular item is stopped on the futures exchange, the spot price for that commodity continues to fluctuate. One case that demonstrates this occurred in May 1994. Volatility in the price for rice began to heat up on the Shanghai grain exchange, so the China Securities Regulatory Commission, the State Planning Commission, and the Ministry of Internal Trade, among other entities, joined together to conduct an investigation. At the time, the type of rice called "polished round-grained non-glutinous rice" was trading on the futures market for around RMB 2,200 per ton. The team investigating the situation announced that this was already in a dangerously high zone. They decided, through agreement, to suspend trading on some positions and later they temporarily suspended trading on the commodity altogether. When futures trading in this commodity had already stopped for a year, the spot price nevertheless continued to go up. Right now, it stands at RMB 2,800 per ton, much higher than when the trading in futures was suspended.

Another example relates to the suspension of trading in refined sugar futures. In May 1994, the futures price was RMB 4,100 per ton. By June 1995, the spot price had reached roughly RMB 4,600 per ton. What the above facts tell us is that the market identified a rising trend in prices but did not actually "discover" the extent of that price rise due to the cessation of trading. People complained about the market, but in this case without just cause. The futures market did not accomplish what it could not in fact do, which was not its fault.

One thing that a market cannot achieve automatically is balanced economic development among different regions of the country, or common prosperity among all people in society. A great number of statistics show that disparities in income, among regions and among people, actually increase dramatically in the course of "marketizing" an economy. Disparities do not decrease. It cannot be denied that the planned-economy system did indeed serve a historic role in reducing income disparities in the past. Earlier income disparities could be attributed to the unsound economy at the time, the incompetence of government, and an irrational overall system. Examples of how the planned economy attempted to change these included building huge modern factories in parts of the country that had no infrastructure at all to deal with them, enabling what had essentially been primitive "natural economies" in these areas to try to move into instant industrialization. They include implementing different wage categories in different parts of the country, and dispensing subsidies to those people working in remote areas. Nevertheless, we cannot fail to recognize that such measures were also carried out at a great cost of lowered efficiency.

Meanwhile, pricing policies that exploited farmers over a long period of time only served to increase the income disparities between rural and urban residents. This too was one of the great negative consequences of a planned economy. Since the start of reform, releasing the prices on agricultural products and the system by which these products are distributed has brought a marked improvement in the incomes of farmers. In overall terms, this has reduced the income disparity between urban and rural areas. Moreover, the "let some people get rich first" policy has created incentives and motivated people in ways that cannot be erased, and has broken through an old egalitarian mentality that celebrated "one big communal pot of rice." The "opening up to the outside," combined with a policy of enabling regional advantages has allowed the coastal region of China to develop at a fast pace. It should be noted that the resulting differential in economic growth rates between the interior of China and its coastal regions is not because of economic stagnation in the interior but rather because of economic growth along the coast. In absolute terms, the economic growth rate of the interior has not declined. Its relative lack of growth is something that can and will be resolved as the pie is made bigger.

Another thing that the market cannot accomplish spontaneously is equilibrium in aggregate demand and aggregate supply. As described above, the market deals with unbalanced supply and demand through inflation or through economic contraction. It cannot "conceal" imbalances, nor can it exaggerate them, let alone create them out of nothing. One cannot blame the market itself, therefore, for things that are merely reflected by the market. When shoddy goods or counterfeit goods appear in the market, one should not blame the market for being "too free," but should rather find fault with inadequate laws and regulations. When aggregate supply and aggregate demand are out of balance, one should look to macroeconomic measures, financial, fiscal, and trade policies, to find the problems and the solutions.

As we attempt to "institutionalize" our market economy, the second issue that I feel we must come to terms with is what the government can and cannot do with respect to the market.

No matter how complex our economic realities become, there is a simple way of putting this that will hold true. That is: the market should be allowed to deal with whatever matters it can handle. Those things that cannot be resolved by the market should be done by government. The government should indeed only do what markets are unable to do—it can play its most advantageous role when the market itself fails to resolve problems. If the government insists on performing functions that the market can perform, it will create twice the work for itself and derive half the results.

The first thing that the government should do is develop laws and regulations. This is not only a privilege that the government should enjoy, but is a responsibility that the government must fulfill. The "market" as envisaged by Adam Smith is a free market with no government intervention. In this market, a group of unrelated people theoretically creates a stable and orderly society that has no government interference just by having each individual pursue his own greatest interest. However, one also assumes that each individual, as a selfish entity, will be pursuing his greatest interests by using the least possible investment. He will seek to reap gains without any effort, which inevitably will lead to universal behavior that engages in stealing and cheating in the absence of laws to counteract such behavior. The "invisible hand of the market" is clearly powerless to deal with this. Only a tightly constructed set of laws and regulations can keep individual desires from infringing upon the rights of others. Only law can define the proper limits of what is and is not damaging to society.

To return to the question posed above: should a market first be allowed to develop on its own, or should standardized rules first be applied to its future development?

Put in other words, at what time should the government "enter into" or interfere in the market? Should this be in the initial period, or in the latter period? The issue relates partly to one's degree of confidence in "the market."

A market without regulations or legislation set by a government is like a playing field with no rules or referee. The end is such a mess that participants lose all confidence in the game. No matter how "hot" such a market becomes, in the end it will cease to be a market. One can see this in the futures markets and stock markets of some countries that failed to implement legislation—these flourished for a time, but were finally closed down due to the calamitous impact they had on the country. The lessons were quite profound. Naturally, the government is involved in the market as an entity that establishes and enforces legislation. This is not remotely the same as gratuitous interference in the market. Any casual interference by the government in the market will swiftly increase the uncertainty of that market. This will add to market risk and, again, harm the confidence of market participants.

Formulating monetary policy is a fundamental economic function of a government. Inflation, full employment, and economic growth are the three key issues of the macro economy. The government should attempt to maintain a balance between aggregate supply and aggregate demand, and it should strive for the lowest degree of inflation and unemployment while aiming for the highest rate of economic growth. Generally speaking, the government should not involve itself in the pricing of any specific goods or services but rather should focus on the overall price level of all. The government should be firm and unwavering in focusing on the most important objective of macroeconomic policies, namely the control of inflation. Once inflation does occur, the government must do all it can to bring this under control. In that effort, the key ingredient is the confidence of the people in the government's promises. Finally, counter-inflation policies require the coordination of both monetary and fiscal policies.

Public finance is the most fundamental way that a government carries out its political, economic, and social duties. Fiscal revenues and expenditures should, first of all, preserve the completeness or integrity of the government's functions. Right now, a number of things that the government should indeed be handling have been pushed out to people at large to manage on their own. The government lacks the funds to cover these things, and the result has been serious problems. For example, monies paid out to cover the salaries of civil servants are insufficient to "nurture a clean government." As public officials earn income from corrupt practices, brokering deals, and "grey-area business," the government has no alternative but to pretend it isn't seeing these things. This creates considerable leeway for the practice of self-serving corruption that operates in a myriad of ways.

The intent of the government with respect to income distribution and economic growth is made manifest by its taxation policies and fiscal expenditures. Through its own direct investment, the government encourages and supports investment in order to accomplish the objective of restructuring industries and building up regions of the country. At the same time, the government uses transfer payments to accomplish "common prosperity" in ways that even out development among regions and among different classes of society. It does all it can to ensure that low-income earners and those who lack a safety net are covered by social security guarantees.

One of the major ways in which the government intervenes in markets is through industrial policy. This concept was brought to China from Japan after the start of reform, by people in China's economic sphere. Industrial policy refers to the way the government treats an entire industry for the purpose of achieving a specific economic or social objective. Through measures that include industry protection, nurturing, readjusting and improving, the government participates in either proactive or passive ways in the industry's production, operations, and transactions. In addition, the government either directly or indirectly intervenes in the market formation activities of the industry with respect to products, services, and financing.

Actual experience has now proven that Japan successfully implemented a series of industrial policies at various times. The practice was a major factor behind Japan's swift rise after the war. In developing our own market economy, we do need to evaluate Japan's experience, but we also need to make sure that we evaluate it in more than a superficial way, or we will be led to prejudiced conclusions. One of the major differences between Japan and China lies in the underlying system. Japan's government practiced intervention in the market on the basis of a system that already had "private ownership" and that was already a market economy. We, in contrast, are attempting to establish a market economy on the basis of a planned economy. If we carry this out improperly, it is altogether possible that some of our economic management departments will reinstitute planned-economy methods under the name of "industrial policy."

It should not be forgotten that the fundamental principle underlying Japan's industrial policy respects the self-determination of the people themselves, and undertakes measures that use market mechanisms in order to promote activity by the people themselves. In the process of formulating industrial policy, in order to incorporate the opinion of "the people," knowledgeable representatives from both the government and civil society organized all kinds of deliberating committees, and the country then institutionalized the process. When implementing industrial policies, the government presented generalized policy objectives in the form of ideas about industrial structure. Any specific details were given to the people themselves to decide upon. Governmental intervention was kept to the smallest possible scope of activity. In China, on the contrary, "industrial policy" is ubiquitous. Even the securities markets are being asked to get in line with policy measures as required by "the government." (In fact, it is specific departments that are the ones presenting these demands.)

As we attempt to "institutionalize" our market economy, I believe that the third thing we must do is break down the monopolies that exist in certain sectors.

The reason we are trying to create a market economy is in order to bring competition into our system and improve efficiency. Having an adequate number of buyers and sellers is the first and foremost condition for enabling market competition. If this condition is not met, marginal prices cannot be equated to true market prices, nor will marginal social production costs reflect true market prices. When either the buyer or the seller is a monopoly, market mechanisms become ineffective.

For example, market mechanisms will not function unless we open up multi-channel operations to handle our grain business. If we merely release prices on the grain that is handled outside the "purchasing order" system, but do not open up the entire system by which grain is stored, transported, and sold, then market mechanisms will have no chance of being effective. In the "purchasing" link of the process, farmers have no alternative but to deal with one buyer, the State-owned grain system (commissariat system). This system then inevitably becomes the monopoly seller when it operates in the wholesale grain market at anything above the county level.

What this means is that farmers cannot sell their grain at a good price, while consumers still have to pay out a relatively high price. We often note that there are too many intermediate companies in the whole circulation process, and they are the reason intermediary fees are excessively high. In fact, this is a misunderstanding of the situation. Intermediaries in the circulation process represent a kind of service, and the pricing of the service should be determined by supply and demand. If supply is abundant, then naturally the price will fall. In similar fashion, if the service itself is in the form of a monopoly, then the price will obviously be kept at a high level and never come down. The same logic can be applied to the circulation system governing the petroleum industry, the refined oil products industry, and the chemical fertilizer industry.

Fourth, we must break down regional protectionism, local "blockades," as we attempt to institutionalize our market economy.

One important path to market efficiency is through increasing the scope of the market and getting rid of anything that obstructs market transactions. Some analysis has tried to say that the reason we have regional protectionism is that local governments intervene too much in economic affairs. There is some logic to this, but it is not the whole story. One of the reasons for regional protectionism is indeed the fact that "government" and "enterprise" are still one and the same, and not split out from one another. The government's authorities and responsibilities with respect to business affairs are unclear. Other reasons, however, should be noted. Our existing system of taxation strengthens the interests of the local government. What's more, when facing job performance evaluations, local government cadres are evaluated on their economic performance, and the criteria by which they are judged are generally not in line with principles of economic efficiency.

For example, criteria might include the rate of economic growth of a given locality, the total amount of foreign exchange that the place is able to generate from exports, the price index of the locality, and so on. When the price of a given commodity is fixed on a nationwide basis by the central government, however, this may well harm the interests of a specific locality. This locality may then "blockade" its own markets in order to protect its own interests.

In recent years, some provinces attempted to keep rice prices low within their own provinces. They did this by preventing farmers from selling their rice to neighboring provinces at a higher price. Government officials even put sentries on guard at crossing points, in order to seal transportation routes. Other such examples are common, known in short as the "corn wars," the "silkworm wars," the "cotton wars," and so on. As prices have been released (as controls on prices have been relaxed), and as the public finance taxation system has been reformed, the phenomenon of blockaded localities has improved. The central government intends to continue to adopt forceful measures that ensure that the country is able to preserve a nationwide, unified market. Such a unified market is highly significant in both economic and political terms.

The fifth thing we must do as we institutionalize our market economy is to use the process of "internationalizing" to help us create institutions. We should also use the process of institutionalizing the market to help us realize greater international engagement.

It should be recognized that "opening up" the country was a tremendous boost to the whole process of institutionalizing the market. Our proactive participation in international competition and international economic cooperation helped us to make use of our own competitive advantage. Of necessity, it meant that our domestic economic system had to be put on the same track, in terms of standards, as that of international economic practices.

If you want to participate in international competition, you have to be fully familiar with international rules of the game and you have to follow those rules. We cannot imagine that we will be able to shut the door, train up our team by using our own rules, and then send it forth to try to win gold medals. In recent years, we have come up against a lot of disputes in the conduct of foreign economic exchange, and most of the problems issued from differences in systems, regulations, and customs. Because of this, we should accelerate the process of creating market institutions and bringing them into line with standard international principles. We have absolutely no experience in formulating a number of rules and regulations to do with the market. One shortcut that we might consider is adopting those laws and regulations of other countries that are already well thought through, so long as they are suited to our own national conditions.

Sixth, we must deepen the reach of our market economy in a sequenced and incremental way, and in a way that is in line with reality. In terms of economic sectors, this "deepening" includes moving into the spheres of financial markets, labor markets, real estate markets, technology markets, information markets. All of these can be thought of as markets in production factors. In terms of actual "depth," we should set up market rules and sound market organizations, break up all kinds of monopolies, and oppose all kinds of irregular or illicit competition. In terms of levels of approach, we must issue from reality and only gradually, and through pilot projects, particularly as we implement plans for various kinds of futures markets, options markets, and markets in other financial derivatives.

The Party's "Decision" pointed out that we must "make sure that the pilot projects carrying out commodity futures markets in a small number of commodities are regulated in a strict manner." (*The Decision on several issues to do with establishing a socialist market-economy system*, set forth at the Third Plenary Session of the 14th Central Committee of the Communist Party of China.)

This makes sense in three respects:

First, futures markets should be strictly "regular" or standardized. Second, they should be limited to commodity futures markets for the time being. Third, we should only carry forward a small number of pilot projects. These pilot projects should form the basis for all legislation and policies to do with futures markets for a certain period of time into the future. At the very least, we must create the following institutional conditions as we set up futures markets:

1   We must have price formation mechanisms that function in a free market in general terms. The market must be based on a sound and robust spot market. At the earliest time, we should eliminate the two-track system that still applies to certain important production materials, as well as any camouflaged or disguised "mandatory supply and marketing plans" (such as the system that gives preference to the State in ordering materials, and that then enables supply of goods with a guaranteed quantity but not a guaranteed price). Otherwise, it will be hard for the futures market to avoid the gradual seeping in of administrative interference that is currently distorting the existing futures market.

2   We must have an adequate number of market participants who have also been through reform of their property rights so that property rights (ownership and accountability) are clearly defined. In the futures market, participants must be operating on an autonomous basis, that is, must be responsible for their own losses as well as profits. This goes for both producers and operators, and for both those hedging in order to preserve value and those who are speculating. Otherwise, those wanting to hedge to preserve value will be unconcerned about the cost of doing so and will not try to avoid the risk of price fluctuations. Those who are speculating will feel no pressures to make decisions on the basis of knowing they will not survive if they make the wrong call. (We cannot have both sides covered by public funding.) If market participants do not operate under these constraints, then the result will either be that no actual "market" results, or the market is overly speculative. According to surveys, the futures markets currently operating in China are crowded with speculators but have few hedgers. Such an overly speculative market will simply become the wellsprings for a bubble. It will be similar to the bubble that has occurred in China's overly speculative real estate market.

3   We must have a financial system that works in conformity with the futures market, as well as a foreign-exchange control system and a foreign-trade administrative system that conform to similar requirements.

    At present, our "commercial banks" and our "policy banks" are one and the same. Their policy-related business (using State funds) is not divided out from purely commercial business. While bank operating mechanisms have not yet been transformed, it is highly seductive to people if they can use bank loans (State funds) to finance futures trading. The settlement procedures associated with futures trading also present substantial institutional barriers to the business. Our current foreign trade system does not allow for domestic markets and international markets to be interconnected. Price formation is actually set more by administrative elements connected with foreign trade management than any market considerations. It is therefore rather hard for the price discovery mechanism of the futures market to play its intended role. Given that the RMB is not fully convertible, brokerage firms are breaking the law 100 percent when they deal in offshore trading with its foreign-exchange exit and entry requirements. This illegal activity is quite above and beyond the cheating in terms of private settlements that I described earlier.

4   The establishment of the futures markets must be carried out in a staged way, under the unified leadership of a national futures exchange regulatory commission. No other administrative organization has the authority to extend permits, or to set up futures trading locations. Futures trading cannot be conducted under the jurisdiction of any given administrative department. In similar fashion, no administrative entity has the authority to approve the establishment of futures trading brokerage firms. Any application to establish such a brokerage firm must undergo a rigorous examination by a professional organization authorized to conduct this review, and the review should, in particular, focus on credit background. Any State-owned institution or enterprise that engages in futures trading activity must be subject to strict controls.

## Notes

1   Originally published in *Reform*, 1995, Vol. 5. Collected in *The Road to a Market Economy: Comprehensive Framework and Working Proposals* with Wu Jinglian, Zhou Xiaochuan, and Rong Jingben as Editors-in-Chief (Central Compilation and Translation Press, Beijing, 1996 edition, 2nd edition in 2000). Winner of the 1996 Sun Yefang Prize for Economic Papers.
2   Stanley Fischer and Rudiger Dornbusch: *Economics*, China Financial & Economic Publishing House (Beijing), 1989, 20.
3   Macroeconomics is a modern approach to economic analysis catering to data aggregates rather than individual data. It studies overall economic life, the total size, form and role of economic experiences instead of the role of individual parts. More specifically, it analyzes the general level of commodity prices rather than the prices of individual commodities; it is not the revenue of individual manufacturers but gross national products and national income instead; it refers to general employment rather than the employment of individual manufacturers. See the *Dictionary of Modern Economics: A Handbook of Terms and Organizations*, Douglas Greenwald as Editor-in-Chief.
4   John Maynard Keynes: *The General Theory of Employment, Interest and Money*, The Commercial Press (Beijing), 1996, 159.

# 4 The role, responsibility, and destiny of economists[1]

## (1998)

Sun Yefang is, without question, the most outstanding among China's modern economic statesmen. This is not just because he consistently stood at the forefront of the science of economics, serving as a leader, but also because of his strength of character. He was tenacious and steady throughout a life that had to deal with tremendous turbulence. We must look upon his scholarly and theoretical contributions in the light of the times that he lived through, for only then can we understand both their limitations and their highly progressive nature. In evaluating his approach to scholarship and his academic courage, we must have enduring admiration for the example that he bequeathed to us, not only to economists, but to those in any field of endeavor.

As one of a later generation, I did not have the opportunity to learn from him directly or meet him while he was still in good health. I read his limited number of works while studying as a postgraduate student in economics at the Chinese Academy of Social Sciences, and I knew something of his life history, but I very much regret not having had that personal contact. Fortunately, I have been able to work under the direction and leadership of a number of people with whom he did commune in life, including his friends, colleagues, students, and assistants. These included Xue Muqiao, Xu Xuehan, Liu Guoguang, Wu Jinglian, Gui Shiyong, and Zhang Zhuoyuan. From them, I began to understand more about this distinguished gentleman. My understanding did not extend to any great details, but was enough to give me a sense of tremendous respect and admiration for the man.

The Sun Yefang Foundation has asked me to write an article commemorating him. I cannot provide any personal reminiscences in what follows, but I thought I would take the opportunity to use the reflected light of his example to talk about the role and responsibilities of economists in general. In giving serious consideration to this subject, I use the experience of China's reform over these past years, and my own experience. Talking about what economists are able to do in their lives may be the best way for us to pay tribute to our late master.

The first question that presents itself is whether or not the country, and indeed society at large, really needs economists. The question might seem to be superfluous but in fact is not irrelevant at all.

Prior to the Cultural Revolution, China also had economists. Their task at that time was mainly to annotate the classics by Marx and Lenin, as presented in economic texts coming out of the Soviet Union, and to promote the country's economic policy according to required dictates. Economists rarely had their own independent views. Needless to say, they did not conduct any kind of significant research. If they were inclined to have a humble opinion, they had little opportunity to publicize this, let alone the courage to do so. It was impossible for people with real strength of character and a firm point of view to escape from being persecuted and denounced during repeated political movements. Such people included Sun Yefang and his close friend Gu Zhun.

Given this situation, the role of economists in society was to serve as lackeys to those in power, as a kind of adornment to the system. During the Cultural Revolution, economists were treated in the same way as "intellectuals." They were classified as the "stinking ninth category," people who could be criticized and beaten with impunity. Sun Yefang, Gu Zhun, and other economists who had dared to have their own ideas were subjected to an even worse fate.

The process of reform and opening up presented economists with tremendous room to grow and develop. A group of people who had grown up during the "traditional" system now set themselves to revamping their thinking and catching up with the times. They became pioneers in criticizing the old structure and in presenting a more enlightened theoretical basis for reform. An even larger group of younger, next-generation economists now surged forth to take up the challenges as the economy developed. Both older and younger economists attained an unprecedented standing in the eyes of the public and were able to make very positive contributions to the endeavor of reform and opening up.

Nevertheless, respect for knowledge and the pursuit of truth did not in fact become the prevailing sentiment in the country. In the actual conduct of economic activity (business), economists generally came up against ridicule and exclusion. This phenomenon was deeply rooted in Chinese tradition. Doctrinaire beliefs have done tremendous damage throughout Chinese history. This ancient nation has maintained a very practical and empirical approach throughout its past. It has looked down upon "knowledge" (particularly specialized knowledge), been contemptuous of theory (especially applied theory), and ostracized intellectuals. Such unfortunate habits have permeated our very bones and have long held back economic development and social progress.

As with other people in specialized fields, economists have generally been derided as people who lack any practical experience. Any theoretical approach to economic phenomena has been regarded as nothing more than "wasting time on researching the functions of a horse's tail." If the view of any given economist was not to the liking of someone, he could be dismissed quite easily with such comments as, "he has never really done any practical work," or "this is not in accord with China's real situation." In contrast, if an economist's views were indeed to someone's taste, that "economist" would be lauded with praise, never mind that he might never have read a book on economics in his life, or done any research, and indeed worked in any department or institution. We have an example of this in recent years, when a person who had never read economics, or written anything about economics to speak of, was nevertheless crowned with accolades just because the opinions he offered up met various needs.

From looking at the scholarly research conducted by Sun Yefang, we can recognize that penetrating insights into economic reality do not necessarily come from governing a district or managing an enterprise. Many different paths and methods can lead to a better understanding of economics. For example, in thinking about how to formulate economic policy, we must sum up the lessons of China's experiences in the past and also review the experience of other countries, not merely cling to one or two conventional precedents. We must also make use of statistical data that are relevant to the entire situation, and that does not necessarily mean "going down to the grassroots level" (to Party work at the local level). Understanding the whole by analyzing a part of the whole is indeed an analytical method—in poetic terms, it is always described as understanding the passage of time by seeing one leaf fall, and understanding the universe of "cold" by studying the ice in a bucket. However, inferring future trends from existing laws is also a way of understanding and analyzing reality. This too is reflected in the wisdom of Chinese sayings that refer to understanding the past in order to know the present.

I am confident that what I just said will not be misinterpreted as any kind of opposition to "getting down to grass roots" or "getting in touch with the actual situation." What we are emphasizing here is that proper respect should be accorded to the methods used by economists, and to their specific ways of thinking. The relationships among all kinds of modern economic operations are extremely complex. Some relationships are counter-intuitive, despite their importance in terms of both the exterior phenomena and the underlying nature. Understanding these things is precisely where the value of economics comes in.

In doing economic research, or deciding upon economic policy, therefore, it is quite insufficient to draw upon a vague memory of what one learned long ago in textbooks. (This holds particularly if they were classic texts from the planned-economy era.) Fragmentary experience from the past is also inadequate, and even dangerous, particularly if it relates to things that were both mistakes and failures. What is needed, instead, is an understanding of modern economic principles, and then a prudent application of them to practical situations. In essence, being contemptuous of theory is equivalent to being contemptuous of any scientific laws at all. As Sun Yefang famously said in the past, "The laws of economics are not like some minion that one can call upon to serve a particular need, and then dismiss. They have their own objective existence, whether you admit that or not." Basing things purely on one's intuition and personal experience, while rejecting theory and the underlying rules of economics, will lead to tragedy in the end. The law of value has come back at us time and again, to remind us of this. Only after bitter experience have we learned the value of Sun Yefang's contributions and begun to recognize his position in history.

It is said that one reason people look down on economists is that "you will find at least five different points of view among three economists." This naturally exaggerates the situation, but it is indeed true that there are often differing opinions among economists. So long as the economists hold their positions responsibly, and back their words up with data, all sides can be highly useful in formulating national economic policy. All sides should be given full respect by the public.

Meanwhile, economists themselves should attempt to foster an atmosphere that accommodates various points of view.

A variety of factors go into the divergent views of economists. These include different academic training, perspectives, methodology, and life experience. For example, many economists engaged in a fairly heated debate in the early 1980s about whether or not China could achieve the target of doubling gross national product (GNP) and then doubling it again. In some people's estimate, the target could not be realized. They felt that capital and resource constraints would be hard to overcome, particularly given the low levels of China's energy reserves and the country's inability to develop new energy sources. Another point of view, as expressed by Sun Yefang, believed that the difficulties could be overcome. The objective could be reached. Both sides presented reasons to back up their conclusions, as well as a great deal of quantitative analysis. Actual economic results were, of course, to prove that the view espoused by Sun Yefang was correct. In looking at what happened, pessimistic views about economic development by the year 2000 were not in accord with later facts.

Nevertheless, this pessimistic view turned out to be quite useful. It helped alert us to the need to be more proactive in importing foreign capital, and in focusing on our energy constraints. We increased investments and accelerated technological advances in this sector. We also did everything possible to extend support to other bottleneck industries such as agriculture, transport, and raw materials. As a result, we were indeed able to meet our goals.

Estimates of potential economic growth in the future are often determined by looking at such underlying conditions as financial and natural resources, the environment, and particularly energy. Pessimistic appraisals have often been the result in many countries. Oil is one example. Since the early 1870s, experts have underestimated oil reserves. Back then, a geologist in Pennsylvania published a dire warning that said America only had enough petroleum to burn its lamps for four years. Experts later pushed back the time when resources would dry up—first to the 1920s, then the 1940s. In the 1970s, the Club of Rome[2] shocked everyone by saying that existing oil reserves would only be enough for the next 20 to 30 years. Right now, however, we see that reserves are at their highest point in history. The key to this is that the results from technological advances have already been, and continue to be, simply astonishing.

Over the past decade, the average cost per barrel of oil, including both exploration and extraction, has gone down by 60 percent. Meanwhile, proven reserves have increased by over 60 percent as compared to 1985. In fact, such official figures underestimate the amount of underground reserves that are available for exploitation. The petroleum research association called Smith Rea Energy Ltd. (UK), based in London, believes that proven global reserves would increase by 350 billion barrels if we included oil that could currently be exploited with new technologies. This figure is equivalent to the amount of oil consumed on a worldwide basis over the past 14 years. The pessimistic message of the Club of Rome has almost become the butt of jokes. At the same time, I feel that this "divergent viewpoint" has also been extremely helpful to the world. It has helped in getting the world to focus on conservation, environmental protection, and knowledge that will help us create strategies for sustainable growth.

Economic forecasting as done by economists often is not in accord with what actually happens. The public then takes economists to task, which becomes a reason for policy makers to brush economists off as well. In point of fact, economic forecasting is not the same thing as weather forecasting. The weather is a natural, objective phenomenon, whereas economic activity is a highly complex form of human and social behavior. It is the result of an interaction between the subjective and the objective. When economists come up with a bleak prospect for the future, people can adopt measures to avoid the damage by relying on economists' recommendations. Calamities then fail to materialize as predicted. Not only is this not because economists were incompetent, but it proves the point: economists have the ability to make a unique contribution to society.

We should promote the idea that any policy recommendations to do with key economic "guidelines" of the government should be passed along to economists first in order for them to review them closely. The ancients had a saying that I will paraphrase as follows: "when the situation is not ripe to do something and yet people barrel ahead, in the end it will lead to reluctance to carry through. When the public has not given thorough consideration to something, such as reforming a given system, and yet the government barrels ahead, in the end it will lead to reluctance to really change anything." By this, I mean to emphasize the great importance of prudent decision-making. Economists have a vital role to play in this regard.

Economists should think of their own social standing in the proper light. In terms of their own status, they should follow the example of Sun Yefang: have a high sense of social responsibility and a commitment to both the people and the governing authority. Economists should meet professional standards that include professional ethics and rules of behavior. They should be rigorous in applying a scholarly attitude to their work and conscientious in applying the accomplishments of theory, even as they build up their own practical experience.

In recent years, we see a worrying trend developing as economists pursue instant success and quick profits by catering to whatever is popular. People do not set their sights on science, or the truth. Instead, they are obsequious to power. They seek reputation and personal reward. This depreciates the field of economics and turns it into an excuse for doing practical things in this way or that way (i.e. business). Some people devote themselves to attending all kinds of conferences that have little in the way of professional significance, where they "sell" poppycock theories. Some researchers insist upon making pronouncements in fields that they know little about, and they write what can only be described as "fast-food economics." At the worst, some publish papers on the stock market that pretend at analysis, while linking up with relevant entities to carry on stock manipulation at the same time. The wealth that these people earn from such behavior is not equitable or just. Fewer and fewer economists are now willing to carry on serious work, willing to do the solitary hard task of researching theoretical issues. The public and the times are greatly in need of calling the spirit of Sun Yefang back to Earth.

When the country prospers, economists prosper, and when the people are flourishing, economists flourish as well. The destiny of economists has always been bound together with the destiny of the nation and its people. Although there are areas for concern, it can still be said that we economists are living in the best of times since the field of economics began in China. "The responsibility is heavy upon us and the road before us is long."

We economists must do all we can to nurture the spirit of Sun Yefang that still lives among us.

## Notes

1  This article was included in *Economic Research*, no. 9, 1998.
2  The Club of Rome is a global think tank that deals with a variety of international political issues. It was founded in 1968 at Accademia dei Lincei in Rome, Italy.

# 5 On capital markets[1]
## (2000)

The hottest economic topic in China these days is capital markets. People are intensely interested in the subject, from the highest level of the country's leadership to the lowest tiers of society and from highly knowledgeable economists to the common man with a modest level of education. Not only are they concerned about the direction the markets might take, but they have their own opinions about the markets themselves, their benefits, drawbacks, pros and cons.

It reminds me somewhat of the situation in the period after the book *Dream of a Red Chamber* came out (after it was allowed to be read in China again). Chinese literati and intellectuals were utterly immersed in reading and discussing the classic. Since the start of reform and opening up, the country's capital markets have similarly been able to attract the broadest spectrum of public attention for the longest sustained period of time of any topic. These days, if any form of mass media neglects the stock market, it begins to lose readership or viewers right away. And if an economist fails to discuss the markets as a key topic, he himself begins to think that he is simply falling behind. Since capital markets represent the concentration of a large amount of economic resources, a great wealth of human as well as financial resources go into studying them. Among other things, this results in countless articles addressing their various aspects.

Despite all of this, questions about the markets continue to stream forth. They are quite legitimate questions and require the ongoing attention of our entire society. I group them into five areas below in order to present my own understanding of these things.

## Issues relating to the role of securities markets, their functions, and their regulation

After China had resolved the whole issue of whether stock markets should be regarded as "capitalist" or "socialist," the problem remained of defining their benefits and drawbacks. This then became a hot topic among economic theorists. The issue came to the fore particularly after the Asian financial crisis and the multitude of problems that this crisis exposed in China's domestic stock market. Scholarly circles in the country then carried on a debate about how to evaluate not just the stock market itself, but also capital markets in general and the whole field of money and finance. Debate on the "virtual economy" has been carried out against this backdrop. Clarifying the various points of view in this debate will be helpful in our understanding of the current role and function of contemporary capital markets.

### Two totally different interpretations of the term "virtual economy"

For quite some time now, people have been carrying on a ferocious debate about what constitutes a virtual economy. Each person has a completely different concept in mind. The debate therefore goes around in circles, talking about fundamentally different things, no matter whether the points of view are positive or negative on the subject. This has been going on for more than a year, with no answers in sight. It looks as though we must first sketch out a clearer definition of "virtual economy" before evaluating the various opinions being expressed.

The term "virtual economy" was first used in order to distinguish it from the real economy. In traditional textbooks, the term "real economy" (or one could call it the material economy) was in turn used in contrast to the monetary economy. The concept of a virtual economy arose in western countries in the 1990s, as something that represented a "counterpart" to, or as distinct from, the real or material economy.

In China, economists often describe the phenomenon of an economic bubble in the monetary economy as a "virtual economy," however. This type of virtual economy is not the same thing. One is "virtual," the other could be called "fictitious." Two different concepts in English were translated into the same term in Chinese, which has caused some confusion. The ambiguity in the debate going on right now stems in part from this misunderstanding.

In English, the term virtual economy does indeed embody a meaning that is opposite to a "real economy." The term comes from the Latin, "*virtus*," which incorporates the sense that "a thing may be the same in substance even if it is superficially different." Or one could say that "a thing may be consistent in logic and function even if it is inconsistent in form." It is in this sense that the term "virtual" is used in general practice throughout the English-speaking world. For example, a "virtual enterprise" in enterprise management is a new form of enterprise that can accommodate the needs of networking, information-sharing, and knowledge-based business. Computer science uses the term with respect to "virtual memory," and "virtual networks," which have essentially the same functions as real memory and real networks.

In classical economics, a "real economy" is one that is based on "physical capital." A virtual economy is one that is based on "knowledge capital" but that has the same functions as a real economy. This is the first thing mentioned by Peter Drucker in works that discuss the knowledge economy. Drucker pioneered a whole new epoch in the sphere of scientific management, which had the effect of nurturing a group of new-style entrepreneurs. One of his primary works was *The Post-Capitalist Society*, published in 1993, in which he set his first formulation of the characteristics of a "knowledge economy."

Economic laws that pertain to a knowledge economy are different from those of a classical economy in many respects. Because of the complementary nature of knowledge, the basic premise of neo-classical economics becomes invalid, namely that of diminishing returns. It is for this reason that some economists over the past ten years have said that we need to rewrite economics if we are to understand the new phenomena associated with the appearance of a knowledge-based society.

Microsoft has used the capital markets to acquire high-priced "conceptual companies" or "idea companies." Yahoo shares are sought after by the market, even though the company's search engine is fundamentally unprofitable. Hong Kong's Pacific Century Cyber Works (PCCW) has seen its share price soar despite having almost no business at all. These are some concrete examples of the virtual economy. "Capital" is no longer connected to "human labor" in this economy. Instead, it is connected to "knowledge." In the process, the virtual economy is capable of generating enormous economic incentives and financial returns.

From the above, it can be seen the term itself is neutral. It simply describes a developing trend that can be seen in economies around the world. When Chinese economists reject or repudiate a virtual economy, therefore, foreign economists simply shake their heads in dismay.

One reason foreign economists simply cannot understand our debate on this subject relates to misunderstandings that arise from the translation of certain concepts. Many of us take the words "virtual economy" to mean something like what Marx meant when he used the term. That usage more approximated what we currently mean when we say a "bubble economy." When Marx wrote "virtual capital," this was translated into "fictitious capital" in English, and into "fiktives kapital" in German. Either way, the meaning is not remotely the same as "virtual" in English. The original intent of Marx should have been translated into terms like false, or illusory, or imaginary, rather than virtual. If the translators of *Das Kapital* had known that mankind would come up with a completely different usage of the term in the future, they might have selected their terms differently and avoided our current confusion.

In the third volume of *Das Kapital*, Marx describes what he regards as fictitious capital. This includes things that merely "represent" capital, such as interest-bearing commercial paper (bills of exchange), public securities (state bonds, treasury bonds, stocks of various sorts), mortgage certificates relating to real estate, and so on. Marx approached the issue of fictitious capital from the perspective of his research into banking capital. Fictitious capital arose together with a bank's use of credit. This enabled not only currency (money) to "receive" "usage value" above and beyond the actual sum of the currency or money, but the tool of bank credit also received a similar usage value above and beyond the actual amount of money. On the one hand, fictitious capital had an enormous influence on such things as capital accumulation, circulation, and consumption. On the other hand, possibilities for different uses multiplied for such fictitious capital, which in turn increased risk possibilities for both individuals and society at large.

According to Marx, fictitious capital was the product of an increase in bank credit, which distorted capital markets. All speculation, bubbles, and even financial crises were caused by the excessive development of fictitious capital. The only "true economy" was represented by the production of real things and the real economy that handled them. This viewpoint as presented by Marx then became the standard for the way things were expressed in economics textbooks of the Soviet Union. It can be said that, to this day, this standard still represents a shining form of "truth" for some people. I believe that we should understand this approach that dates from over 100 years ago, but we should not be rigid in our adherence to it. At this new turn of the century, we recognize that the world's economy has undergone earth-shattering change in the past 100 years. It is only natural that we should be able to get over and move beyond certain concepts inherent in traditional schools of thought.

The entry for "fictitious capital" in the authoritative *New Palgrave Dictionary of Economics* mentions that not only Marx but others also used the concept, including Friedrich Hayek.[2] In Hayek's view, when investment and saving (as broadly defined) are consistent, or the same, the stability of capital markets is ensured. If savings fail to increase in line with the growth of bank credit, which stimulates enterprises to invest, there will then be a crisis. As the *New Palgrave* says, "Today, economists rarely use the concept of fictitious capital." Generally speaking, Marx and other western economists used the term "fictitious capital" in a pejorative fashion, but they never extended this negative connotation to the concept of a "fictitious economy."

Why have financial assets grown at a far faster pace than gross domestic product (GDP) has risen in recent years? A close examination of the statistical data of various countries shows that this is a necessary product of modern economic development. Financial assets include the value of such "derived" products as futures, options, and swaps, and the value of these things is based on their ability to mitigate risk. In mature futures markets around the globe, the total volume of physical transactions comes to between 1 and 5 percent of the value of the futures market. This does not mean that the other 95 to 99 percent of all futures trades are meaningless speculations. Without the participation of speculative capital in the market, the 1 to 5 percent of physical trading volume would run up against major obstacles. Speculative capital serves a function in price discovery and risk avoidance precisely because it is willing to take on risk itself. Without it, trades in physical goods would have to take on enormous risk. The Nobel laureate James Tobin showed this in his research back in the early 1950s, as confirmed by empirical results. Naturally, the situation was greatly complicated by the appearance of financial index futures and options, but the fundamental principles and functions underlying these derivatives have not changed.

As Marx pointed out, the production of commercial goods (goods to be sold) requires a kind of breathtaking acceptance of risk. Indeed, without ways to moderate risk, it would not happen. Human cooperation has always involved risk, including both moral risk (moral hazard) and natural risk. If there were not some way to disperse that risk, and tools by which to avoid it, the scope of human cooperation would remain highly limited. Specialized division of labor would not proceed. Economies of scale would not be possible, costs would not be constantly lowered, and economic and scientific progress would not move ahead.

Stock markets, for example, provide liquidity and an exit channel for investors. Without stock markets, venture capital would not be willing to invest in innovative scientific ventures. The unbelievable advances in high-end science and technology would be unthinkable without the "irrigating" function of the wellsprings of large amounts of such capital.

Therefore, it is an oversimplification and somewhat superficial to think that the expansion of the monetary economy (financial activities) is leading to complete disassociation with the underlying real economy. Not only can we not do without finance, but we cannot fail to operate by international rules of the game in conducting our own finance. We should frequently remind ourselves that the systems built up by mankind over generations are extremely valuable, and we should keep ourselves from rushing into hasty decisions. It may well be that we cannot take in and master all of the systems right away, but we should not treat them lightly in the meantime.

Financial crises can occur in any society that makes use of financial instruments. After the eruption of the Asian financial crisis, we saw a wave of criticism within China that argued against going further with financial reform or with "financial innovations." As it happened, once the crisis passed, Asian economies have already gradually been restored through the use of institutional reform and restructuring. Now that things have cooled off, most people will be willing to admit that financial crises are something nobody likes, but they are inescapable at times and can be educational. They are the cost that society must pay in the process of economic development and institutional improvement. Of course, one always hopes that the cost will be as low as possible. In brief, one cannot imagine that any market can avoid financial risk altogether if it wants to become more mature.

Given that financial instruments have become so important in helping mankind expand the scope of cooperation, and given that financial assets are closely tied to the speed of information flow as well as to people's expectations, it is understandable why the market value of these things has grown at multiples of the growth rate of GDP. This is particularly true for economies in the stage of "monetization." Naturally, we do not want to see financial bubbles caused by psychological factors in our financial markets. This can be extremely damaging to the underlying physical economy but it nevertheless is a universal phenomenon. Controlling bubbles and countering crises is a matter of "moving one step backward and two steps forward." It is a matter of proper handling of the relationship between opportunities and challenges as an economy develops. It is something that no purely ideological approach can be of any help with.

A second consideration here is how to evaluate the phenomenon of a disconnect between the two tiers of prices, one in the monetary economy and the other in the physical economy. As noted above, finance and actual goods are two sides of the same process by which humans cooperate with one another. The price signals that each of these systems generates are signals of the same process as seen from two different perspectives. Although they may frequently deviate from one another, they are intimately interconnected. Deviations are determined by the channels through which and the speed at which information flows.

For example, once credit expanded greatly, a temporary deviation could then exist between the pricing of a company's shares and the measurement of its results. The reason is that a certain period of time was required for a company's internal information to be brought to the light of day. Right now, in mature financial markets, the time required for such information to "catch up" with the market is around three months. (This is the result of the quarterly nature of corporate results.) That is, it takes three months for the financial markets to reflect the underlying physical economics. In a market such as China's, the deviation between market price and the underlying actuality in an enterprise is much greater, given the ubiquitous practice of falsification of financial reports. The length of time that the deviation lasts is also fairly long. No matter how listed companies cover up their data, however, or how securities firms "package data," in the end such deviations must necessarily disappear and the price of the shares must return to a level that is in line with reality.

Finance is important to humans since it can relieve uncertainties and mitigate risk in the process of enabling humans to cooperate with one another. We agree with certain colleagues when they note and take issue with the deviation or difference between the virtual economy and the physical economy. However, we do not agree with the idea of trying to create a better system to achieve the same ends, just because of this difference. Given the limited knowledge of humans, we do not think it wise to try to create an ideal system that is purer than pure, for that certainly would lead to even greater institutional distortion.

Reform brought with it the introduction of capital markets into China. The primary aim was to help optimize resource allocation and further improve operations within enterprises. It was not done merely for the purpose of enabling enterprises to raise funds, and it certainly was not to create a place where people could gain profits that were disassociated with any underlying production activity. Nevertheless, given people's hallucinatory approaches to making money, the moment you have a capital market, you will have people who use it for speculative manipulation in order to make a profit. Speculation is a natural companion to capital markets. No matter how tightly you define regulations that pertain to the market, it is impossible to stop up or block off all speculative activity. No market exists without some speculation and that goes even more for capital markets. If we do indeed aim to have capital markets, then we must accommodate a certain amount of speculation. Naturally, such illegal behavior as manipulating the market and insider trading is a different subject altogether, and cannot be allowed. It must be attacked and suppressed with all force of disciplinary action and laws.

Statistics indicate that the current "financial expansion effect" is directly related to the "high tide" of aging populations in western countries. In the past decade, western countries, and particularly the United States, are seeing a wave of retirement of people born just after the war. Trillions of dollars worth of pension funds are flowing into the capital markets. An excess of capital is madly seeking limited opportunities for investment, leading to an ongoing rise in the global stock markets. This kind of demographic factor, that is, age structure, is necessarily impacting the speed at which financial markets are expanding, and is something we have to accept as an objective fact. Some economists predict that after the peak of the aging population declines, after 2010, share prices in mature market economies will greatly decline. This is the basis for the "demographic theory" of those who are predicting a huge bear market.

With respect to the role and function of modern finance, we cannot fail to mention a "heretic" in America who became influential in Chinese intellectual circles for a brief period of time around the year 1996. Lyndon LaRouche claimed that humanity had caught what he termed "financial AIDS." This was an extremist view of the rapidly expanding financial world. The predictions of LaRouche did in fact coincide, by chance, with the eruption of the Asian financial crisis in 1997, although he won no credibility as a result. In order to enflame people's emotions, LaRouche greatly exaggerated the negative aspects of financial activity, and called for a return to prehistoric societies when people simply exchanged physical goods. He warned repeatedly about the coming collapse of human society in the midst of financial crisis. No person in his right mind takes any note of such talk. Meanwhile, human society appears to carry on, albeit in a circuitous way that is not without its problems.

### *Defining the functions of capital markets, and concepts relating to how to regulate those markets*

Among countries that are "shifting tracks" from one system to another, China is the only country in the world to introduce securities markets without first going through major privatization measures. The significance of stock markets to China is that they enable more effective allocation of resources. It is obvious that using a securities market to allocate resources is more effective than using State planning departments. Securities markets are an important component of a property rights system, however. Therefore all legislation regarding them must be in compliance with clear rules and regulations regarding property rights. Such legislation must protect the rights and interests of all investors, but in particular of smaller investors.

Securities markets require information flows that are public and transparent. If that is achieved, price information moves at a lower cost and higher speed than in any other market. Innumerable unrelated investors rely on this information to determine how they want to invest, and this greatly reduces the costs of their transactions. Given that capital markets stimulate competition, they also mobilize people's intelligence to achieve results. Capital markets enable the transfer of risk by allowing those who want to take risk to use financial instruments to achieve their aims. Capital markets have powerful property rights restraints, so that anyone who wants to participate must take into full consideration the potential returns on his investment of capital. Anyone who wants to make a profit must take into consideration the risk involved, and his responsibilities for paying back the funds. Professional brokers in the stock market provide a fairly uniform standard for evaluating performance of underlying companies. Managers of those companies are motivated to improve their performance, and this then creates social benefit as well as the ability to accumulate capital.

For the above reasons, securities markets have been adopted by most countries in the world. China has achieved initial success with its own markets, which are showing very considerable vitality.

Our problem today, however, is that people now have overly high and unrealistic expectations of the capital markets. They do not lack adequate understanding of the role that markets can play, but they need to understand that there are many things markets cannot do. Capital markets will fail if the demands on them are unrealistic. For example, capital markets cannot provide capital for free. The idea of fund-raising via capital markets was over-emphasized in recent years. One of the starting points for having a market was indeed that some companies lacked funding sources. Many companies then undertook shareholding reform for the sole purpose of allowing them to participate in the market and raise funds. This is indeed important for China right now, given its structure of aggregate savings. The markets serve as a way to transform net savings into a source of funding for both the government and enterprises. However, if people over-emphasize this fund-raising function of markets, the results can distort the mechanisms and very image of the stock market.

One rather common perception right now is that State-Owned Enterprises face operating difficulties because of their excessive debt-to-asset ratios. Their debt burden is too great, including the interest they have to pay on that debt. If they could only get into the capital markets, they could then reduce the amount of interest they have to pay and lighten their load.

This misperception is tied in to the fact that such publicly owned enterprises lack a responsible "owner" who is accountable for losses. People within the enterprise naturally look to their own interests. To owners (the public), however, capital also has opportunity costs. The opportunity cost of their capital is equivalent to what their capital might gain if it were used in other places. At the very least, therefore, the opportunity cost cannot be lower than what the capital would make off interest in a bank account. If owners are not in fact making a return off their capital that is higher than such interest rates, then the owners have not used their capital wisely. They have not received the highest possible returns. A simplistic point of view that thinks an enterprise can benefit by reducing debt and increasing capital as derived from capital markets is simply mistaken. It fails to diagnose the problem correctly, and it fails to come up with a workable remedy.

Another misperception relates to what the government can and cannot do with respect to markets. Even though the real economy is much more complex, the old saying that applies to it also holds for the capital markets. Whatever the market can do should be done by the market, while government should perform only those functions that the market cannot perform. When the market becomes ineffective for any reason, then and only then should the government step in, and only then does a government do any good. If the government insists on doing things that should be left to the market, problems will multiply while results will be cut in half.

The first thing that the government should indeed do is to set up a system of laws and regulations to preserve market order and to protect the rights and interests of small investors. The government not only has the authority to do this but it should fulfill this obligation. The market as envisaged by Adam Smith was one of no government intervention at all. In this market, a group of unrelated people theoretically creates a stable and orderly society that has no government interference just by having each individual pursue his own greatest interest. However, one also assumes that each individual, as a selfish entity, will be pursuing his greatest interests by using the least possible investment. He will seek to reap gains without any effort, which inevitably will lead to universal behavior that engages in stealing and cheating if there are no laws to counteract such behavior. The "invisible hand of the market" is clearly powerless to deal with this. Only a tightly constructed set of laws and regulations can keep individual desires from infringing upon the rights of others. Only law can define the proper limits of what is and is not damaging to society.

Another responsibility that the government must fulfill relates to macroeconomic regulation. Such regulation should indeed be undertaken, but right now our economic management departments want to involve themselves in far too much. One could say that economic management departments fail to handle what they should be handling, or they handle it badly, yet they involve themselves in matters that they should not be handling. The most glaring example is the fact that the government has not put sufficient effort into managing macroeconomic issues while it is still involved in the micromanagement of details. Moreover, the trend in this direction is increasing.

The most fundamental principle of market economies is that of "self responsibility." In a market economy, an individual (a term that includes a legal person) is fully responsible for his own gains and losses in the market so long as he complies with rules and regulations. It is not up to others or to the State to get involved. Even if the desire "to help" stems from the best intentions, therefore, when government departments take responsibility for things that should be the sole responsibility of individuals and enterprises, this does nothing but hurt the sound development of a market-economy system.

In the securities and futures markets, the government's most fundamental responsibilities are to preserve market order, and ensure an open, equal and fair market. What the government should not do is interfere in the profits and losses of any given participant due to price changes of either securities or futures. That the government does in fact interfere in this way is the most notable indication of the immaturity of China's markets. This over-stepping of the bounds of authority is reflected in the regulatory work of the government and also in the general consciousness of the great mass of market participants. Many investors in China lack adequate understanding of risk. They are, psychologically as well as financially, unprepared to take a loss. As a result, they take their case to the media and to government officials, and use every means to have their losses recouped through governmental "administrative intervention." Their aim is purely to protect their private interests. In looking at past situations, many of these cases present information that is partial or even untrue. So long as the people make sufficient noise, however, they generally are able to achieve some results. They capitalize on the psychological weak points of government departments. When they make money, that is only right and proper, but when they lose money, the government owes them money. Regulatory bodies have trouble with this, but at the same time they generally bow to the pressure of interest groups. They take measures to influence market prices, consciously or unconsciously bailing out the interest groups under the pretext of "saving the market." In the short run, such measures might relieve problems. In the long run, they distort the market and also habituate individuals and enterprises to the idea that they will be bailed out. This only incubates greater problems in the end.

Naturally, the government is involved in the market as an entity that establishes and enforces legislation. This is not remotely the same as gratuitous interference in the market. Any casual interference by the government in the market will swiftly increase the uncertainty of that market. This will add to market risk and, again, harm the confidence of market participants.

When China's stock markets were just being set up, in the early period, it was impossible to rely completely on the spontaneous role of the market and government participation was indeed necessary. If the government continues to involve itself unduly in market affairs, however, this will be detrimental to raising risk awareness among investors. Examples of undue interference include having the government decide how many shares should be issued, and to whom they should be allocated. They include auditing companies and then deciding upon which can be listed, deciding upon the method of distributing shares, having the authority to hire and fire senior personnel in listed companies, and deciding on how shares are internally allocated.

Too great an involvement in the stock market will put the government itself under great risk. The securities regulatory departments of the government should be responsible only for regulating the market and for investigating and punishing illegal practices. They should not interfere in the prices of the stock market, so they also should not have any responsibility for individual stock prices. If tremendous volatility erupts in the market, this may very likely be blamed on government behavior.

A classic case of this might be the following. When prices start to fall, investors blame it on the government for enabling listed companies to issue too many shares. They then ask the government to stop the share expansion or to slow down the pace of having the company be listed. When a listed company distributes shares as a bonus, and the quantity is not satisfactory to some individuals, or when company results are poor, investors come running to complain to the government. Why? Because the State owns controlling shares, and the process of listing on the market was reviewed and approved by the government. In short, the more administrative management departments get involved in stock market affairs, the more susceptible the government is to the charge of corruption. Investors are given plenty of reason to be upset.

In order to ensure the normal functioning of the market, it is necessary to take full advantage of the role of mass media and of "supervision via public opinion." Government regulatory agencies and the primary market entities, such as listed companies, securities companies, investors, and so on, should form a kind of interrelated system with mass media, in that each supervises the other. Securities regulatory departments absolutely must not go over and above their lawfully bestowed authority, or place themselves above market participants or mass media. They should allow newspapers to disclose negative news on the market and not just news that is in line with their own opinions and evaluation of companies. Otherwise, this will have a negative impact on the sound development of the securities markets. Creating a sound market is not merely a matter of asking regulatory departments to "regularize" market participants and mass media, but a matter of asking these agencies to "regularize" themselves.

## Issues to do with listed companies

### *Listed companies must not regard the securities market as a path to easy money*

A thorough analysis of the behavior of listed companies first requires a brief look at the process of China's reform of its State-Owned Enterprises. In the early period of reform, we carried out the following two reforms to do with capital and profit distribution, based on our very rudimentary understanding of the defects of traditional State-Owned Enterprises.

First, we implemented a reform called "devolution of authority, and granting of profits." This meant that State-Owned Enterprises had greater autonomy in decision-making, while profits were divided between State and enterprise in certain percentages. This was to address the former situation in which State-Owned Enterprises had no capital at all with which to carry out autonomous operations. The traditional system had involved "incoming and outgoing funds" that were centrally determined.

At the time, people thought that the great drawback of the traditional planned-economy system was that State-Owned Enterprises lacked their own independence in making decisions. Most importantly, they lacked the authority to distribute profits or to utilize capital as they themselves wished. If State-Owned Enterprises were to have their own self-determined capital, so the thinking went, those managing the enterprises would operate them according to market demand. They would carry out technological upgrading and they would expand production capacity. The reason State-Owned Enterprises lacked any vitality, people thought, was that their production was not matched to market demand. Enabling them to have their own capital would quite naturally make this problem disappear.

The second reform that the country carried out therefore involved capitalizing enterprises. What originally had been "allocations" of public funds from the State were changed into what were now called bank loans (which came from State-owned banks). This was intended to change the situation whereby enterprises used State funds for free. When this reform was carried out, the thinking of people was that the traditional system allowed enterprises to receive State allocations without giving any consideration to return on investment. This was one reason that funds were used so inefficiently. Once State-Owned Enterprises had the right to allocate a portion of their profits, themselves, and once "allocations" had been changed to "bank loans," enterprises themselves would pay more attention to their cost of capital. They would also be subject to constraints imposed upon them by the banks making the loans. Not only would they have to return the loans, but they would have to pay interest on the loans. This would force an improvement in the efficient use of capital.

The above two reforms were also carried out in other traditional planned-economy countries, namely the former Soviet Union and Eastern Europe. They were undertaken in different years and in differing forms, however. The results were generally rather modest, mainly because the process did not impinge upon the basic contradictions of the traditional system. Reforms had to be carried out repeatedly as a result.

The reforms in China also failed to achieve the desired results. The specified percentage of profits that a State-Owned Enterprise was authorized to keep now generally went into paying bonuses and payments to individuals. Having been granted by the State, there was no real "ownership" of the entity that had paid out the money, and therefore no ownership constraints. The funding that enterprises needed to increase production now generally relied upon bank loans but the reform of banks themselves was then delayed. This meant that restrictions that a normal bank might have imposed upon enterprises, as originally planned, did not materialize. Banks made loans without corresponding payback requirements and, again, there was no "owner" who could be held accountable.

As a result, enterprises universally took on excessive amounts of debt. According to State statistical data, the average asset-to-debt ratio among State-Owned Enterprises nationwide was 71.4 percent (excluding land assets). The figure was 59.9 percent including land assets. Since the asset-to-debt ratio of small- and medium-sized State-Owned Enterprises was somewhat higher, authorities estimated that some 80 percent of all State-Owned Enterprises in China had asset-to-debt ratios that exceeded 80 percent. These figures applied prior to the reform that then "transformed debt into equity."

Now, while all levels of government in China were no longer obliged to pour capital into State-Owned Enterprises, they also had no capacity to fund newly-founded enterprises. As a result, local governments relied upon the practice of "commanding" banks and other financial institutions to make loans for "project" funding. From the very start of these new enterprises, therefore, they operated "for free," as it were. State-owned commercial banks and other financial institutions had no authority to decide upon projects. All they could do was follow government by making loans to enterprises that put up no collateral whatsoever, and that had no assets or capital of their own.

Since banks and financial institutions were "forced" to issue these command loans, and were only following orders, they naturally could not be responsible if the loans were not repaid. In fact, banks and institutions rarely even gave a second thought to carrying out this kind of responsibility. Instead, they watched as their risk grew higher and higher. Bad debts, and loans not yet classified as nonperforming loans but headed in that direction, mounted by the day. Asset quality constantly deteriorated.

In fact, the reason many banks and institutions put such weak controls on loans was that most enterprises were able to say that projects had been set by "the government." Whether or not a given project had good results was the responsibility of "the government." Once a project was unsuccessful, the enterprise was not only unable but also not inclined to return any capital together with interest to the bank.

If an enterprise had been set up entirely on the basis of bank loans, its managers could regard it as something that belonged neither to the government, which had not put in any real investment, nor to the kind of bank that absolutely required payback in the end. Managers perhaps thought that the enterprise belonged to the "entire body of workers." This enabled a considerable lack of clarity about property rights. The result was that the heads of enterprises were able to allocate profits of the enterprise as they wished, but could put all of the risk for debt repayment onto the banks. This was naturally detrimental to enterprise reform as well as banking reform.

All of this made people begin to reconsider. They realized that it was going to be impossible to transform the operating mechanisms of State-Owned Enterprises by relying on any constraining principles of State ownership or any rules about creditor's rights of banks. Given major changes that were already occurring in the pattern of how national income was distributed, it was also going to be impossible to rely on public finance to pay the operating costs of State-Owned Enterprises.

Calculations done in recent years show that of total net savings in the country, citizens held 83 percent, including rural and urban residents, all levels of governments held 3%, while enterprises of all kinds held 14 percent. Among enterprises, State-Owned Enterprises held no more than 7 percent. Clearly, it was going to be impossible to depend on public finance to bolster the capital of existing enterprises, not to mention new enterprises, and the accumulated capital of State-Owned Enterprises was inadequate as well. The problem of excessive debt levels of State-Owned Enterprises, and their lack of operating capital, was going to be a perpetual problem.

The problems described above could be summed up by saying that China had to figure out how to set up new mechanisms for enterprises to accumulate capital once the old mechanisms, which relied on the State, had been dismantled. Counting on indirect financing via banks was not going to work. One problem was unclear ownership of property rights in enterprises, so that no "owner" put any restrictions on how the money was used. Meanwhile banks assumed huge levels of risk. The other problem was that reform of bank mechanisms was not moving forward and banks had no effective way to monitor the loans they were making to State-Owned Enterprises.

Given this situation, economists within China came to the universal conclusion that the country had to develop new ways to finance business through direct financing.

The country had to use securities markets as a way to transform the savings of the public into investment. The hope was also that this would encourage enterprises now listed on the market to set up effective corporate governance structures. It can therefore be said that the formation of China's stock markets was forced upon the country. The "waters were forced into a particular channel" at a certain stage in the course of reform.

The problem was that stock markets were like not some minion that one could command at will, nor were they a tame horse that was easy to ride. Only by enabling a stock market to proceed according to its own inherent laws could that market have any enduring benefit to society. If the market was simply a place for companies to make an initial hit of money when they were listed, any spark was going to produce momentary heat and the market would then subside.

The fundamental principle of a market economy is freedom of choice in buying and selling, with both sides willing to make a transaction and both sides taking responsibility for the results. Only when two sides both agree there is mutual benefit in doing trades on a market will that market be able to carry on. If a market consistently allows only one side to benefit, without compensation, it will soon cease to function.

It was clear, therefore, that one could not expect State-Owned Enterprises to receive ongoing financing from a stock market as a way to extricate them from their problems if those enterprises did not in turn pay back a reasonable return to investors. The problems that State-Owned Enterprises have recently come up against in overseas stock markets are a strong warning signal to us in this regard. Prior to listing on a market, many of our companies are merely thinking of how to get an initial sum of money by issuing shares. They rarely take into consideration any issues of credibility, or any real responsibility to investors. Some listed companies do not in fact use funds as they have promised in their prospectuses. Given that enterprises fail to deliver on the returns to shareholders that they have promised, shareholders in turn are unwilling to hold onto the shares for any length of time. They become traders, taking advantage of any profit to be made in price changes, which leads to radical differences between the share price of an enterprise and its actual results. It also leads to extreme volatility in the market.

### The problem of "insider control" in listed companies in which the State has a controlling interest

In the initial period of reform, steps taken to "release decision-making authority down to lower levels and allow profits to stay with enterprises themselves" did indeed prove successful at first.

Before long, however, the managers of State-Owned Enterprises soon discovered that it was far more lucrative to hide profits and use them for internal distribution than it was to increase profits and "hand them over" to the State. This enabled managers to benefit personally. It also allowed them to gain the support of their workers. As a result, the problem of "insider control" became universal in State-Owned Enterprises. Both managers and workers controlled the authority to allocate profits. This was an internally generated problem that soon appeared in the course of "switching tracks" from one type of economy to another, as State-Owned Enterprises became "corporatized."[3]

Naturally, people inside the enterprise realized that the more capital they could get hold of to help generate profits, the better off they would be. At the start of reform, the idea was to change money formerly dispersed by the government into loans dispersed by banks. This was meant to alter the planned-economy system by which enterprises were able to use public funds for free. Unfortunately, reform overlooked the distinction between constraints on property rights and the constraints of creditors' rights. This left enterprises in a condition of not having any funds with which to operate, but also not being subject to property rights constraints. As described above, merely "switching allocation into debt," switching from State allocations of money to bank loans, was not sufficient to improve the efficiency of using capital. On the contrary, it generated a whole new set of problems.

The current thought is to "switch debt into equity." This at least indicates that the concept of property rights is beginning to get attention.

In this process, however, we must guard against the idea that enterprises do not need to pay back any return on equity. They cannot simply receive money from the stock market for free without the obligation of paying dividends to those who purchase shares. We will have made a huge circle and come back to our starting point for reform if this does in fact prove to be the case. Intentionally or not, by approving plans to turn debt into equity, we will have allowed this reform to take the wrong course and we will benefit only the interests of insiders.

Up to now, shareholding systems in China only allowed for "incremental" capital to be securitized. (Original capital came from the public at large as the State-Owned Enterprises were first established.) That is, only shares issued for such additionally-added capital are liquid or tradable. State-owned shares are not liquid, nor are the shares of "legal persons." These latter types of shares constitute the absolute majority of shares in a given corporation, however. This system therefore guarantees that this shareholding structure will not incentivize managers to perform, nor will it provide a supervisory role in regulating their activities.

At present there are over 900 companies that have been listed. These have issued some 300 billion shares. Of these, the State holds 110 billion, and legal persons hold roughly 80 billion. Together, these constitute over 60 percent of shares. Translated into market value, the non-traded shares come to something approaching RMB 2 trillion.

By current regulations, neither State-owned shares nor legal-person shares can be traded on the market. The problem is that all of these listed companies were "born" out of State-Owned Enterprises. In a short period of time, it is extremely difficult to eradicate the old governance structures under which they formerly operated. What's more, in the course of reform this problem of insider control has made an appearance. As the "representatives" of the State's shareholdings, managers of listed enterprises can simply disregard opinions of common shareholders. As insiders, they can also disregard the will of the major shareholder, namely the State. Not only are they in a position to hurt the interests of small shareholders, but they are also in a position to hurt the interests of the country at large. Given this situation, simply listing on a market is not an effective way to strengthen controls on property rights or to reform corporate governance.

When we are analyzing this situation of insider control, and its problems, we should not be simplistic in thinking that control by outsiders will be any better. We should not thereby conclude that we should go back to the old ways of having outsiders control enterprises. We should be particularly careful to avoid the kind of "irregular" oversight that administrative departments exercise over enterprises. This can easily coexist with the problem of insider control that infringes upon the rights of investors. We should attempt to design a system that allows for the mutual support and balanced control of insiders and outsiders, and corporate governance systems that are appropriate to China's specific conditions.

Corporate governance systems of various countries differ, given their origins in different cultures, traditions, and legal systems. For example, the great majority of publicly-listed companies in Japan still maintain relationships with a "primary bank." In Germany, banks can not only own corporate shares directly, but they are the custodian of the shares of other tiers of shareholders with the authority to vote their shares. They therefore play a key role in the corporate governance structures of corporations. In the United States, on the contrary, laws originally strictly forbad banks to hold shares in publicly-held companies. Still afraid of breaking the law, banks are reluctant to interfere in the internal operations of corporations to which they have loaned large amounts of money. As a result, they have little influence on corporate governance.

China's corporate governance structures in turn have their own particular features during this transitional period, and opinions differ on how this should develop in the future. People in academic circles are inclined to think that future corporate governance systems should lie somewhere in between those of the United States and those of Germany. According to conventional principles, there should be a clear delineation of property rights, and there should be a sound trustee (fiduciary) relationship between the shareholders' meeting and the board of directors. There should be a sound proxy relationship between the board of directors and the managers of the corporation.

In addition, China must improve the systems by which operators of the stock market are evaluated and approved and it must ensure that the managers and staff of enterprises fulfill their rightful duties. Only then can companies expect to enjoy long-term growth, and provide shareholders with adequate "surplus income." In addition to establishing effective incentives for corporate managers, we must place them under the proper constraints of market competition. These include the evaluation of companies by the capital markets and market competition for the jobs of managers themselves. In this regard, the volume of trading of a given stock and its market price is extremely important. Any stock market that deviates from the role of evaluating and measuring corporate performance is not functioning in the proper way.

Important measures that can be taken to improve the way stock markets evaluate corporate performance include standardizing the disclosure information required of companies and improving the transparency of corporate operations. In addition, we should increase the ability of intermediary companies to analyze corporations, and improve the professional capabilities of analysts themselves as well as their professional integrity. In order for investors to make intelligent choices about what to invest in, we must ensure that measures of corporate performance are available that evaluate each corporation from different perspectives.

### Hidden dangers in a stock market that has experienced high price-earnings ratios for a long period of time

China's stock markets are currently exhibiting a peculiar phenomenon. People are addicted to seeing the market go higher and higher, and greatly pleased at seeing this wish come true for now. As everyone knows, however, a market that goes up must come down. This is as inevitable as inflation if a government continues to print money. Thinking otherwise is simply a delusion. Nevertheless, authorities continue to make all concerted efforts to pass policies that are supportive of the market and keep it up. What's more, the "dosage" of their prescription continues to increase. Eventually, things must come to an impasse. At the end of the day, the level of the market is determined by the underlying performance of listed companies and by macroeconomic fundamentals. Using supportive policies to stimulate the market is short-term behavior that mortgages the future. Sooner or later, the bill comes due.

The question then becomes how to determine what the proper value of the market should be. Right now, the Shenzhen market is trading at around 40 to 50 times earnings. Before 1993, the New York Stock Exchange traded at an average P/E ratio of 16. The Nasdaq traded at an average of 18. The markets in the US have now reached a new level and we have to bring new theories to bear on this to understand it. Internet shares can trade around 100, high-tech telecom stocks at around 40, and computer stocks between 40 and 50. Biotechnology shares trade at around 22, but traditional industries are still trading at P/E ratios of 16 to 18.

The Hong Kong market generally trades at P/E ratios below 20, although this dropped to under ten after the Asian financial crisis. State-owned H shares on the Hong Kong market trade at P/E ratios that are below ten, while B shares inside China, aimed at foreign investors, trade at P/E ratios that are under five. Some people explain this by emphasizing the specific nature of share ownership in Chinese-listed companies. That is, shares that are allowed to be traded (liquid shares) only constitute some 70 to 75 percent of all equity. This enables the market to keep trading at consistently high P/E ratios.

In fact, one only needs to look at the relationship between the prices of H shares and B shares to know that this reasoning has no logic to it. Otherwise, A shares, traded inside the country, could drop in value by more than half, and it would still seem reasonable. If this were to happen, however, social stability would be strongly affected. It is obvious that high P/E ratios not only have a hold on the market, but also on all of society.

High P/E ratios should be the result of high growth of the corporation in question. In this regard, the high level of the market right now lacks any kind of supporting evidence from corporate performance. Not only have earnings been universally low among listed companies in China, but they continue to decline every year. As the saying goes, "results in the first year are excellent, in the second not so bad, and in the third pretty awful." The Shanghai stock market rose from an index of 96 in 1990 to 1,756 in 1999. During this period, the average return on every share dropped from RMB 0.35 in 1993 to 0.20 in 1998. Return on net investment went from 14.6 percent in 1993 to 7.79 percent in 1998.

Strangely enough, some companies with high P/E ratios have continued to demonstrate poor performance and growth prospects for years, while companies with relatively good performance have lower P/E ratios. This is closely related to how media coverage of companies is manipulated. It also relates to how brokers (agents) manipulate share prices. Although this is broadly recognized, people seem surprisingly unconcerned about this since they themselves stand to benefit.

Some people hold that it is wise to keep the level of the market high in order to attract more investors. This helps enterprises raise funds. In fact, the higher a share price is, the more expensive it is and the less it has further investment value. Consistently high P/E ratios in China over a long period of time are in fact having the effect of distorting investors' behavior as well as the behavior of listed companies. Money comes easily to the listed companies, and is therefore used as though it were cheap. It is not used prudently. Listed companies rarely give cash dividends to shareholders, and shareholders do not seem to find anything wrong with that. They have a trading mentality. They focus exclusively on price differentials in the market and rarely pay any attention to the underlying performance of a company. Investors have thereby lost the ability to play a supervisory role in monitoring the behavior of corporations, a role that by all rights they should play.

Sooner or later, the inevitable result of all this will be a substantial decline in the market overall. We can only hope for a soft landing. We hope we are not incubating the makings of a market disaster. The only proper course of action when something does happen, however, will be to let the normal level of the market reassert itself and not do anything to intervene.

### *Pushing forward measures that enable State-owned shares to be traded on the market, in line with our reform principle of doing things on a selective basis*

The most obvious "unique feature" of China's securities market is that shares owned by the State-owned sector, the majority shareholder, are not in circulation.

They cannot be traded. The drawbacks of this equity structure have become more and more apparent in recent years.

As listed companies grow and need more capital, publicly-owned shares are in an increasingly awkward position. Depending on need, it may be that a company needs massive infusions of capital, which means that the percentage that the public sector must contribute is substantial. As a result, the "frontline" of the State-owned sector becomes more and more attenuated as it has to fund more and more corporations. The burden on it becomes heavier. If capital needs are such that a proportionate amount of funding cannot be put in, then the State suffers an enormous dilution of its equity.

At the same time, the illiquidity of State-owned shares means that State-owned assets earn no returns from the market and the controlling shareholder is therefore not highly concerned about their market value. That shareholder is also not highly concerned about the operating performance of the listed company, since the underlying performance does not affect the value of State shares. As noted above, listed companies in which the State holds controlling shares universally exhibit the problem of having no accountability—that is, they all have the problem of "an absent owner." If we are to set up and strengthen mechanisms that allow for adequate performance evaluation of listed companies and their managers, we must allow for the trading of State-owned shares.

This may be achieved in a number of ways. One is "transfer of share rights through negotiated agreement." This is already taking place. The other is allowing for actual trading on the market. Obviously, if negotiated transfer is undertaken only among different publicly-owned entities, this may help in restructuring and asset reallocation but it is detrimental to any transformation of corporate operating mechanisms. Therefore, we should not only allow but also encourage the non-publicly-owned sector to participate in this kind of negotiated transfer of State-owned shares. If non-publicly-owned investors do not in fact participate actively, leading to healthy price competition and a strict discipline of weeding out enterprises that are less capable, this will be extremely damaging to the normal operating of the market. Investors' faith in the market will not be restored.

In fact, we are already conducting pilot projects that allow State-owned shares to be traded on the market. We carry this out in line with the policy directive of "moving forward on a selective basis by doing some things but not others." This practice represents a major breakthrough in the history of China's securities markets. State-owned shares are the largest block of "wealth" that the country can mobilize for its uses at the current time. Enabling them to circulate by being traded on the market is an enormous step in enabling the State to undertake strategic economic restructuring. Through selling some State-owned shares on the stock market, the government can smoothly withdraw from certain competitive-type industries. Through shifting investment, it can strengthen certain infrastructure-type industries, and it can also fund deficits in social security funds.

A number of things should be taken into consideration as we formulate proposals for making State-owned shares tradable. The results should ensure that State-owned assets "maintain value and appreciate in value." The results should benefit the smooth functioning and sound development of the stock market. They should give adequate protection to normal investors and especially to the lawful rights and interests of smaller investors. We must make all efforts to prevent the tendency of local governments and government departments to rush to sell their shares out of a desire for immediate profit. We cannot have short-sighted behavior that pays no consideration to how selling shares may affect the value of State-owned assets. We must prevent shocks to the market that might result in a precipitous decline of share prices.

Because of this, we must ensure that the process of making State-owned shares tradable is a controlled process yet not fully an administrative action. It cannot be based solely on government determination without any regard to market expectations. Given this, there must be a framework within which certain conditions and rules must be met. State-owned entities that hold controlling shares must abide by strict rules and yet have a certain leeway in how they operate. At the same time, information must be disclosed to all investors, together with risk advisories.

## Regarding intermediary entities in the securities market

In recent years, the work of disengaging financial institutions has accomplished notable success, as conducted by relevant authorities according to the guidelines of the central government. Such "disengagement" refers to separating out the operations of securities companies from banks and credit investment companies and enabling securities companies to carry on independent operations. Meanwhile, the securities exchanges and futures exchanges have been separated out from local government and departmental jurisdiction and made into "membership" organizations. Intermediary organizations such as firms that do accounting, appraisals, and legal work have been separated out from the entities to which they reported before. They are now partnerships.

Ever since being established, securities investment funds have put forward standardized, defined relationships with owners (of shares) and proxies for those owners. Currently, the biggest problem is that the regulatory agencies handling the majority of industries in China regard those that they are regulating as something like subsidiaries, entities that they have the right to "manage." Regulatory agencies still wear two different hats. They still combine "government" and "enterprise" in one entity, so that governmental affairs become intertwined with business. This old problem has therefore appeared now in a new guise. The problem may well be hard to rectify in a short time, but sooner or later it will be resolved.

### As the cornerstone of the capital markets, securities firms are highly unreliable

First, in terms of the letter of the law, our laws and regulations governing those operating in the field of securities are very strict. Some indeed feel that it is hard to get work done under such rules. Therefore, behavior that breaks rules and laws is universal. Cases of noncompliance are ubiquitous, to the extent that it is easiest just to handle them leniently or not prosecute at all.

Our "Securities Law" was set up under highly chaotic conditions in the securities market, when there was an urgent need to get something written. It was natural at the time to think that greater severity would be helpful. What happened was that the great majority of institutions and individuals behaved in a way that was illegal. If we went after every single violator, the market would have to shut down. Authorities have no choice but to pretend they don't see what is going on.

Those entrusted with enforcing the law are therefore currently being allowed to make their own decisions. Whether or not to go after people is up to them. They have a great deal of extra-legal latitude, "special privilege," in deciding how to operate. Regulators even use the practice of enforcement as a way to moderate the market. They relax controls when the market is too quiet, but catch a chicken or two to frighten the monkey when things are too hot. This kind of extra-legal privilege makes securities companies and their employees feign compliance while doing what they please. They have a devil-may-care attitude when it comes to securities institutions and their personnel.

Second, when the very first securities companies were set up in China, one or just a few people sat on the preparatory committees that started them. Knowledgeable expertise in securities was hard to come by at the time, and it was impossible to be too picky about people's qualifications. Since conditions were tough, it was also hard to burden them with too many constraints. As a result, the management of securities firms is generally opaque. One person generally calls the shots and the others go along in an atmosphere of being "brothers in cahoots." The primary person in charge is never rotated out, so it is very hard to prove illegal activity or corruption. In daily activities, when there is a conflict of interest between an individual or small group of people and the company, it is very hard to protect the company's interests.

At the very least, it can be said that unlawful transfers of interests and unlawful transfers of State-owned assets are not a unique occurrence in securities companies.

Third, when it comes to the brokerage business, kickbacks are a very serious problem. The practices of allowing overdraft transactions and payback of commissions are far from being eradicated. Every securities firm engages in the practice of embezzling the margin money of customers—the practice is so prevalent that they no longer even try to cover up this fact. A certain degree of progress has been made in addressing it, but prior to the clean-up movement, 90 securities firms in China were engaged in the practice, as well as in embezzling the funds for the settlement of customers' trades, illegally taking in funds from the public, and engaging in a large amount of non-securities-related business. Some were even carrying out business "off the books," creating an enormous potential risk in the process. By now, only 35 securities firms have returned the clients' margins that they took and had their illegal "borrowings" dealt with. There are still 50 firms who have not returned margin money, while their poor asset quality and illegal operations have not yet been resolved. In some cases, the margin money that was taken from others comes to multiples of the money of the securities firm itself. Enormous losses have built up in the meantime, creating a massive amount of hidden financial risk.

Fourth, insider trading and market manipulation are commonplace. This is particularly true of brokerage firms that are operated on a proprietary basis. Some listed companies set up a securities company to serve the function of a kind of banker in a gambling game—in Chinese, known literally as the banker (*zuo zhuang*). Seldom is this investigated. Operations on one's own behalf generally exceed the trading limits as called for in the *Administrative Measures for Proprietary Securities Firms*. It is widely known that these firms use personal accounts for carrying out business, they illegally serve as agents for others in managing their money, and they commingle the accounts of funds entrusted to them with their own funds. All of this hurts the interests of the firm, the firm's clients, and market order. Since these practices are ubiquitous, the problems are serious.

Securities exchanges should have a self-regulating role. They should not be a tool for manipulating market prices.

One of the problems facing securities exchanges and futures exchanges (in the recent past) was the corrosive competition that immediately developed between exchanges. As a result, they simply disregarded the rules of regulators and openly broke the law. Regulatory agencies generally could do nothing about it. At the time, one person responsible for one of the exchanges directly repudiated the jurisdiction of the agencies.

By now, exchanges are directly under the authority of regulatory agencies and the executives of the exchange are assigned by or controlled by them. Securities regulatory agencies are able to command exchanges directly. On receipt of orders from the securities regulatory agency, the exchanges convey them on to securities dealers. In this way, exchanges are one of the tools that securities agencies can use to intervene in the market. The so-called "membership system," meanwhile, exists in name only.

### Problems regarding securities investment funds

In 1998, people were highly enthusiastic about "securities investment funds," since these seemed to be suited to the common investor. The funds appeared to provide "professional wealth management," and regulatory agencies felt that trading them would help the market become more stable and reliable. By the end of last year, however, the average return on 12 different funds that had been set up for more than half a year was only 15.57 percent, while the stock indexes of the Shanghai and Shenzhen agencies had risen by 19 percent and 17 percent, respectively. Funds had not outperformed the board. If you further deducted out the "subsidized earnings" meant to assist new issues in the market, the performance of these funds was not worth talking about. Meanwhile, it was highly debatable whether or not securities investment funds had any stabilizing effect on the volatility of the market.

Even more problematic is that the real situation regarding these investment funds is more mystifying than what the accounts seem to show. It is strange that wealth managers fail to beat the market when the board is consistently rising, yet they themselves make huge amounts on commissions and percentages from new issues. This goes on even when the markets are in a slump, and even though their funds go to levels that are below face value. The total "distributable profit" of the 12 funds described above, who had been operating for at least half a year, ranged between RMB 5 billion and RMB 6 billion. Yet somehow these funds were forced to sell shares for cash, losing money in the process, when it came to declaring dividends. Their profits lay primarily in dealing in the shares of just a few major entities.

Our disappointment with these new funds is concentrated in two main areas. First, the people handling them have not behaved professionally. Second, the funds have not set an example of using "best practices" investment philosophy. Below I describe my reasons for these two impressions.

First, the relationship between the new funds and big securities dealers is far too close. It is easy for fund managers to worry more about their parent companies than they do about the performance of the fund itself. Close observers have discovered a kind of investment preference among new funds. They like to buy in shares which their own companies have issued and with which they have an intimate relationship (all of these new funds were started up out of the major securities dealers). Not only did funds get set up by securities firms, but the managers of funds were once the very backbone of the securities firms. When securities firms either face losses or are forced to take large positions in the secondary market as new securities are issued, the funds generally don't think twice. Whether or not they will have a profit or a loss out of it, they take these shares in to their portfolios. This helps the securities firm out by sharing the burden.

Second, new funds lack any way to mitigate risk. On the one hand, it is hard for investors in the funds to exercise any regulatory supervision over operations. On the other hand, the compensation paid to managers of the funds is not tied in to the funds' profits or losses. Their compensation is figured as a percentage of the net value of the funds, which does not equate closely to business performance. Fund managers therefore can use the funds of investors to do "favors" for others at little cost to themselves.

Third, too much preferential treatment has been showered upon these new funds, to the extent that they face little competitive pressure. Allowing funds to buy newly-issued shares on the secondary market is not a fair and equal practice. Yet the income of new funds currently derives primarily from such new issues. As new issues become more and more common, the portion of new issues that funds are able to buy will be increasingly small. At the same time, after we reform the way in which new issues are priced, there will be a smaller differential between the price of newly issued shares and existing shares on the secondary market. When prices of newly issued shares fall below the level at which they were initially offered, funds will be facing hard times.

Fourth, the illegal manipulation of share prices by securities investment funds is quite serious. It has not been dealt with as it should have been. We often hear that the fund managers of securities investment funds carry out private business through what is called "rat trading" (front-running). They transfer the fund's assets through irregular trades into their own pockets. Such "rat trading" is sometimes done in association with friends and relatives, and sometimes it is done more blatantly through false identity accounts that the fund manager has set up for himself. Some funds also ally with securities dealers to manipulate the market through various ways. Some artificially increase the volume of business for a dealer by trading between their own two accounts, and then take a kickback in commissions from the dealer. This last practice has basically become an open secret.

Finally, the hidden risks that are accumulating in securities investment firms may not be exposed until several years later. From information released on the positions held by some securities investment firms, holdings focus heavily on certain shares. Some even constitute as much as 30 percent of a given portfolio. The prices of these shares are, to a great extent, determined by the price quotations of the fund itself. When the fund decides to sell off its position, the value of the stock may go far below the value that the fund currently has on its books.

### On venture investing and high-tech issues

In the following section, I would like to compare some things I have learned about Silicon Valley to China's own situation, particularly with respect to how venture capital works and how it has led to the extraordinary development of Silicon Valley.

*The force attracting capital into high-tech areas has relied on private*
*initiative and not on a government that does it all*

Venture capital is the economic engine driving the development of high-tech industries. It has generated the success of a number of enterprises, including Hewlett Packard, Apple, and Yahoo in Silicon Valley. Unlike traditional industries, high-tech areas necessarily carry a high degree of risk. The reason is that any given technology can often only have one winner, not two. All of the contenders below #2 find it hard to get enough market share to survive, and therefore become the losers in market competition. As a result of this, venture capital that is invested in high-tech areas has specific characteristics. First, it is expensive capital. Innovative enterprises that seek venture capital must pay a high price for it. Second, it is capital that is highly professional in how it is managed. It adheres to high standards of specialization in any given field. Third, it is private funding that is handled through one-on-one negotiations, and therefore it must provide adequate incentives to fund managers and also adequate constraints on them.

In Silicon Valley, venture capital can be divided into three types. The first is "angel investment," where an individual himself puts in his own money as seed money for the initial stages of an enterprise. This is a one-time investment that comes to anywhere between USD 50,000 and 500,000. The second type is investment funds that specialize in innovative industries, with sums ranging from USD 500,000 to five million. These funds generally come out of pension funds, mutual funds, foundations, insurance companies, banks, as well as affluent families and individuals. The third type is strategic investment funds. These are set up by very large companies to invest specifically in areas that are related to the interests of the company.

Many of the people handling venture capital investment funds in Silicon Valley are engineers by training, with the ability to make informed decisions about the innovative potential and the market prospects for certain products. Decision-making in the venture capital field has to be fast, but the selection process is extremely rigorous. Any given venture capital field might receive 5,000 applications in a year. Out of these, only 200 people might be invited to come and give in-person presentations, while only 20 applications might finally be approved for funding. Naturally, of those only a few are successful in the end.

The expensive nature of venture capital does not relate only to the difficulty of getting funded. The price that the founder of an enterprise has to pay often includes losing control of his own company. Venture capital is not an "all in one" type proposition. First, the investor generally asks for a controlling interest. Second, the investor pays great attention to the management team of the enterprise. Since the founder often is not a professional manager, the investor often hires such a professional manager to replace the founder in this position. From the founder's perspective, what he receives is not only capital but also the opportunity to revamp systems, reconstitute a management team, learn new conceptual approaches, operating strategies, and management models.

In 1994, AnnaLee Saxenian, at the University of California at Berkeley, published a book called *Regional Advantage: Culture and Competition in Silicon Valley and Route 128*. In this, the author compares the development of high-tech companies in the vicinity of the Route 128 beltway around Boston to that of companies in Silicon Valley. Before the 1980s, high-tech companies around Route 128 were far ahead of those in Silicon Valley. They were surpassed by Silicon Valley companies after the 1980s. The author concluded that the reason was that large companies could not operate as nimbly as smaller ones, in terms of how acutely their R&D efforts responded to change.

In relating this conclusion to our own situation in China, when our large State-Owned Enterprises decides to start up or shut down a particular scientific research project, the process is long and arduous. It involves discussions, reports, and approvals. Small companies can mobilize a project any time they wish. They can also be washed out by the market at any moment. What this tells us is that venture capital is not only not appropriate for large enterprises, but the entity doing the investing absolutely should not be the government.

The reasons for this are simple. First, those deciding upon what to invest in must have adequate incentives if they are to put the necessary effort into project selection. These are not possible within funds set up by the government. Second, it is impossible for the government to set up adequately stringent procedures to prevent "moral risk," while at the same time allowing fund managers to accommodate more than 90 percent of investment failures. Third, the habitual tendency of relevant departments to intervene in decisions via what is called "administrative interference" is something fund managers would find it very hard to contend with. Even against their own conscience, fund managers might find it necessary to make improper decisions. Fourth, the government's very long and tedious "review and approval process" for projects is fundamentally unsuited to the ever-changing nature of high-tech projects.

Right now, quite a few local governments in China are setting up their own venture capital funds. Some Silicon Valley people have said the following to me, with some sarcasm in their tone, "Certain government-invested projects involving fundamental research or national defense may be successful, since they do not require market approval and the government can disregard the cost. Venture capital that is going into marketable products is quite different. Such projects absolutely must not depend on government financing. Local governments are putting together considerable sums of money right now for venture investing, but these are certainly at the expense of the people in those areas. After a few years, when the time comes to see the results of those investments, the people's money will be long gone." This may have been said sarcastically, but it is worth thinking over.

*The destiny of entrepreneurial high-tech ventures should be decided*
*upon by the market and not by the government*

I have come to the profound understanding that individual initiative and creativity is the fundamental reason behind success in Silicon Valley. Silicon Valley could never have been born out of a rigid planning system. Only a system that was oriented toward free competition and decentralized decision-making could have created such a miracle. High-tech is not something that springs fully developed out of people's minds. Instead, it grows out of vague concepts that occur to many people independently. These concepts are brought to fruition by the concerted efforts of individuals, only one or two of whom may be successful. "High-tech" is built up out of the failures of countless others. In this process, the ideas of one individual cannot replace those of all the others, but nor can discussions force a consensus of everyone's thinking before forward movement takes place.

For this reason, if the government attempted to be the primary entity in venture investment, not only would this reduce the rate at which failures occurred but it would vastly increase risk. When individuals go forth to try out innovations, they disperse risk. They also shift risk so that it is born by the public at large.

We have to admit that our government personnel have strong suits that do not necessarily match those needed by high-tech entrepreneurship. They may have significant academic records, and substantial knowledge in their own right, but their talents lie in the direction of administrative management. The Chinese government's "review and approval procedures" will absolutely delay any progress in China's high-tech endeavors. As one Chinese student who was studying abroad put it, "Just think about it. Bill Gates, Steve Jobs—these people did not even graduate from college, let alone have higher degrees in engineering. If they had applied for permission to start a company in China, do you think any of our departments would have given permission?!"

The role that the government does play in the capital markets relates directly to the destiny of venture capital. The capital markets represent the "exit strategy" of venture capital. They are a key part of the circulation of venture capital. When an entrepreneurial venture approaches maturity and the high income associated with high risk begins to shift into normal income, venture capital is cashed out and again seeks investment in other opportunities. It enters the next cycle in the process. In Silicon Valley, the period of time between when an idea is formalized as a company, and that company is launched on the market, tends to be around 18 months. The great majority of companies are not profitable when they are listed on the market, mainly via the Nasdaq. The Nasdaq exchange has facilitated the rapid growth of venture capital in the United States. There is a second way in which venture capital exits a given company. The company is either sold or it is merged with another. Venture capital is then released to start another cycle.

In either case, the process requires highly efficient capital markets. The function of governments in such markets is to supervise and regulate, while "review and approval" procedures should be kept to a minimum. We are currently considering setting up a "board" that would exclusively deal in high-tech issues. It would be called the "high-tech board." The problem is that we have unwarranted faith in the discerning capacities of the government. All an enterprise has to do is pass "review and approval procedures" of relevant government departments and it can be declared a "high-tech company." It can then have preferential treatment in being listed on the market. Who can guarantee that such "confirmation" by the government not only is correct but that it is fair? At the same time, who can say that a legitimately high-tech company will pass the hurdles and the illegitimate company will not? The process is very akin to "catching the right fish in muddy waters."

The Hong Kong Exchange has a secondary board called the "Growth Enterprise Market" or GEM. The sole purpose of this is to enable start-up companies to be listed as a way to raise capital. The very name of this exchange is meant to indicate the high-risk nature of investment in such companies. Our "secondary board," however, is defined as including only those companies that have gone through government approval and that are qualified to be listed on the market. This necessarily gives investors the mistaken impression that the government has provided these companies a kind of stamp of approval. They are in one way or another guaranteed by the government. Investors overlook the risk involved. The moment the enterprise runs into problems, investors will be presenting indignant complaints to the government.

As everyone knows, the government's "review and approval procedures" are an imperfect process. They can weed out projects that put forth information honestly, but not those that are dishonest. They work for gentlemen, but not for scoundrels. The feasibility studies that are a part of investment projects are in fact simply reports written in such a way as to make a given project pass the rules. Most "redundant projects" in China (the kind that create too many factories which all put out the same thing) are projects that passed the rules and got approved. Most fake companies that have been listed were, in similar fashion, projects that passed "stringent" rules and got approved.

"Review and approval procedures" for traditional projects are typically a sham. Given this, procedures for high-tech projects will be even more so. We should be delighted to have the market itself conduct the selection procedure on projects. It is open and fair, and it saves us a lot of work.

*Rather than have nothing at all to do with the high-tech sphere, the government should perform its own functions properly*

The key to this issue is revamping our ideas about what that proper role should be.

In the high-tech arena, it is not as though the government's role is limited to "review and approval procedures." There are plenty of other things that the government can and should do, including the very important task of stimulating and protecting the positive energies of entrepreneurs. Such things include, for example, relaxing allocation policies, protecting intellectual property rights, allowing the technological advances made by individuals to qualify for shares in a company. They include allowing the issuing of warrants (authority to hold shares) to both employees and managers, and allowing enterprises to be "transferred" (sold). They include creating the right conditions for enabling entrepreneurial firms to list on the secondary board. They include creating policies that enable more overseas students to return to China to work, that ensure their freedom to go back and forth and that protect their cooperative efforts with entities overseas.

From the example of Silicon Valley, we note that one of the primary reasons venture capital has developed so well and had such remarkable success is that it operates in a beneficial investment environment, which includes a fairly lenient legal environment. The United States passed the *Small Business Investment Act* back in 1958. This encouraged the establishment of small- and medium-sized companies through preferential treatment in the areas of taxation, fund-raising, and low-interest loans. California's legal environment is particularly conducive to small high-tech companies, especially with respect to when people change jobs ("jump out of the groove"). As an overseas student has pointed out, all states in America have laws to protect industrial secrets. When a person is hired at a company, he signs a contract that prevents him from disclosing commercial or industrial secrets when he leaves. In states other than California, these laws are overly stringent so that a person who has "jumped out of the groove" is often taken to court and loses the suit. In California, this is not the case, which has the effect of promoting greater mobility of talent.

As the government aims to further its role in promoting scientific and technological development, one of its key considerations is conceptual. Right now many local governments are very zealous in promoting high-tech development and have put together funds that come to a billion RMB in some cases. Few of them take time to think of the actual circumstances of their area, however. They put on airs, and focus on form rather than substance. At best, this will stay at the level of boasting, but at worst, it can lead to a substantial waste of financial resources in the end. For example, once Shenzhen held a "High-tech Expo," many other places immediately started competing to hold similar activities of their own. Chinese overseas students in Silicon Valley were fairly scathing in their comments about this. They noted that conventional products are already sold on the Internet, given the whirlwind advances of technology. To use a conventional "booth" procedure to try to sell high-tech is simply laughable. It is also rather pathetic. If one has to wait for a year to sell high-tech at a booth at an annual trade fair, the "dish will be cold" before it gets eaten.

The most important and pressing thing that the government should do to encourage high-tech development is to bring back overseas students from abroad. How to do this, and how to ensure that people feel fulfilled and accomplish what they want to do in their careers is a problem that requires conceptual revamping.

## On issues relating to capital markets, including innovative approaches and opening up to the outside

On the eve of China's entry into GATT (the General Agreement on Tariffs and Trade, renamed the World Trade Organization (WTO)), China's financial industry faced an unprecedented challenge. Given that the country's financial and securities industry was in the very early stages of development, pressures on it from potential outside competition were particularly apparent. In order to stand up to intense international competition, it was imperative that China's securities industry should create new institutions and improve the overall competence of its practitioners.

In order to be more aligned with development trends in international finance, China now has to initiate a number of measures as follows. The country must strengthen laws relating to securities regulation and raise the caliber of those involved in regulatory departments. On a pilot-program basis, it must begin to trade in new financial instruments, including derivatives, once adequate laws and regulations are set up. In the initial stages, finance will continue to be operated as distinct individual categories (departments), and regulated on that basis, with separate regulatory bodies. In successive phases, we will integrate aspects of banking, insurance, securities, and asset management. This will improve the capacities of industries that serve the securities industry, as well as improve their profitability and ability to withstand risk. Finally, China must pick up the pace of training people involved in securities within China, while also importing foreign talent to contribute to the effort.

### On a pilot-program basis, gradually start trading new financial instruments, including derivatives

Given that China's economic system is in the midst of switching tracks from one structure to another, it is premature to involve the financial industry in the trading of derivatives. We must recognize the current state of our economic institutions and laws. Nevertheless, the country is also no longer a "blank sheet of paper." Markets that trade in futures already exist. What's more, in order to avoid risk, the country's institutional investors are highly in need of means by which they can preserve value or "cover themselves" through hedging. We need to face reality, therefore, and adopt guiding policies that allow for an integrated approach to "cleaning up and rectifying" what is being done improperly, while proactively making use of what can be done properly. Futures markets are, after all, an integral part of a market economy. Since they are already appearing in China, we should regulate them properly and do our best to ensure that they operate in a sound and healthy way.

The most alarming thing is that futures markets are operating in China before anyone has any clear idea of what they really are and what their contribution may be. Since people are operating in a fog, it is altogether possible that the markets will shut down by the time the fog lifts. We feel that this would be most unfortunate in both economic and political terms, whether the markets are shut down by human actions or simply die from natural causes. It should be recognized that derivatives are being traded all over the place, under one guise or another, via "underground" exchange. The trading has the makings of a disaster. Once the conflagration happens, however, and the situation calms down, the embers will simply start up again.

It may well be that we have insufficient human resources to deal with this rampant activity, whether we try to regulate it effectively or simply forbid it. It operates outside the bounds of legitimate systems, so that coordinated actions to deal with it are difficult. International experience indicates that a somewhat more successful approach is to try to guide energies that undeniably exist into more legitimate, regulated, channels. By getting them to operate within the system, it becomes easier to reinforce their positive nature and get rid of their shortcomings.

In order to meet the challenges of joining the WTO, we therefore must research the whole issue of new financial products, including derivatives.

### The formation of "financial groups" is the global trend

In the past, such countries as the United States and Japan maintained a strict segregation of different aspects of the financial industry. Given developments in recent years, however, including the diversification of financial services, the internationalization of finance, and financial innovations, such countries are permitting changes that allow for the financial industry to form "groups." They are allowing the formation of comprehensive financial groups with banking, insurance, and securities operations contained under the umbrella of a core financial holding company that maintains a controlling interest. This increases the international competitiveness of each group.

In 1996, Japan implemented a financial reform policy that allowed for the integration of banking, securities, and insurance businesses within a financial holding company or via its subsidiaries. Since 1998, the United States has accelerated the process of modernizing its legislation with respect to the financial industry.

In quick succession, Congress passed the *Financial Services Act of 1998*, and the *Financial Services Modernization Act of 1999*. Most recently, the country repealed the *Glass-Steagall Act*, which had been in effect for more than half a century. The country now permits financial holding companies to carry on banking, securities, and insurance operations at the same time. A number of financial holding companies have quickly taken advantage of the change, including Citigroup. Meanwhile, European countries that had long since practiced an integrated form of full-service banking, such as Germany, have seen an intensification of banking mergers and acquisitions as the result of the formation of the European monetary union. The size of the resulting groups is constantly increasing. Clearly, the "megatrend" around the globe is encouraging the formation and ongoing growth of such groups.

Almost all of the financial services organizations that have come into China have the backing of a sizeable comprehensive financial group. Each group has a very powerful competitive advantage. As China joins the WTO, and as the pace picks up for international entry into the various stages of China's financial "opening up," our financial industry is in a highly unfavorable position. We feel that we should learn from international experience in this regard. We should select several financial institutions that have the proper qualifications in terms of management and good business performance, and then restructure them to form integrated comprehensive financial groups. This should have very significant practical consequences.

For one, the formation of integrated financial groups may serve to address the problem of size that we face today. We currently have securities firms that are far too small, indeed that "try to fight a war with just one soldier." The internal resources of a group can be at the disposal of the entire group, which greatly reduces costs and allows for price advantage. At the same time, integration allows for greater investment in R&D, and enables a higher vantage point in our "information age." Second, integrated financial groups have a greater ability to withstand risk, given that they wield far greater capital resources. Third, the controlling interest in such groups can make decisions based on a comprehensive view of the overall interests of the whole, and can therefore formulate strategic development plans, allocate resources on a unified basis, and realize economies of scale. Finally, such groups have an easier time of attracting human resources and cultivating a cadre of professionals.

In China, given economic growth and increased opportunities to choose among different financial products, customers are demanding ever greater diversification of financial services. The practice overseas should therefore be adopted here as well. Customers should be able to source all kinds of low-cost financial products and services through just one extremely well-known brand. International groups are finding this a very effective way to beat their competition. Right now, China can offer only a small selection of securities products to customers via the existing securities firms. Once financial businesses are consolidated, many more opportunities will become available to satisfy customer needs.

Lowering risk and improving results should also result from integration. The small scale at which firms currently operate has become a major factor constraining further growth of China's financial industry. The launch of financial groups is a necessary route to take if we intend to create a powerful financial industry in the country.

Problems with this approach, or considerations we must address, include the following:

### Modernizing legislation that relates to the financial industry

At present, China's legislation draws upon the earlier period of western laws on the subject. We have not done sufficient research into how new changes are affecting the financial legislation of all countries in the world. We must renew efforts to understand how these changes affect financial regulation in particular. We should understand the history of how things changed, and what effect the changes are having. We should make timely adjustments to our own laws and modernize our own financial legislation.

### How to form financial groups via appropriate methods

To start with, we may first select one or two financial institutions that have adequate internal control systems and good results as pilot programs in setting up financial groups. Once the conditions are suitable, we can then gradually extend the practice. In terms of methods by which we actually form groups, we should mainly lend support to securities firms that are already well endowed with a sufficient foundation in securities and asset-management capabilities. Companies that have relied on their own efforts to grow, and that have grown according to their own development needs, generally have a more unified corporate culture, more standardized business norms, and better systems to counter risk. It is easier for them to accommodate greater economies of scale.

In addition, we should improve relevant laws and regulations and create an environment for fair competition. Through mergers and acquisitions, and other market-oriented measures, we then enable those corporations that are adequately competitive to grow more quickly. We enable them to become powerful enough to engage in international competition. It should be noted that we must avoid using simplistic administrative measures that simply "stick" companies together, as we develop comprehensive financial groups.

### Setting up the regulatory framework for effective supervision of financial groups

After financial groups are established, regulation of each different industry in the group must still be conducted by the regulatory institution handling that industry, given our current principle of industry-specific regulation. Banking, securities, insurance, and so on will be a separate subsidiary and will be handled accordingly.

The benefits of handling things this way are as follows. First, regulation is done by an institution that is familiar with the field and with its legal rights and legal limitations. Second, different regulatory methods can be applied to different sectors of finance, given their specific characteristics. Third, dividing up regulatory responsibilities by industry will reduce conflict among regulatory institutions, as well as overstepping of jurisdiction and the resulting disputes. Fourth, we will be able to break through the way a given financial institution believes that it is responsible only to one regulatory agency—that is, the old framework for handling things. (The way in which vertical jurisdictions and authority applied to regulatory activities is not in line with the principles of a market economy.) In these ways, we will create a better environment for fair competition among enterprises.

As for the holding company itself, it must be subject to regulatory oversight by its shareholders, on the one hand. On the other hand, it must be subject to unified guidance and leadership by central authorities, as well as to management by the local government of the place in which it resides. Since a financial group will be able to engage in different kinds of financial business via subsidiaries, it must be subject to effective means of avoiding risk. The regulatory authorities involved must set up adequate channels of information sharing, and must strengthen mechanisms that allow for discussion and cooperation.

## Notes

1 This article is written to commemorate the 70th birthday of Mr Wu Jinglian. It consists of several short essays, which may lead to some inconsistency in style. I would like to extend my thanks to Wang Dingding, Qian Yingyi, and Lin Yixiang who have helped me to finish the different parts of this article, respectively. This article has been included in my book *At the Forefront of China's Market-based Reform* (Shanghai Far East Publishing House in 2000).
2 Friedrich Hayek: *Profits, Interest and Investment: And Other Essays on the Theory of Industrial Fluctuations*, G. Routledge and Sons Ltd. (London), 1939.
3 Masahiko Aoki (ed.): *Corporate Governance in Transitional Economies: Insider Control and Roles of Banks*, The World Bank (Washington DC), 1995.

# 6 China's reform and opening up, and the establishment of clean government[1]

## (March 30, 2000)

I am highly honored today to be asked to participate in this international conference, called to discuss the subject of "A new epoch of ethical leadership that meets challenges and creates opportunities." I extend my appreciation to the co-organizers of the conference, the Independent Commission Against Corruption (ICAC), and the Civil Service Bureau of the Hong Kong Special Administrative Region.

In line with the subject of the conference, I would like to take the opportunity to introduce China's situation with respect to setting up a clean government, given China's economic development and reform. I will describe my own personal views on this, in the hopes that it will help people in the audience understand China.

Given China's size and population, and the fact that it is in the midst of transition, many friends around the world are acutely interested in what is happening with respect to the country's economic growth and its "reform and opening up" process. All eyes are particularly on China as a result of the Asian financial crisis of 1997 and the floods that the country had to deal with in 1998, both of which caused considerable economic hardship.

In fact, for quite a few years now China has been encountering a host of problems. These are unique to our situation and unprecedented in our experience. They are unlike the Asian financial crisis, which many surrounding countries have had to cope with as well. In the past, we suffered the trauma of shortages for a long time during the planned-economy period. Since October of 1997, however, we have seen the national retail price index drop for 20 consecutive months. This indicates that China has said goodbye to an era in which all consumer goods, across the board, were hard to get. This is a highly significant change, one with historic importance. However, what we now face is insufficient demand, across the board, and an over-supply of goods. This too puts pressure on economic growth. It puts pressure on corporate profits as well as people's employment and income levels. One unavoidable result is that it has a negative impact on social stability.

We have had fairly extensive experience in how to deal successfully with inflation. We have not had to deal with deflation in the past. We are feeling our way forward, gathering experience. In recent years, the Chinese government has adopted a whole set of effective measures, including proactive fiscal policies. By increasing investment, expanding domestic demand, and strengthening social security systems, the national economy has maintained a positive development trend with GDP growing at an average annual rate of over 7 percent. The value of the RMB is stable and foreign exchange reserves are growing. At the same time, not only have we not slowed down the pace at which we are implementing economic reform, but we are achieving new breakthroughs in the areas of banking and finance, public finance, medicine, pensions, State-Owned Enterprises, and government institutions.

At the end of the day, the reason China has been able to maintain more than 20 years of high-speed economic growth, the reason it has overcome the problems caused by this most recent financial crisis as well as the floods, is that it has consistently adhered to the policy line of reform and opening up.

Reform and opening up has vastly increased China's comprehensive national strength and the standard of living of its people. By now, the escape from poverty and the drive for prosperity have become a "tide of history" that cannot be held back by any force. Every single person has an acute personal understanding of how market-oriented reform has improved his own interests and how it is the only correct path to prosperity for the country overall. People are by now thoroughly aware of this truth.

Naturally, negative phenomena are bound to happen in the course of reform and opening up. At the same time, reform is constantly readjusting people's interests, and how they relate to one another. In a given stage, it may damage the interests of some people who then express their discontent. Overall, however, for the great majority of people, reform represents an improvement in their immediate or their long-term interests. This is universally understood and has become an enduring social consensus. Even though reform will be impacting the interests of an even larger number of people in the future, therefore, as it penetrates to deeper levels, the overall approach is not going to be reversed. We remain fully confident of China's economic reform and the prospects for the country's ongoing development.

As humankind takes its leave of the last century, and greets the start of the next millennium, the ancient scourge of greed and corruption continues to plague many governments around the world. This surfaces to differing degrees and China's government is among those that cannot avoid the problem.

To the Chinese people, dealing with greed and corruption is not only a modern topic but one that has existed throughout history. In the thousand-year chapter of our civilization, the ancestors of the Chinese nation bequeathed to their descendants a valuable spiritual heritage. This heritage includes a tremendous amount of decency, uprightness, and honesty, and a desire to oppose corruption and support clean government. For the past half-century, from the day the People's Republic of China was founded, the Chinese government has been engaged in a sustained battle against corrupt behavior. In the past 20 years, in the process of shifting from a planned-economy to a market-economy system, the problem of corruption has been plain to see by each and every Chinese person. It has been the focus of considerable attention and reflection.

Some feel that corruption is driven by a desire for money. Since a market economy respects the principle of individual interests, it also stimulates the wellsprings of that desire for money. In order to purify social mores, they claim, we should therefore turn reform away from its market orientation. We should yet again strengthen administrative controls and planned management of the economy. There are other points of view, however. Another holds that, in implementing a planned economy, each person should be allowed to pursue his individual interests and that, to a certain degree, the existence of corruption should be tolerated. Both of these points of view draw a link between a market economy and corruption.

My own view is that both of these views contain extremely mistaken ideas about a market economy.

The fact is that no economic system, throughout human history, has completely eliminated corruption. During the planned-economy period, even under a situation in which supply was achieved through allocation of physical goods, the phenomenon of greed and corruption was not eliminated altogether. The view that corruption can be attributed solely to the rise of a market economy is simplistic and lacks any kind of rational analysis. One could point to developing countries after the Second World War. In the course of implementing marketization and economic takeoff, they too saw the universal appearance of large amounts of corruption. The degree of corruption in each country and region was quite different, however, and the difference was closely related to the speed with which the country marketized. The faster and more thoroughly a country or region was able to marketize, the less it experienced the phenomena of corruption. Corruption was less severe in marketizing countries, while it was more extreme in countries that retained the old system of special privilege for administrative departments in the government.

China has experienced high-speed growth over the past 20 years, with GDP quadrupling over the period. At the same time, its market economy remains in the early stages, as the planned economy and the market economy serve to "push and pull" one another. On the one hand, the market is immature and the rules and fairness of market order still have to be established. On the other hand, the old planned system still exerts a very strong influence. Administrative authority and interests continue to exert widespread interference in microeconomic activities. Given that this double-layered system coexists, a great deal of economic activity has indeed been monetized and "commodified," but "administrative review and approval procedures" and allocation of goods via the plan have also been retained to a very large extent.

In the meantime, we have market prices that are determined through supply and demand, but we also have fixed prices, determined by administrative controls. These are considerably lower. Anyone who has the authority to buy goods in the low-price system can turn them around and sell them in the high-price system for a very high profit. Such corrupt "flipping" or reselling, also described as "rent-seeking activity," is ubiquitous as a result.

Naturally, in trying to ensure a stable transition process, China's reform has opted for what it calls a "sequenced and incremental process." Because of this, it becomes difficult to avoid the simultaneous presence of two different systems for a fairly long period of time. There is definitely a price to pay for this. In objective terms, the coexistence of two systems presents opportunities that corrupt people will obviously take advantage of. They will take advantage of the assets that the planned-economy system has put in their hands, whether that is a commodity in short supply, quota allocations, permits or licenses, or land allocations. With these, they will make a trade: your money for my authority to grant what you need. Money for power. This is the root of rampant corruption during this period of transitioning from one track to another.

As reform proceeds, market prices have already been basically released from controls over these years, and the tyranny of required administrative permissions is weakening to a degree. The legal system is gradually being set up and improved upon, doing away with many of the loopholes that allowed corruption to fester. From these things, it can be seen that the corruption of the early days of reform was not an inescapable consequence of a market economy. On the contrary, it was the consequence of incomplete market reforms. In order to prevent corruption, not only should we not let anything shake our determination to keep on with market-oriented reform, but we must go further in accelerating and deepening marketization reform.

We realize quite clearly that creating equal opportunity in the market, creating rules that govern competition, will have the effect of reducing "rent-seeking" by reducing the opportunities for corruption. Corruption will not, however, in and of itself, go away naturally. Corruption will always arise in the empty areas that are not touched by the law and regulatory control. A market-economy country that is not governed by a sound and complete set of laws will always be a country in which corruption wreaks havoc.

The socialist market economy that China is implementing is a market economy based on the rule of law. This system has the potential to integrate the goals of ensuring social fairness and also improving economic efficiency. Although we will not be able to control corruption completely for the time being, or for a fairly long time to come, we still consider any kind of corruption at all to be intolerable. It goes counter to the value orientation of a socialist market economy, to ethical standards, to efficiency principles and to the spirit of the law.

Whether or not we are able to prevent and punish corruption depends not only on the success of reform, but it depends on who is in power. The Chinese government puts very considerable weight on the issue of setting up a clean government. In recent years, it has intensified its efforts to combat corruption. A large number of cases have been examined and decided upon, and some high-level people have been convicted and given the most severe sentence possible. This is only one indication that the Chinese government is firm in its determination to combat corruption.

"Rule of law" is the essence of China's democratic politics and also the basis for China's socialist market economy. Since the start of reform and opening up, China has made tremendous progress in setting up and improving upon a system of laws and regulations. The Chinese government requires that members of the government go through a process of education on ethical and idealistic concepts. It asks them to serve the people with heart and mind, to respect and obey the law, to be self-disciplined and morally clean. At the same time, the government has strengthened regulatory oversight and is strictly enforcing the law. No leniency is allowed, no matter who breaks the laws. The Chinese government encourages the media to report on major cases as a way to help publicize the effects of supervision and send a warning to others.

It is only a matter of time before China joins the WTO. The efforts that the Chinese government has put into this process make it clear that China will continue with its opening-up policies. Not only will the great gates to China not be shut, they will be opened ever wider. As we all know, entry into the WTO will present China not only with opportunities but also with challenges. The challenges are already putting pressure on enterprises to transform their mechanisms and improve their operations, but the process is also providing forceful impetus to the government to improve itself and raise its own efficiency. We have a sense of urgency that is greater than ever before, and a conscious sense of alarm. We must accelerate reform of all unreasonable systems that impede economic growth, that stifle the vitality of enterprises, and that hold back the enthusiasm of workers. We must be prepared to meet the great wave of economic globalization that is upon us, and the demands of a knowledge economy.

Faced with the challenges of a new century, there are simply too many issues that China must resolve through reform, including economic and social. The framework of the new system is just beginning to take shape in China, while the defects of the old planned-economy system have not yet disappeared. The government still interferes too much in corporate affairs, and corporations still rely too much on government. Irrational administrative licensing procedures, price controls, and market protectionism remain. Although we have made astonishing progress in the sphere of economic development, social stability will not have any kind of firm foundation to rest on if we do not persevere in reform. It will be hard to keep economic growth moving upward if we do not ensure that laws are sound, people are cohesive, and corruption is being dealt with.

In carrying on with reform, we have a tough road ahead of us. If we do not reform, however, we will have no way out at all. Only through ongoing adherence to reform will we be able to build a government that is clean, diligent, practical, and efficient. And only will that kind of government be able to lead the people in meeting the challenges of the new century.

## Note

1　This speech was given at the luncheon of the opening day of Turning Challenges into Opportunities—Ethical Leadership Forum held at the Hong Kong Convention and Exhibition Centre. The author took part in the forum at the invitation of the Independent Commission against Corruption.

# 7 Going beyond the labor theory of value[1]

(November 15, 2001)

We view Marxism as a science, rather than a religion. Given this stance, we must admit that any of its scientific theories are always going to be conditional and relative, not absolute truth. If this were not the case, Marxism would be deprived of any value to us at all. It would lose its value as a theory as well as its connection to common sense.

From a scientific standpoint, no theory is immune from reexamination, discussion, improvement, and further development. Nor indeed, is it immune from being cast out and superseded altogether. The great accomplishments of reform and opening up over the past 20 or so years, as well as the bitter lessons learned from Eastern European upheavals and the dissolution of the Soviet Union, have taught us that clinging to doctrinaire beliefs is a dead end. Only by breaking out of closed thinking, constantly innovating, can we develop, become powerful, and move forward at the cutting edge of our era.

In the past, any questioning of the (Marxist) classics was absolutely forbidden and would bring about political retribution. (That has now changed.) In his "July 1 speech," President Jiang Zemin emphasized the following: "Moving forward with the times is an innate quality of Marxism. If we disregard the realities of a situation and the specific times we are in, and instead stay stuck in the times that applied when Marxist classics were written, then our thinking will become divorced from reality. We will fail to advance smoothly. Our theoretical approach, as well as our specific policies, may even make serious mistakes."

The President's words had the effect of transforming and "liberating" people's thinking, and the great majority of comrades supported his views. Nevertheless, when the time comes to examine specifically which theories and "policy line" may not be in accord with the realities of our changing times, many comrades now begin to equivocate in their own views. It may be that they are simply timid, and lack the courage that it takes to analyze and discuss these things. Or it may be that they do not really think things through, but rather have a reflexive response that says "oppose," or even "attack." This is a mental attitude that has become entrenched over many years. If we do not overcome this way of thinking, then we will not be able to push forward reform without resistance.

My own opinion is that there are quite a few theories in traditional political economy that require discussion and reevaluation. (The labor theory of value is one of them.) President Jiang points out, "The labor theory of value, and theories regarding labor in capitalist societies, exposed the basic contradictions of specific capitalist production methods at the time, as described by the authors of Marxist classics. Today, as we develop our socialist market economy, we face conditions that are vastly different from those that founders of Marxism confronted. We should take our new situation into consideration and incorporate it into a deeper understanding of 'social labor under socialism' and the 'labor theory of value.'"

How we define the "labor theory of value" has, in fact, become a stumbling block to our ongoing reform. We should now take the subject under serious consideration and try to overcome the hurdles and break through the problems.

## Traditional political economy is no longer able to guide the actual practice of setting up a socialist market economy

Starting with the Soviet Union, all socialist countries, without exception, began to set up planned-economy systems in the early part of the last century. By now, essentially all of such purely planned-economy type systems have disappeared as the result of their deadlocked operations and low efficiency. In the past, we modeled our highly centralized planned-economy system after that of the Soviet Union, summing it up as the "Stalin model." Indeed, the highly circuitous path we had to take since then had a lot to do with regarding the Soviet Union as the example to follow. Nevertheless, we also need to recognize that the establishment of our own system relied on the theoretical underpinning of the Marxist classics.

In the early period of reform, we generally put the blame on the Soviet Union for making us take the wrong path. This took advantage of an aversion towards the Soviet Union that had been building up for years, and the recognition of Stalin's mistakes. It was helpful in reducing the obstacles to reform that were presented by the planned-economy system with its traditional set of concepts. It dispelled the concerns of most people, enabling them to participate in reform with a positive attitude.

We have always explained our decision to set up a planned-economy system as a necessary choice at the time. China was facing an economic blockade by the capitalist world and was in the midst of war. At the start of the establishment of a proletarian ruling authority (with the "asset-less class" now holding political power), it was felt that there was no other course. As a further argument, moreover, we said that this kind of highly centralized planned economy could help overcome the problems we faced in restoring the economy and establishing a country with its own form of industrialization.

History does not allow for redoing the experiment. It is very hard to say whether or not we could have made a more intelligent choice at the time. By now, however, it is apparent that the planned economy model lost out in the contest with a market-economy model over the last century. This is simply a fact that we must confront and come to terms with.

By now, the political and social situation allows for a more thorough discussion of these issues. These days, we can calmly ask a variety of questions. Why did the planned economies of essentially every socialist country encounter such major setbacks? Why did these economies ultimately become deadlocked, stopped in their tracks, when they did in fact have a brief period of glory? Can the failure be attributed to specific mistakes in policy? Why have all the Communist parties in socialist countries been able to maintain power while deciding, one after another, to implement reform and opt for a market-economy system? These questions now require some very clear-minded theoretical thinking.

It is useful to refer to the relevant parts of the classics. Marx was not very specific in his ideas about a socialist society, but he was quite penetrating and thorough in his criticism of capitalism. The classics in traditional political economy believe that a market-economy system will inevitably lead to capitalism. The logic behind the argument is as follows. The twofold nature of commodities, the "cells" of capitalism, is what gives rise to the labor theory of value. The labor theory of value in turn leads to the theory of surplus value. The theory of surplus value exposes the exploitation of capitalist societies. Marx believed that the transition from a feudal to a capitalist society could be characterized as having labor become a commodity, and having money become "capital." Based on this, he constructed a series of "revolution theories" with respect to the "class without assets," that is, the proletariat. Scholars of traditional political economy believe that Marx not only provided the ethical basis for overthrowing capitalism, but also discovered a "natural law" with respect to social development.

In similar fashion, although Marx only provided a very rough sketch of what a socialist society might look like, his determination of the nature of such a society was quite explicit. The classic works of traditional political economy believe that the system underlying such a society must be a planned economy. In these classics, market economies are the highest and final stage of capitalism. The demise of the capitalist system must necessarily lead to the demise of market economies, and the only thing that can replace them is a planned economy that is based on public ownership. In the conceptual system of traditional political economy, it is unimaginable to think that a market economy could exist in a socialist society.

This explains why it was so extraordinarily courageous for Deng Xiaoping to say that "capitalism also has plans, and socialism also has markets." This was a revolutionary statement that went beyond the bounds of traditional political economy. It "sublated" some extremely tactical aspects of Marxist theory, that is, redefined them from a different perspective. In speaking of a socialist society, Deng Xiaoping was no longer using the term in the traditional sense, but was referring to socialism with Chinese characteristics, something that was definitely not defined in Marxist classics. Looking back on it now, once the Party confirmed this conceptual approach to "socialism with Chinese characteristics" and a market economy, and once people universally accepted the approach, it was only a matter of time before traditional political economy would be transcended.

One of the key tactics used by Deng Xiaoping to push forward the idea of reform was his use of "no debate." This helped save time in the early period of reform. It reduced internal dissension and endless scholastic haranguing. As we proceed with innovative changes to our systems and as we explore the path for reform, we should continue to respect this principle of "no debate."

Nevertheless, our reform faces a fundamental risk that can crop up any time. At any point, people can use specific "theories" of the elders to attack reform and opening up. They can even repudiate Deng Xiaoping Theory. We will not be able to respond to this threat with any credibility if we are inadequately prepared, and in the end it will lead to a reversal of reform. When the political situation allows for it, therefore, we should clarify our own viewpoints on several fundamental theoretical issues. We must defend the results of "reform and opening up" and of Deng Xiaoping Theory. Indeed, we should initiate a whole new "socialist political economy" for our Party.

## The labor theory of value is a stumbling block in the way of ongoing reform

Marx's labor theory of value as a system in its own right is a continuation and further development of the results of classic economic theory coming out of England. Capitalist classes (the bourgeois) welcomed this classic school of British economics, since it helped oppose the feudal interests at the time, and met the needs of their rising class. It represented the development needs of the most advanced production forces and could be used as an effective weapon against feudal landowners. Marx constructed his own theory of labor on the foundations of a critical assimilation of this classical economic theory. He turned the theoretical weapons by which the capitalist class opposed feudal forces into a way to attack capitalist production methods. This was indeed a tremendous accomplishment of Marxist economics and was to play a revolutionary role in history.

Marx's labor theory of value grew out of and expanded upon the ideas of Adam Smith and David Ricardo. Ricardo's theory of labor was regarded as revolutionary at one time, but it contained contradictions in logic as well as the drawback of regarding itself as "absolute." Ricardo insisted on the idea that labor is the source of all value. He derived the law of exchange from the *a priori* assumption of a primitive exchange of material goods, and he insisted that this was an unchanging and perpetual law. He believed that labor and capital were necessarily exchanged at equal value, which made it impossible to explain the existence of profit. It was impossible also to explain why, no matter how much labor was used, the same amount of capital could result in the same amount of profit. As a result, the actual application of his theories to practical economics came up with irreconcilable contradictions. Ricardo's banner flew high during the time of the industrial revolution, but his reputation swiftly and irrevocably faded after the capitalist classes themselves were in power. In the end, the school (or faction) supporting his theories dissolved, but some of his ideas became fatal flaws in the logic of other theoretical systems. One could conclude that his ideas were divorced from the needs of the times, but it is more accurate to say that the public simply outgrew them.

In the Preface to the second volume of *Das Kapital*, Engels presented an authoritative comment about the bankruptcy of the Ricardo school. He not only pointed to the inconsistencies in Ricardo's theories, but asserted that Marxist theory could resolve these contradictions. More than a century has gone by since *Das Kapital* was born into the world, however, the history of economic thought has shown that intense debate continues to question whether or not Marx did in fact resolve Ricardo's logical inconsistencies. In this debate, the critical opinions of many well-known economists are worthy of our consideration. Today, Marx's labor theory of value still shines with the light of considerable wisdom, but many of its limitations, as discussed below, make it unsuitable for guiding the realities of a socialist market economy.

First, the assumptions and underlying premise of Marx's labor theory of value are long since a thing of the past. The social environment that Marx had in mind utilized the most primitive kind of exchange of material goods, as practiced in the very beginning of the history of mankind. Such a mode of exchange existed only in prehistoric societies. It meant that neither money nor capital was involved in the exchange of goods. It meant that only labor was compensated in the course of exchange, whereas no other factors, such as land, came into consideration and therefore were free. Labor itself was regarded in its most simplistic sense, in terms of physical exertion, and did not incorporate anything like science and technology or management. Any theory derived from such a premise obviously could not serve as a universal and perpetual truth.

Second, in defining the labor theory of value in the first volume of *Das Kapital*, Marx measures the exchange of goods according to "labor that is necessary to society I," but he takes no consideration of the factors of supply and demand. In order to explain the laws that determine price formation in the course of competition, Marx then raises the idea of "labor that is necessary to society II," as described in the third volume of *Das Kapital*. His point is to say that labor that determines value is not only necessary to the producers but also must be in line with the needs of society. At the same time, however, Marx immediately and decisively rejects the possibility that supply and demand relationships determine price. Because of this, Marx does not allow for the idea that the value of labor, in the end, transforms "value" into "prices." Prices are, in fact, the core issue at the heart of a market economy.

Third, in his research into the labor theory of value, Marx used the arithmetic mean in his mathematical approach. He excluded production factors in his models, and ignored any constraints that might be posed by demand. He adopted the assumption that there was no scarcity of resources. This kind of simplification related to the mathematical tools that he had at his disposal. Compared to later developments of economics, the analysis is highly superficial and indeed is divorced altogether from the realities of economic life.

For example, later developments produced "marginal economics," one of the foundations of modern economic theory, which uses calculus as a primary mathematical tool. This has enabled mankind to have a much more profound understanding of the laws of economics. Developments in mathematics have stimulated tremendous advances in economics. Due to ideological constraints, however, we ourselves continued to use highly simplified analytical tools as we researched socialist political economy.

For a long time, not only did we fail to appreciate more than a century's worth of tremendous advances in western economics, but our attitude was to reject western economics out of hand, to oppose it. Western economists were already transforming the labor theory of value into a "production costs theory of value" at a time when Marx was proposing his labor theory of value as a successor of classical economics. As the "marginal theory of value" began to take hold, both the labor theory of value and the production costs theory of value were subjected to critical thinking. In the end, Alfred Marshall, among others, integrated these into what became known as neo-classical economics. This unified the theory of value and the theory of prices. The "supply and demand equilibrium theory of value" has become the foundation of modern microeconomics. Western economists have continued to move forward in their thinking, with a multitude of contending schools of thought and towering figures over this past century coming up with impressive results. The success of theoretical results has continued to guide the western world at each stage of its economic development.

It should be noted that the labor theory of value continued be a topic of vigorous scholarly debate in western countries after Marx himself was gone. In socialist countries, in contrast, the theory was "fixed in stone" and stayed as it had been when first proposed by Marx. As a field of study, it failed to advance at all in socialist countries. In point of fact, any such "advance" was prohibited. Marx himself built his system of thought on the foundation of the ideas of others who had come before, and he never ceased to revise and correct his own ideas while he was still alive. Why is it that we ourselves ended our ongoing exploration of "truth" the moment that Marx died?

It is highly unfortunate that some of the inheritors of the Marxist mantle turned it into a closed system that rejected any interaction with other schools of thought. They turned it into an ossified system that forbad any possibility of changing with the times. In our traditional thinking, only an extremely small number of senior leaders were qualified to undertake any further development of Marxism. The fact is, however, that a theory will retain its relevance and vitality only if it is constantly subjected to the careful evaluation and innovations of generations of people. If this does not take place, it will fade away, no matter how revolutionary and advanced it might appear to be.

China's reform and opening up can be regarded as a very great step in the history of the socialist movement, but even more importantly, it can be seen as a form of liberation for socialist political economy. Since the start of reform and opening up, we have in fact been able to surmount the traditional labor theory of value. In this regard, we might look back on the debate over price reform in the early period of reform. At the time, the majority of our cadres had ideas that issued from the perspective of the traditional labor theory of value. They felt that it was absolutely imperative that we not allow prices to be determined by the spontaneous workings of supply and demand (they applied this thinking to the majority of commodities, and to the greater part of commodities in categories that were exempted). Prices should change only through government controls and structural adjustments. Not only that, but the government was fully capable of determining prices and weaving together a plan.

Based on this, these cadres refused to relinquish any hold on a planned economy and resolutely opposed a commodity economy (never mind a market economy.) In their eyes, a commodity economy (or a market economy) was equivalent to taking a "capitalist-roader path." Those who persisted in arguing for reform at the time, however, believed that it was impossible for the government to be in control of sufficient information to determine prices and maintain any kind of balance in supply and demand. Any kind of economic "plan" was therefore the product of subjective delusions. As the first step in instituting a market economy, the government must fully "release its price-control system" (fully remove price controls).

Official confirmation of price system reform came when the Communist Party of China issued a decisive statement during the 14th National Congress: "The Market plays a fundamental role in allocating resources." Price reform was the first step in surmounting the labor theory of value. Reform of the allocation (distribution) system was the second step, and one that was even more courageous and difficult to take.

Out of the best intentions, some comrades suggested that this second reform could be undertaken within the framework of the traditional labor theory of value. They took the attitude that bits and pieces of Marx could be adopted for the purpose. They therefore tried to incorporate all kinds of factors within the scope of "labor," for example, capital itself simply represented an accumulation of labor. Management and so on was also equated to labor. The substance of the term was extended at will so that almost anything could be included. The rationale for this was that it would avoid bumping up against and going against traditional economic theory, and it would also enable reform at a time when resistance to reform was fairly minor. It could detour around considerable political problems. If that had been true, of course, we would have saved ourselves considerable trouble.

The problem is that this kind of explanation was not in accord with what Marx originally thought. We believe that distorting the classic Marxist texts by interpreting them in creative ways is no different from twisting them around to suit one's own ends. This is not the attitude with which our Communist Party members should treat the classic works of Marxism. For years now, a rather vulgar trend has appeared in society, that turns academic discussions into contests to show how many memorized quotations one can spout out. The practice was perfected to an absurd degree during the period of the Cultural Revolution. It is unfortunate to see that it persists to this day. If a contestant is unable to find the right quotation to back him up, he seems to think he has lost the point.

In arguing that "factors" should be able to participate in allocation, therefore, some people search through Marx to find the right phrase. They know full well that Marx explicitly opposed this, but they keep up the futile search. The results of such efforts are not ideal. For example, "operations management" is a development associated with mass production of goods. At the very least, it came into being with the early stages of capitalism. To equate "operations management" with labor, however, and argue on its behalf from the perspective of the traditional labor theory of value, is rather forced. If one tries to redefine "capital" as "accumulated labor," that too simply turns the theory on its head.

Looking to the classics for answers to every issue not only belittles science, but it makes a mess of things. Deng Xiaoping put it best: "Marx died over one hundred years ago. How we understand and develop Marxism today, given the changes since then, is something people are not too clear about. We cannot ask Marx to give answers to things that happened more than a century after his death, let alone several hundred years. Same goes for Lenin. We can't expect him to take on the task of presenting us with ready-made answers to things some fifty, one hundred years, after he died."

It is imperative, therefore, that we go beyond the labor theory of value for a second time as we analyze how to reform our system of distribution.

### Going beyond the labor theory of value by using a "theory of distribution according to factors" as a way to organize socialist income distribution

Over years of practical experience, our Party has already gone beyond the traditional theory of labor to confirm the legality of having factors participate in distribution. This conclusion required a gradual and incremental process. In 1993, the Third Plenary Session of the 14th Central Committee of the Communist Party of China put forth the document known in shorthand as the "Decision." This stated, "With respect to distribution of individual income, we adhere to the principle of 'to each according to his labor' as the dominant approach, while allowing diverse other methods to coexist... The State, as per laws, protects all lawful income and wealth of both citizens and legal persons. It encourages rural and urban residents to save as well as invest, and it permits the capital that is owned by individuals to be considered a part of 'income distribution,' as well as other factors of production."

In 1997, the Report of the 15th Central Committee of the Communist Party of China went a step further. It stated, "We adhere to the principle of distribution according to labor as the mainstay, while also allowing for diverse other forms of distribution to coexist. We integrate the two forms, distribution according to labor and distribution according to factors of production." This Report said, as well, that the State "Protects legitimate income as according to law, and permits and encourages a portion of people to get rich first through honest work and legal means. [The State] allows and encourages capital, technology, and other factors of production to be included in income distribution."

We now need to go further in modernizing our existing terminology. For example, "labor" itself is a kind of factor of production so it should be an inherent part of "distribution according to factors." Saying that we need to integrate the two things is just an expedient way of putting it but not terribly accurate. Nevertheless, for us to have reached this kind of consensus among all Party members in the past few years is already a major breakthrough. This is because the labor theory of value only allowed for a single mode of distribution, purely and simply "according to labor," in a socialist society under a system of public ownership, that is, ownership by "all the people." The problem now is that "ownership" is being diversified. As we move into establishing a socialist market economy, property rights are not solely owned by "all the people." So long as we admit the legality of a diversification of ownership, we cannot deny the legality of income which results from capital. It becomes essential for us to break out of "distribution according to labor" as the sole legal mode of distribution in the country.

It should be noted that we will make an enormous advance in replacing substituting the theory of "distribution according to labor" with the theory of "distribution according to factors." The "distribution according to factors theory" says that income should be calculated according to the contribution that each factor makes in the process of production. The size of that contribution should be determined by the availability of that factor (scarcity) and by its price as determined by supply and demand in the market. As defined here, the supply-and-demand price refers to the marginal price, not the average price.

If we are to use the theory of factor distribution in setting up and rationalizing distribution relationships in a socialist market economy, I believe we should address the following three urgent considerations.

1   The first consideration is our need to advance or improve the market.

    One very vivid way to describe social economic activities in prehistoric societies is paraphrased by saying, "labor creates value." The phrase is both symbolic and yet approaches reality at the same time. As production factors developed, however, and societies advanced, the role of other types of production factors became more apparent in the creation of value. By the information age, and the age of a "knowledge economy," such things as science and technology, operations management, and capital stand in a more decisive position. Once the great majority of people in western countries began to own shares, and pension funds had become the dominant institutional investors in economies, it became impossible for us to use outmoded concepts in discussing problems of "exploitation." Given the existence of production lines that operate without people at all, we can no longer say that a living human laborer is the sole source of creating value. Refusing to accept the theory of distribution by factors, therefore, is equivalent to closing one's eyes and denying that the world has progressed since prehistoric times.

2   The second consideration is our need to continue on the track of reform and opening up.

    Since the start of reform and opening up, we have actively sought to import foreign capital while also releasing domestic controls and allowing diverse types of ownership among businesses to develop. Because of this, it is now simply necessary to extend legal standing to income that is derived from capital. This applies both to our theoretical approval and to the actual practicality of the situation. If, in the real world, we say "the more foreign capital the better," and "the more domestic investment being done by private individuals the better," but we do not give explicit recognition to this in theoretical terms, it is illogical and it prevents people from having confidence in the environment for their investments.

3 The third consideration is our need to ensure social stability.

Having gone through the Cultural Revolution, people in China are universally aware of the fact that poverty is not the same as socialism. Indeed, it is impossible to ask people to follow the Party in wholeheartedly "taking a socialist path" when people are living in poverty for a very long time. China has an old saying, "Those who own property tend to be moral and responsible." This principle can similarly be applied to our current society. If we want to preserve social stability, it is imperative that we enable the great mass of people to have an adequate standard of living. Moreover, they must be able to spend their own individual assets as they wish. In creating a social climate in which labor is lauded as both honorable and profitable, and in which returns from investment too are recognized as proper, we must set up a legal system that protects private property. Only if we make sure that people's assets cannot be infringed upon can we be sure that society is stable and the ruling power will endure.

The main criticism of the theory of distribution according to factors derives from income disparities.

It is absolutely undeniable that the fundamental goal of socialism is to preserve and promote social justice and create common prosperity (prosperity for all, or inclusive prosperity). In this regard, for over 50 years our Party has led the people to astonishing success. The process has been tough and has taken a very circuitous path, but the results have won high praise from the global community. In a country with a population of 1.3 billion, we have been able to provide a basic standard of living for all—people have enough to eat and drink and a place to live. At fairly low cost, we have enabled the nation to reach a fairly high standard of health. The per capita life expectancy and infant mortality rate are at levels that match those of middle developing countries. These are major events in the history of mankind.

We therefore need to analyze the problem of income disparities with an attitude of "seeking truth from the facts." Our overall assessment right now is that ideas of "egalitarianism" and feelings that we have "an excessive income gap" coexist in society. "Egalitarianism" is in fact the main disposition of people. An excessive income gap, moreover, is not generally seen to be the consequence of distribution according to factors.

Some people point to the Gini coefficient in saying that the polarization of China's income is already at alarming levels. This is somewhat too simplistic. In making international comparisons, one must always take into consideration differences in size. Populations in smaller countries enjoy greater mobility, which has the effect of reducing income disparities among regions. Larger countries have the problem of regionalization. Different regions encompass different ethnicities and religions, which leads to different customs and ways of living. Superficially, there may seem to be no borders in China, but the reality is that there are very real geographic hurdles that are hard to surmount. It is hard for people from backward areas to migrate to more prosperous regions, while prosperous regions find it hard to shift investment to more backward regions. Meanwhile, China's urban–rural household registration system means that the Gini coefficient is, to a large extent, caused by the disparity between urban and rural populations. One cannot attribute these disparities to a theory of "distribution by factors," since many are caused by history, by other systemic considerations, and by the urban–rural registration system. If one calculates the Gini coefficient within just one province, or one city, the resulting income disparity is not as dramatic.

Only by analyzing the above causes of our existing income disparities will we be able to apply the right remedy to the disease, and implement measures that truly resolve the problem. At present, the policy that central government is undertaking in "opening up the West" is aimed at reducing the disparities among regions with respect to economic growth. Additional proactive policies include pushing for the urbanization of rural "towns," encouraging cross-regional mobility of populations, and getting rid of all kinds of policies that keep rural populations and rural industry from moving into cities. At the same time, we should increase our investment in rural areas and in agriculture, adjust the structure of agricultural production, and put major effort into improving the living environment of farmers. In urban areas, in addition to setting up and improving upon social security systems, we should make every attempt to increase employment and raise the standard of living of low-income people.

In formulating distribution policies, we should be clear minded in recognizing that a strong streak of "egalitarianism" still exists in China. People would rather see everyone get the same amount than allow for some making more than others and enabling everyone to get more as a result. This is a kind of petty farmer mentality that espouses "universal poverty." We cannot simply give in to this demand and use methods that "kill all the rich and distribute the loot to the poor." Doing that would affect the efficiency of economic growth as well as the positive energies of individuals. All countries of the world that study tax reduction and preferential-treatment policies conclude that they should encourage the rich to work hard and put their earnings into investment. Only then, through policy guidance and ethical persuasion, should they ask the rich to pay greater taxes and make charitable contributions, give a portion of their wealth back to society. This is an approach that we might want to adopt ourselves.

What people are really discontent about is not that people have earned wealth. They are not concerned about successful investors. On the contrary, in conceptual terms they have long since accepted the policy of "letting some people get rich first." What people are resentful about is that a group of "mafia-types" have become rich overnight through using their official authority to gain profit and by "eating up" the wealth that rightfully belongs to the public. Using our institutions, we must close the loopholes by which such profiteering takes place, and we must propose effective ways and means to attack economic crimes and punish corruption.

One thing is worth pointing out—using the theory of factors as a way to allocate income under socialism is not some kind of purely academic topic that can be put aside and considered at some point in the future. As noted above, both price reform and distribution system reform represent two important means by which we can move beyond the labor theory of value and enable two key stages of reform. Price reform resolved the question of how to allocate the means of production. Distribution reform will resolve how to provide incentives for and also constraints on the primary players in the economy. One could say that price reform built a high-speed highway for China's economy to move toward modernization. "Distribution reform" built a high-powered engine for the nation's economy. Obviously the two supplement and help create one another and one could not exist without the other. The tides of time cannot be held back. Reform is now anticipating the second phase of moving above and beyond the labor theory of value.

Moving beyond the labor theory of value is not the same as repudiating Marxism. Rather, it is representing Marxism as it really is. In a letter that Engels wrote to friends, in which he commented on how Marx was being misinterpreted, he said, "All these gentlemen think they are practicing 'Marxism.' In fact, this is the Marxism you were so familiar with ten years ago in Paris, of which Marx himself said, 'All I know is that I myself am not a Marxist in those terms.' In a similar vein, Marx would very likely have repeated the words that Heine said to his imitators, 'I have sown dragon's teeth, and what I have managed to reap are fleas.'"

Every "deep believer" in Marxism should take what Engels said in this letter to heart.

## Note

1  This article is from a speech made at a symposium.

# 8 Various thoughts on rural employment, rural finance, and rural public healthcare[1]

(December 18, 2001)

The central government has consistently placed rural issues at the forefront of its economic work. Through speeding up the building of infrastructure in rural areas and increasing rural incomes, it has been able to accomplish notable results in recent years. Nevertheless, it is impossible not to note that reform in rural areas has not advanced all that much since the implementation of the contract responsibility system (*cheng-bao*), and particularly once the focus of national reform shifted to urban areas in 1984. Despite the fact that we have resolved basic subsistence problems for the rural population over a brief 20 or so years, something that China had never done in the past, the gap between economic levels in urban and rural areas has been greatly increased by a stagnant rural economy and a rapidly growing urban economy.

Naturally, there are many reasons for the rapid growth in urban areas. One of the more important is that reform measures have led to the nation's focusing resources in this area. The results of reform are mainly evident in urban areas. Examples would be the introduction of foreign investment, the growth of capital markets, the elimination of planned controls over industrial products, the State-Owned Enterprise reform that transformed debt into equity, the establishment of a social security system, and so on. All of these created a powerful engine that drove forward urban economies, whereas they had essentially no effect on rural areas.

Generally speaking, the growing disparity between urban and rural areas was due to policy orientation but also the market itself. It is therefore a mistake to think that simply increasing government investment will be enough if we also do not push forward further reforms. In the same way, if we merely push reform without increasing investment that too will be misguided. Only if we "fly on two wings," so to speak, will China's rural areas break out of the current stagnation and begin to soar.

To avoid duplicating what other comrades will be covering in their speeches, I would like to focus on just three topics here that relate to my own research over these past few years. They concern rural labor, rural finance, and rural healthcare.

## We must take a new approach to "shifting" rural labor into non-agricultural work

International experience has shown that it is essential to shift rural labor into non-agricultural occupations if a country is to modernize. China has a large population on a small amount of land, with farming that operates on a very small scale. Given this reality, we can put enormous effort into making structural adjustments and improving yields but the only real solution is to release (or liberate) the great majority of farmers from the land.

During the 10th Five-Year Plan period, the country's goal is to shift 40 million rural workers off the land.[2] Naturally, this kind of shift is not something derived purely from our subjective desires. A shift in rural labor toward non-agricultural industries is both an engine for economic growth and the result of economic growth. It is constrained by a variety of objective factors. Nevertheless, government conceptual approaches and policies can have a major influence on the speed and scale of the process. As things change, I believe we must revise our old conceptual framework if it hinders job growth in any way, and we must erect a new way of thinking on that basis.

President Jiang Zemin noted in the Sixth Plenary Session of the 15th Central Committee of the Communist Party of China, as well as the Central Economic Work Conference, that the guiding policy line is to give preference to the economic development goal of increasing employment. To accomplish this, and make employment grow at a rate beyond the normal pace, we must correct our understanding of the following things.

During the 9th Five-Year Plan period, we said that we should transform our mode of economic growth from one that is "extensive" to one that is "intensive." The significance of this lay in the idea of raising the quality of economic growth. Unfortunately, quite a few people took this idea of "intensifying" or concentrating to mean substituting capital for labor. Indiscriminately substituting such things as new technologies for labor clearly is not going to help us with increasing jobs. It also departs from a proper understanding of China's current stage of development.

Departing from our current stage of development is the same in substance as getting out of touch with China's masses of people. For example, we have had some explosions in mines recently. Those who were fortunate enough to survive have said that if the mines reopen, they will gladly go back into the pits, and the reason is that they need the work. Meanwhile, those breaking the law in how they operate these mines are seen by local people as capable people who are giving them a helping hand. Not only is this heartbreaking, but it makes one wonder about what is best. Naturally we have to go after people who break the law, jeopardize people's lives, practice mafia-type business, and we must be ruthless in cracking down on them. If that's all we do, however, close some mines and put people in jail, without providing alternative employment to people, how are we in fact representing the real interests of the people? What are those farmers going to think about their government and their Party?

I believe that we should put considerable effort into coming up with basic standards for such things as environmental protection and occupational safety. This can be done for very little money. Then we should encourage private capital to participate in resource development. If, on the contrary, we set the standards too high (and sometimes those standards are rather vague), and we rely exclusively on State investment for large-scale resource exploitation (while making any alternatives illegal), not only is this detrimental to job creation but it is detrimental to fostering competition among diverse forms of ownership.

The dynamics of modern economies are extremely complex. Some of the most important economic relationships are not obvious on the surface, nor in their underlying nature. Indeed, some economic principles behind them are counter-intuitive. This is precisely where the value of economics comes in. Some things that appear to be reasonable on the microeconomic level are not necessarily correct at the macroeconomic level. For example, it may seem that reducing personnel will increase results, but several issues must be examined more closely before coming to that conclusion. I discuss them below.

First, is the cost of labor the primary problem in terms of how China manages its State-Owned Enterprises? According to data in a World Bank report called "World Development Report 2001," the average annual labor cost of a worker in China was roughly 1/40th what it was in the United States (USD 729 in China versus USD 28,907 in the United States). It was roughly 1/43rd what it was in Japan (USD 31,687), 1/33rd what it was in England (USD 23,843), 1/46th what it was in Germany (USD 33,226), 1/48th what it was in Italy (USD 34,859), 1/15th what it was in Korea (USD 10,743), and 1/29th what it was in Singapore (USD 21,317).

At the same time, the "value added contribution" of a worker in China was USD 2,885, roughly four times the cost of that worker. In the United States, the figure was 2.8 times (USD 81,353), in Japan it was 2.9 times (USD 92,582), in England it was 2.3 times (USD 55,060), in Germany it was 2.4 times (USD 79,616), in Italy it was 1.5 times (USD 50,760), in Korea it was 3.8 times (USD 40,916), and in Singapore it was 1.9 times (USD 40,674). Clearly, the productivity of China's labor is not so low. It is therefore an oversimplification to think that low competitiveness is purely the result of having too many employees.[3]

Second, the government's task is to increase employment, while the task of the enterprise is to try to make a profit. Each has its own function, and a mutual balance between the two can be most effective in pushing forward economic growth. Policies that the government formulates should encourage enterprises to use as much labor as possible, but it should be up to the enterprise itself to decide upon how much capital it invests and how many people it hires. So long as enterprises are the primary entities functioning in an economy, they will make rational decisions on how to allocate capital and labor. It is not our function in the government to worry too much on their behalf, or to get involved in things that are up to the enterprise to handle. Otherwise, we run the risk of allowing things that we should indeed be handling to fade from our sights.

Third, China now has serious production overcapacity, due to the amount of redundant construction that has been going on in recent years. During deflationary periods, this overcapacity has the effect of intensifying economic contraction and creating a downward spiral. Overcapacity leads to layoffs of excess personnel, which leads to a decline in consumer spending. This leads to a further contraction in productivity and to ongoing increases in unemployment.

People's income expectations decline once layoffs begin, due to factories operating below their capacity, or stopping production or going bankrupt altogether. People's purchasing power declines which leads to even further overcapacity. Once deflation appears, therefore, it is highly possible we may experience this downward spiral if we allow enterprises to lay off workers in the name of efficiency. In such cases, not only must the government not allow the market to play its spontaneous role, but the government must take concerted action and intervene. It should expand spending and take measures to increase employment in order to break out of the vicious cycle.

Naturally, it is ridiculous to think that we should go to extremes, hire people to dig holes and then fill them up again, as the saying goes. What we need is the wealth-creation type of employment. For this, we must get rid of the factors that segregate urban and rural areas, we need capital investment, and we need the participation of entrepreneurs.

First of all, we must pay heed to what President Jiang Zemin said at the Central Economic Work Conference: "Allowing mobility of rural labor is necessary if we are to connect urban and rural economies and develop our market for factors. That means enabling rural people to move from one region to another, and into cities, to find jobs. Every local government in China must align itself with this trend and must accept it. Each government should improve the ways in which it guides and manages the process. It should not simply wall itself off, protect its own markets, nor should it adopt discriminatory policies against others."

Second, we must respect the management talents and entrepreneurial spirit of entrepreneurs and provide incentives for these to be fully utilized. We must provide adequate protections for the legal rights and interests of investors. We must provide a sound operating environment for their business activities, as well as fair political treatment. We should institute the principle of "distribution according to factors," which means regarding investment results as a fair return for taking risk. We must enable people to have the courage to go out and invest and thereby create job opportunities for others.

Finally, we should put major effort into developing small- and medium-sized enterprises that engage in labor-intensive production. We must enable market mechanisms to improve capital allocation, so as to earn a higher return. State-owned capital should withdraw from business fields that are suited to private investment. From now on, it is not realistic nor is it wise to think that China will address its employment problems by setting up new State-Owned Enterprises.[4]

## We must apply a new model to financial reform in rural areas

A variety of proposals have been set forth as ways to revitalize agriculture. They include setting up companies and farmers cooperative organizations, as well as restructuring what is being planted and farmed. Realizing these things, however, will require technical as well as financial support. Given the current financial situation in rural areas, however, neither the systems nor the services are in place to do the job.

Since 1996, when rural credit cooperatives were separated out from the Agricultural Bank of China, the Agricultural Bank of China gradually withdrew from rural areas. The task of providing financial services basically fell to the cooperatives. The financial situation of these, however, is barely sustainable as it is. By the end of 2000,[5] their nonperforming loans came to RMB 517.4 billion on a nationwide basis. (This included RMB 267.2 billion in doubtful assets, not yet declared as nonperforming, RMB 158.2 billion in loans now due, and RMB 92 billion in overdue loans.) The cumulative loss over years came to RMB 102.2 billion. The face value of owner's equity came to a negative RMB 29.1 billion. Even though cooperatives located in fairly prosperous areas might appear to be doing well, their actual situation might well be worse than what their accounts indicate.

The most urgent task before us, as we aim to improve rural financial services, is to put the systems of rural credit cooperatives in order. First, we should reconsider the idea of whether or not these cooperatives should keep having what, at least in name, is a "cooperative" structure.

Since the 1950s, we instituted three major "cooperative" systems in the countryside. These were "agricultural cooperatives," "supply and marketing cooperatives," and "credit cooperatives." This was suited to what, at the time, was a very closely-knit management system devised in order to run a planned economy. It totally controlled the rural economy, from production to circulation of goods to financing.

The system played an enormous role in accumulating sufficient capital for the country as a whole during its early period of industrialization. At the same time, it created long-term fluctuations and general backwardness in the rural economy. China's economic reform started with the dissolution of people's communes (rural cooperatives) and the rural household responsibility contract system. This had the effect of releasing productivity in a major way.

What remained, however, were the supply and marketing cooperatives and the credit cooperatives. The situation with these was distinctly bad. In recent years, a national system has been reinstituted for the supply and marketing cooperatives. Since the "shingle" that declared these to be government cooperatives had not changed in the slightest, this permitted local officials to carry on the habitual practice of interfering with or controlling business affairs. Not only have supply and marketing cooperatives functioned poorly over these years, but they have dug themselves into a massive pit of losses.

From the very day they were born, rural credit cooperatives have never truly functioned as cooperatives. For a time, rural credit cooperatives were under the jurisdiction and management of State banks and indeed became the grassroots organizations of those banks. At present, the capital for the rural credit cooperatives is composed primarily of accumulated capital after the cooperatives were separated out from the banks, as well as from share capital of cooperative members. The funds that were "transferred over" from the banks do not have any explicit owner. The funds derived from share capital are minimal, with widely dispersed ownership. Dividends are essentially nonexistent. "Members" of the cooperatives pay little attention to the operating situation of cooperatives since they have no incentive to do so. In the past, farmers indeed had no real authority in the management of cooperatives. Now that the cooperatives are well and truly bankrupt, it is illusory to think that we can pass responsibility for them over to farmers and restore any kind of "cooperative" character.

Some comrades among us feel differently. They say that cooperatives are a kind of economic organization used around the globe and that China should continue to keep them. Because of this, they have come up with the argument that we must preserve their "cooperative" character. I feel that this simplistic kind of comparison is most inappropriate. At the very least, the following things should not be overlooked in recognizing the differences between our situation and those of other countries.

First, most of the successful cooperative systems abroad were started up voluntarily by people, and were self-run. They were not simply put together on their behalf by governments, nor were they managed in an absolutely uniform and controlled way, from top to bottom. Second, successful examples abroad operated under fairly complete legal and regulatory systems, and under traditions that allowed for democratic management. Third, there is in fact no precedent abroad for a successful cooperative system that came out of or was "transferred over from" a State-owned, official-led system.

As a result, I personally believe that there is no rationale for our stubbornly adhering to a "cooperative" system that is anything but cooperative except in name. With a more progressive mindset, we should now think of reforming what we call our rural credit cooperatives.

Right now, the "positioning" of the functions of rural credit cooperatives is rather unclear. On the one hand, the government requires that they serve the "three agricultures," that is, support policies related to farmers, farming, and the rural economy in general. In compliance with this request, the cooperatives undertake loss-making business without any "policy subsidies" to make up the difference. On the other hand, cooperatives undertake commercial activities with the aim of making a profit. They constantly expand the scope of these business activities, to the extent that rural capital is invested into cities. The experience of history has proven that government subsidies will face a bottomless pit any time you have an economic organization that is allowed to carry on "policy-related" and "business-oriented" activities at the same time. (It will demand subsidies to fulfill policy goals, while spending those on its own commercial goals.)

Both of these factors, as described above, have led to increasing losses in rural credit cooperatives. Every year, the government must issue "basic money supply" just in order to maintain liquidity in their operations. In fact, however, the demand of local people for normal loans is not being met at all, even though farmers might have the capacity to repay the loans. This situation simply cannot be allowed to go on.

Naturally, there are tremendous differences among rural credit cooperatives in various provinces and cities. These include differences in assets, loan structure, economic results, client structure, caliber of personnel, and operating mechanisms. Differences can be enormous even within a given province or city. What this means is that it is hard to find a universal solution to the question of reform. Institutional reform can only proceed from the real situation. Not only do we want to reform the existing systems and organizations, but we cannot completely disengage from them in the process. In some cases, we want to make use of existing forms. The key thing is to enable rural credit cooperatives to become market participants in their own right with clearly defined ownership, or property rights, and to make them participate in the market according to market rules.

In line with our principle of "guiding" the situation according to specific categories, we might think of dividing rural credit cooperative reform into two different types. One includes cooperatives in economically advanced regions. These can take in share ownership investment from local businesses, from both "*ge-ti*" or privately-owned industry and commerce and town-and-village enterprises. They can become financial institutions operating under a shareholding system. Enhanced regulatory oversight by the People's Bank of China will prevent a minority from manipulating their affairs and protect the rights and interests of small shareholders and households. In this way, rural credit cooperatives will become true market participants.

The second includes cooperatives in poorer parts of the country. In these areas, capital and business results are fundamentally inadequate to support any kind of commercially viable financial institution.[6] In these areas, farmers' need for capital can be addressed only by "policy-type" financial institutions. Because of this, local governments will have to provide a certain amount of subsidized "policy-type" financing in cooperatives where economies of scale are inadequate. This would include a minority of impoverished counties and townships. These cooperatives would maintain their existing structures but their operations would be standardized. They would be responsible for their own profits and losses, as the basis for obtaining government-approved subsidies.

From now on, rural credit cooperatives operating according to the existing system should implement shareholding-system reform. So long as their level of business permits, and they are able to attract enough capital, they should turn themselves into financial enterprises.

One thing worth looking into is the fact that China has an unending stream of private financing activities going on right now in the countryside, and has had for some time. Some of this undeniably involves financial scams, aimed at cheating people out of their money. But some of it is legitimate enough to have become an irreplaceable source of funding for rural business, private enterprise as well as agricultural production. What's more, such private financing shows every indication of growing ever more powerful.

Could we therefore not think of applying a new model to rural financing, one that uses reform in a selective way where needed? That is, we do not need to require areas to keep rural finance cooperatives as an organizational form. Instead, where conditions are suitable, we could permit the legal existence of private financing. Private financing can develop in a sound way so long as adequate laws and regulations are in place. Given that China has already become a member of WTO, we can see that the global trend is towards a diversity of forms of ownership that engage in financial activities. We simply must be willing to face reality and go along with the flow.

## Rural healthcare endeavors must have a new starting point[7]

In the 50 years since the country was founded, China has maintained a healthcare policy that was in line with the actual conditions in the country. It has built up rural healthcare organizations, developed healthcare "teams" at the grassroots level, worked on improving the cooperative medical system, and been proactive in promoting primary healthcare. This has basically addressed the problem of inadequate healthcare and medicine in rural areas, and health standards of rural residents have greatly improved as a result.

Nevertheless, it is worth noting that the speed at which rural residents' health is improving has begun to slow down in recent years. This is now severely impacting rural economic growth and various social (or community) initiatives. In a sizeable number of villages, people do have food, and children go to school, but healthcare and sanitation conditions are deteriorating.

In my own investigations on field trips, I have noticed that living standards in rural areas are much better than when I was sent down to the countryside to work. At the same time, the conditions in village healthcare clinics are far below what they were before. In some places, clinics that existed during the period of people's communes are now dilapidated and falling down, posing a danger to people. One can still see how large they were back in those days, however.

At the same time, healthcare and medical resources are gravitating toward urban areas, and the contrast with the shortages and shabbiness of healthcare in rural areas is extreme. In its *World Health Report of 2000*, the World Health Organization ranked 191 member countries in terms of certain standards. China ranked 139th in healthcare expenditures per capita, and 188th in the "fairness" of healthcare funding. Although some people feel that the methodology used to come up with these rankings was questionable, and that the materials used were inaccurate, the rankings do serve to present us with a very important warning.

At present, the outstanding problems associated with rural healthcare are the following.

First, health standards in rural areas are relatively low and the disparity between rural and urban areas in this regard is growing. At present, the health conditions of urban residents are approaching levels in developed countries. In cities, the life expectancy at birth is now over 72 years. In rural areas, it is not even 65 years. Levels of health in rural areas continue to belong to categories of less-developed nations and particularly in impoverished parts of rural areas. Starting in the mid-1990s, the rate at which some key health indicators in rural areas were improving began to slow down or stop.

In 1994, the maternal mortality rate in rural areas of China was 1.9, while the infant mortality rate was 2.9. By 2000, maternal mortality had tripled, and infant mortality had increased 3.4 times. In 2000, the incidence of underweight children in rural areas was 4.6 times what it was in urban areas. The incidence of stunted growth in rural areas was 7.1 times what it was in urban areas. The situation in impoverished parts of rural areas was even worse: underweight children—6.8 times urban areas; stunted growth—10.6 times urban areas. All of these rates are notably higher than in other developing countries.

In some impoverished rural areas, more than 60 percent of newborn babies are not given any kind of health examination. And 59 percent of pregnant women either did not give birth in a hospital or did not undergo any kind of prenatal or postnatal health examination.

Second, infectious diseases and endemic diseases are still a severe threat to the health of China's rural inhabitants. Although the incidence of infectious disease has fallen dramatically in China in recent years, overall, this is not the case in rural areas and especially impoverished rural areas. Some key infectious diseases are failing to come under control, and even showing signs of resurgence. This is a significant factor influencing people's health.

The threat of endemic diseases has not been effectively controlled. Such things as iodine deficiency disorders, Kaschin-Beck disease, endemic fluorosis, schistosomiasis, and so on are found primarily in rural areas, with western China containing the most heavily hit areas. The incidence of disabilities resulting from these diseases is extremely high. The resulting loss of labor resources in rural areas is severe.

If we are unable to control these problems effectively, they will become a severe threat to social stability, economic growth, and also our strategy for developing the western region. Kaschin-Beck disease is an illness that leads to crippling disabilities. It is found in its most active concentrations in China's western regions where it threatens a population of more than 16 million people. As many as one-third of all those who get the disease are left with disabilities.

In 1999, 1,289 districts in China had people that had contracted endemic fluorosis. This meant that a population of 110 million people was susceptible to the disease, while over 2.7 million people were already suffering from it. Meanwhile, China has a very high rate of viral hepatitis. In 1999, the incidence of this disease was 68.9 out of 100,000 people, a number that rose by 4.8 percent over the year before. Viral hepatitis is particularly severe in rural areas. In recent years, tuberculosis has been increasing rapidly. The number of cases rose 4.9 times between 1982 and 1999. Tuberculosis too is occurring mainly in rural areas.

The epidemic situation with respect to the plague ("rat disease") has also been dramatically worsening in recent years. Source locations are expanding in size every year. Person-to-person transmittal of the epidemic is also occurring, leading to an increased risk of epidemic expansion.

Poverty brought on by getting sick, and a return to poverty as the result of being sick, is increasing daily among rural people. Many farmers are unable to bear the costs of being sick. All they can do is try to survive, if the illness is not severe, and "wait to see Yama, King of Hell," if it is severe. Surveys indicate that some 33 percent of those who should see a doctor do not. Among those who do not, 36 percent fail to see the doctor because of economic hardship. Among patients in rural hospitals, 45 percent leave at their own request prior to being discharged, and among these, 60 percent leave because of economic hardship. The situation is even worse in impoverished rural areas. There, 72.6 percent do not see doctors and 89.2 percent of those are due to financial hardship.

Among children under five who die in rural areas, 57.3 percent die at home. Among these, 22.1 percent have never received any kind of medical care at all. According to the results of a typical survey carried out in Anhui province, 88.5 percent of people who died due to some kind of illness died at home.

Among impoverished households in rural areas, 21.6 percent are poor either because of illness or because illness forced them back into poverty. In certain provinces, including Henan, Shaanxi, and Sichuan, the percentage rises as high as 40 to 50 percent. Illness has become a major factor influencing economic growth in rural areas. It also holds back the policy that the country is espousing of "moderate prosperity," getting out of poverty and moving towards a life that is better off.

Among the many causes of these problems, I note some of the most important below:

1  Investment in rural health issues has been insufficient for a long time, and there are no guarantees or safety-net system for public health and prevention services.

   At the national level, rural healthcare expenditures occupy a rather low percentage of total national health expenditures. What's more, that percentage is declining every year. Experts have calculated that total nationwide expenditures on healthcare in 1998 were RMB 363.925 billion. Within this amount, the rural component came to RMB 90.753. That is to say, 75 percent of the population of the country was using only 25 percent of healthcare money, and this figure had gone down by 10 percent since 1993.

   In terms of government investment in healthcare, in 1998, the government invested RMB 58.72 billion in healthcare. Of this, only 9.25 billion was spent on rural areas, or 15.9 percent of the total. The per capita expenditure on healthcare endeavors in rural areas was a mere RMB 9.9.

   Given the inadequate investment by the government and by local collectives, 90 percent of the compensation of rural healthcare organizations comes from business income. This leads to a situation in which such organizations have no alternative but to put their energies into providing services for money. They are incapable of taking care of public health issues that do not receive compensation, or for providing any preventive services. This means that the three levels of rural medical service that provide a "network of care," at country, township, and village levels, are in fact nearly at the point of collapse. Their "comprehensive service capacities" and their "networking capacities" are feeble at best. Actually accomplishing any public healthcare or preventive services at the rural level is hard.

2  The mission of protecting and promoting rural health is hard, given the inadequacies of rural healthcare services.

Township hospitals and village clinics are the main providers of health services in rural China. At present, the majority of these have primitive basic equipment, low-tech methods of treatment, and one uniform system to deal with things. Competition is lacking, operations are inefficient, and services are inadequate. These hospitals and clinics are far from being able to satisfy the health needs of rural citizens.

After the country started implementing a system of public finance whereby management was handled at different levels of government, township hospitals came under the jurisdiction of the heads of township governments. Given that the finances of townships are universally in the red right now, funding has gone down for the majority of hospitals. Their very survival is in doubt. Town clinics, meanwhile, have lost the support of collectives, that is, the "collective sector" of the local economy. Village committees frequently are powerless to do any good. These clinics are basically therefore either contracted out to doctors in the village, or they have broken up into different parts that are trying to manage on their own.

In the last ten years, 82.74 percent of township hospitals have been renovated through the policy initiative called the "three construction projects." Together with upgraded equipment, this has had a positive effect on the work environment of rural healthcare. However, some 41.68 percent of the investment has been achieved by taking loans from banks (RMB 10.094 billion out of a total of RMB 24.218 billion.) A large portion of the country's township hospitals have taken on a heavy debt burden as a result and it will be hard for them to repay this debt through their own efforts.

Surveys indicate that a considerable percentage of China's rural hospitals lack the basic facilities that are necessary for examinations and simple procedures. Some in the most impoverished areas have nothing more than instruments for measuring blood pressure, taking a temperature, or measuring a pulse. Among village clinics, 13.2 percent still cannot even measure blood pressure and 40.5 percent have no sterilizing pan.

With no funds to train people or to attract qualified personnel, most healthcare technicians in rural institutions have quite a low level of education. According to a study done by the Ministry of Health in 1998, only 1.4 percent of technicians in these places had a bachelor's degree or above, 36.4 percent had only a high school degree or below. Training is at even lower levels in village clinics—in terms of basic education, 9.2 percent of personnel have only a grade-school degree, 67.8 percent have only a middle-school or high-school degree. These levels are even worse than they were during the Cultural Revolution.

3  Lacking a sound preventive healthcare system, rural people are susceptible to the risk of disease.

At present, any kind of effective preventive healthcare system has not yet been set up in rural areas. In the past, cooperative medicine played a major role in addressing rural healthcare issues. As rural economic structures changed, however, the cooperative medical system disintegrated in most places. Efforts were made to resuscitate it, but this proved a hopeless cause. By now, it covers, at most, some 10 percent of the rural population.

Lacking the support of funding from the government and from the "collective" sector of the economy, cooperative medical institutions that still remain are operating mainly on private funding. The healthcare services that they provide are at a low level and they are not able to deal with severe illnesses at all. The cooperative medical system that was set up under the prior historical conditions now has serious drawbacks that lower people's trust in the system and they are increasingly reluctant to join in. The remaining 10 percent of the system is facing the danger of shutting down altogether.

The healthcare problems of the rural population have become an extremely grave social issue to the country at large. Some of our cadres are oblivious of this. They live in cities and are indifferent or even arrogant when it comes to the hardships faced by farmers. Meanwhile, the situation leaves farmers feeling helpless and frustrated, and wishing they could return to the old days. Their discontent is growing by the day in the more impoverished areas. If we mishandle the situation, we run the risk of incurring a people's revolt.

Our Party had certain practices in the past that were effective in winning the trust of local people. We sent out medical teams to visit and treat the poor in newly-liberated areas, as well as in what we called "old revolutionary base areas, ethnic, border, and poor areas." This made people aware of the compassionate concern of the Party. Caring for the health of the great mass of China's rural population is an expression of our Party principles. It confirms the prestige of the Party, and is a major part of winning the support of rural people. All levels of government and society at large had better start paying attention to this problem. We had better begin to fulfill our responsibilities in earnest. We should pull together a firm resolve to enable our rural population to receive the most basic of medical and healthcare services.

In order to do this, I propose that we carry out the following work.

First, we should go further in explicitly setting forth the responsibilities of each level of government for rural healthcare. The responsibilities of the government should include: protecting the basic rights and interests of each rural inhabitant with respect to health, reducing the disparity between urban and rural residents in terms of health, and raising the level of fairness of China's healthcare system.

Each level of government should incorporate goals for improving rural healthcare into its overall objectives for economic and social development. Each level should institute policies that emphasize healthcare work and that strengthen organizational leadership in this respect. Combined with its establishment of public finance systems, the State should set forth projects that ensure a minimum level of healthcare services in rural areas. In line with this, the State should mandate minimum spending requirements of each level of government with respect to healthcare. This includes minimum levels of basic salaries for healthcare personnel and minimum expenditures for healthcare operations. In the tax reforms associated with rural areas, the State must ensure that the necessary costs of rural healthcare are incorporated into government budgets.

Second, we should adopt a diverse range of measures to ensure the health of the rural population. At the current stage, in line with our principles of voluntary participation and targeted solutions, we should continue to develop the cooperative medical system as a private initiative with the government supplementing as necessary. In this regard, adequate government investment is a prerequisite in order to encourage people to participate. This means strengthening supervisory regulation and increasing the transparency and openness of the cooperative medical system as a part of the initiative to have open village administration and self-governance by rural people.

We must be proactive in exploring a variety of ways to ensure health and to implement health guarantees. These might include insurance that is targeted at specific groups; they might include setting up community healthcare services that contract with households to ensure healthcare by providing a minimum level of basic medical services.

In coastal areas of the southeastern part of China, as well as medium-sized cities and their surrounding areas, we should employ medical insurance systems that cover major illnesses. These should be funded by individuals themselves, as well as collectives and local governments at all levels. The emphasis in the central part of China should be put on developing cooperative medicine, with funds raised primarily from individuals, collectives, and all levels of local government. In the western part of the country, the emphasis should be put on setting up medical relief measures for particularly vulnerable populations. I suggest that project funding for this come from the central government as well as governments at the provincial level.

Third, through ongoing reforms, we should raise the efficiency with which health resources are put to use. Public health departments must strengthen the organizational leadership in this regard. By the means of more in-depth reforms, departments should explore different channels for raising funds. They should enhance the ability of township-and village-level healthcare organizations to take charge of their own development and to raise the comprehensive service capacities of rural healthcare.

Township hospitals must adopt competitive mechanisms. Through reform of personnel systems, they should begin to institute a "hiring system" (as opposed to an appointment system) for all employees in order to raise efficiency and lower the percentage of personnel who have no technical training. In a planned process, they should eliminate positions that do not require such training. Using realistic measures, we should get people working in the medical profession in urban areas to undertake healthcare work in rural areas.

In order to strengthen the management of the entire rural healthcare industry, we should define responsibilities for healthcare positions in counties, townships, and villages. We should have standardized and consistent requirements that apply to personnel, facilities, and expenditures, in order to ensure their reasonable allocation and ensure that we maximize the sound functioning of rural healthcare institutions.

Fourth, we should increase spending in rural areas on projects specifically targeted at healthcare. In line with our principle of giving weight to the most outstanding needs, including those in the western region and among impoverished areas, during the period of the 10th Five-Year Plan, we should not only carry through with projects that are already line items in the budget but we should invest a certain amount of funds in additional projects. These should focus on resolving issues that most seriously affect rural health in the central and western parts of China and that most seriously impact rural economic development. First, we should improve the training of healthcare personnel in these areas. Second, we should improve the basic healthcare facilities of clinics in impoverished regions. Third, we should control major infectious diseases and endemic diseases. Fourth, we should continue to lower infant mortality and the rate at which women die in childbirth. We should institute a program specifically targeted at lowering the incidence of malnutrition among children.

## Notes

1 This is the outline of a speech delivered by the author at an internal symposium held from December 24 to 25, 2001. It was originally published in *Comparative Studies* no.7 by Citic Press.

2 Statistics show that since the 1980s China's economy has been growing faster than employment. During the eighties, China's economic growth rate was 9.3 percent while the employment growth rate was 3 percent; during the 1990s, the former was 10.4 percent and the latter dropped to 1.1 percent. According to a World Bank study, China needs to create eight to nine million new jobs every year, which gives a great contrast to the 5.5 to 6.5 million new jobs and 8 percent of economic growth each year during the past five years.

3 When comparing domestic and foreign enterprises, some of us hold on to the limited understanding, gained from overseas study trips during the early years of reform and opening up, that the problem of our enterprises is "more people than jobs." This opinion fails to recognize the gap of management structure between domestic and foreign enterprises. In some cases, the irresponsible State-Owned Enterprise leaders also use overstaffing as an excuse for their wrong decisions or failing management.

4 By the end of the year 2000, 355 million people worked in primary industry, and at least more than half of them were surplus labor, meaning 178 million needed to be transferred. With the current unemployed laborers and new members of urban workforce each year, China is facing rising employment pressure. The grave problem can by no means be solved by the government alone.

5 Statistics here are from the relevant materials of the People's Bank of China.

6 With the 2 percent spread between the deposit and lending rates, and RMB 30,000 of cost apportioned to each Rural Credit Cooperative (RCC) employee, the employees should each loan at least RMB 1.5 million (and absorb RMB 2 million deposits considering margins, provisions, and doubtful and bad debts). And this can barely keep a ten-person financial institution running in a poor township. Take Shanxi Province as

an example, which is not the least developed region across the country. In 1999 regular workers (excluding contract workers) of the RCCs in Shanxi took in deposits of RMB 1,670,000 and loaned RMB 1,120,000 per capita. However, only RMB 480,000 loans could be repaid with principal and interest, resulting in per capita accumulated losses reaching RMB 230,000, with the annual per capita loss in 1999 of RMB 40,000.

7 The statistics cited in this section, unless otherwise specified, are all from the Ministry of Health of the People's Republic of China.

# 9 Financial innovations, financial stability, and financial regulation[1]

## (April 2003)

Our current situation includes an excessive amount of (business) investment, bank loans that are growing too fast, and the piling up of financial risk. Given this, it is extremely practical and relevant to focus on what we can do to guard against economic overheating and to mitigate financial risk.

## The relationship between financial stability and financial innovations

All countries have experienced enormous change in their financial systems over recent years. Economic globalization, technological advances, and financial liberalization have led to a profusion of financial innovations, in terms of both products and services. It could be said that such financial innovations are already the oil that greases global economic growth. One could perhaps call them the financial engine that propels growth. If China is to participate actively in international economic competition, we too must be ready to meet this trend by accelerating the reform of our financial systems, getting up to speed in terms of our understanding of these things, and improving the efficiency of our financial systems.

At the same time, we are highly aware of the risks that financial innovations can incur. I remember the analogy made by Harvard President Larry Summers when he said that economic innovation is like an airplane that is an excellent vehicle for travel so long as it stays in the air. Once it crashes, the results can be tragic. He went on to say that airplane crashes have not, however, prevented mankind from searching for ever-faster ways to get from one place to another. The reason is that any country that goes back to the old way of getting around will soon find itself beaten out in global competition. People's efforts are therefore devoted to figuring out how to minimize the chances that a plane might crash.

In similar fashion, in the sphere of finance, not only must we try to minimize economic crises that may be brought on by ever faster and better financial innovations, but we must also be prudent in managing the chronic problems brought on by an economic system that has low efficiency and high costs. Following the old ways is as damaging as it is to take risks in the hopes of instant profits.

In China, a variety of reasons have led to already scarce resources flowing into loss-making industries and enterprises, making it hard for certain economic sectors and enterprises with any life to them to get the necessary funding. Such reasons include ways that financial institutions are governed, how incentives are arranged, unsound and inadequate regulatory structures, and how all of these distort financial policies.

If the situation is allowed to persist, and not corrected, in essence what we have is a kind of chronic financial crisis that is not readily detectable. For example, the large amounts of nonperforming loans in our banking system were generated by the "hunger for investment funds" in the planned economy, and the expansionary fever. Low efficiencies and waste were brought on by the "soft constraints" on China's traditional State-Owned Enterprise budgets. Abnormal ethical conduct was brought on by lack of any conceptual understanding of the rule of law.

As a result, as we look into how to ensure financial stability, not only must we guard against the financial crises brought on by financial innovations, but we must look at the long-term negative side-effects that our backward and deadlocked financial system can have on the national economy. We must pay strict attention, in particular, to any attempt to postpone reform. A good financial system is no absolute guarantee against financial crises, but a deficient system will inevitably lead to financial instability.

## How to coordinate financial regulation in the context of an industry that is currently regulated according to each part of the business, and how to mitigate financial risk in this situation

If one could describe China's process with respect to financial reform in one word, that word would be "separate." We are using all kinds of separate or discrete measures to move the process forward. Some of these are fundamental, but some are of a distinctly "transitional" nature.

At the start of reform, a new "Industrial and Commercial Bank of China" was spun off from the People's Bank of China. The People's Bank of China then gradually began to perform the functions of a true "central bank" of China, whereas before it had been an arm of the Ministry of Finance, simply accounting for the ins and outs of public spending. This significant move heralded the start of China's financial reform.

After this, the Construction Bank was gradually transformed into a real commercial bank, whereas before it had in fact also been a part of the Ministry of Finance, handling financial accounting for basic infrastructure projects. The country's rural credit cooperatives were similarly split out from the Agricultural Bank of China. In 1994, "policy-type business" was removed from what were now regarded as commercial banks, while three policy-type banks were set up to handle loans in support of government policies. All of these steps were taken as the objectives of our financial reform gradually became clearer and more defined.

Massive growth in China's financial sector came in the late 1970s and early 1980s when a "mixed" form of operations began. At that time, commercial banks set up numerous "trust investment companies" and "securities companies." Due to unsound and incomplete financial laws and regulations at the time, as well as poor financial regulation and insufficient risk control systems within financial institutions, a number of problems were the result. In 1992, a fever to invest in both the real estate market and the stock market meant that banks, insurance companies, and securities firms flowed into "hot" industries via various means including interbank loans. This led to a loss of control over financial markets and utter chaos in financial order.

To bring the situation under control, the Central Committee of the Communist Party of China and the State Council put forth documents in 1993 that explicitly called for "separating out" the different parts of the financial industry. They called for "separate operations" of each industry and "separate regulation" of each industry. Starting in 1995, a sequence of laws and regulations were put out including the "Law on Commercial Banks," the "Law on Securities," and the "Law on Insurance." These set forth the basic legal framework and principles for administering different parts of the financial industry. It should be said that the principle of "separate administration" of these industries was appropriate given the situation at that time. It ensured the stable functioning of not only China's financial system but even of its entire economy. It also contributed to China's smooth entry into the WTO in a major way, and so played a historic role at the time.

Once the Securities Regulatory Commission and the Insurance Regulatory Commission were split out from China's central bank, regulatory functions that addressed China's banks were also split out from the central bank in the beginning of 2003. A Banking Regulatory Commission was set up to focus exclusively on regulating and supervising China's banks. By 2003, therefore, China had taken the initial steps to set up a framework for separate operations and separate regulation of its financial sector.

During this same decade, the great majority of countries around the world were taking steps to move away from separate management of their financial businesses and towards mixed operations and comprehensive regulation. Since the 1980s, financial liberalization has kept pace with the globalization of economies and financial systems. Financial innovations have proliferated, regulation has relaxed, while business among financial institutions has intensified and become ever more interpenetrating.

In November of 1999, the United States passed the *Financial Services Modernization Act*. Congress abrogated the *Glass-Steagall Act*, which had placed restrictions on and maintained a separation of firms dealing in banking, securities, and insurance. This was an acute reflection of trends that were to continue in the twenty-first century in global finance. Under the impetus of ongoing financial liberalization and the unified integration of global financial activities, more and more countries similarly abandoned previous policies that had required separate handling of different parts of the financial industry. The international trend to set up full-capacity financial groups was now irreversible.

In China, despite the intent to have separate operations, integrated or mixed financial operations began to emerge anyway. The first indication of this was a strengthening of cooperative activities between banks and securities companies and banks and insurance companies. For example, both banks and institutions dealing in securities were allowed to enter into interbank market operations and debt repo operations. They were allowed to participate in interbank borrowing and lending transactions. Qualified securities institutions were allowed to use a percentage of their own shares and investment funds, those that they held on their own account, as collateral for bank loans. Commercial banks, meanwhile, were allowed to package and sell derivative products. They were allowed to engage in investment-bank type businesses including financial consulting. The relationship between banks and insurance companies included having banks serve as agents in selling insurance products, and enabling them to collect premiums and make payments on behalf of insurance companies. This then formed a new kind of business cooperation which led to further levels of interconnected interests.

Another example of the de facto "mixing" of financial sectors relates to financial groups. These are currently the most outstanding expression of how financial operations are in fact combined in one entity. A number of financial holding companies have been set up in China, in one form or another. One form comes about when a State-owned commercial bank creates such a holding company through either sole investment in or joint venture investment in other financial institutions. Examples are the China Holding Company ("BOC International Holdings, Ltd.") that holds the Bank of China, the China International Capital Corporation Limited that holds the China Construction Bank, and the Industrial and Commercial East Asia Financial Holding Company that holds the Industrial and Commercial Bank of China.

A second form of mixed financial operations comes about when an industrial group forms a financial holding company. Examples are the groups formed by Haier, Shandong Electric Power Corporation, and so on. A third form relates to the financial holding companies set up by non-financial institutions. Examples are the CITIC Holding Company, the GuangDa Group ("China Everbright Goup"), and the Ping'an Group, among others. Financial holding companies are the most realistic option for China right now, given the country's "mixed financial operations" under a system of separately administered financial businesses.

Because of this new situation, it is obviously of crucial importance that we figure out how our central bank and our three regulatory agencies handling different parts of the financial world cooperate and work together.

Financial stability has always been a priority of the Chinese government. At the end of 2003, the Standing Committee of the National People's Congress passed the revised draft of the *Law on the People's Bank of China.* This formally set up a central bank (the People's Bank of China), and gave it the function of ensuring financial stability. This is consistent with international trends. No matter how financial regulatory institutions are set up, or what functions they are given, any central bank has the natural and indisputable task of protecting a country's financial stability. It is absolutely vital, therefore, that China clearly define and also strengthen its own central bank's functions in this regard.

At present, China's several financial regulatory agencies are beginning to set up cooperative mechanisms for coordinating with one another. They have signed a memorandum of understanding and hold joint conferences on a regular basis. The problem is that China is likely, at any given moment, to run up against financial activities that are not defined as being a part of this or that agency's functions or responsibilities. There are, inescapably, lacunae in regulatory controls as well as areas that overlap. When areas overlap, this leads to a conflict between authorities. When things fall in the cracks, there is in fact no regulatory oversight at all. This exposes the entire system to an explosion of financial risk.

We urgently need to set up institutional mechanisms for cooperation among the various departments involved, including the central bank, the regulatory agencies, the Ministry of Finance, and others. Long experience shows that officials in China's government departments are more accustomed to reporting "up" to more senior levels than they are to cooperating with others in an inter-departmental way. Although the Law of the central bank, as recently amended, sets forth the functions of the bank with respect to maintaining financial stability, if the bank is not also endowed with the corresponding power to coordinate actions, then this function will remain an empty phrase. We particularly need to implement a set of coordinating mechanisms that is well in place before we confront sudden events and crises.

Even in the course of daily regulatory activities, as well as macroeconomic management, there is a need for constant exchange of information and frequent consultation. Only with such routine cooperation will we be able to avoid overlapping responsibilities, regulatory lacunae, and also redundant and conflicting policies. China still, therefore, faces a number of challenges in the practicalities of how it goes about ensuring financial stability. There is still a great deal of work to do.

## On taking advantage of the lessons provided by international experience, in how we ourselves go about coordinating mechanisms for financial stability

In the international arena, a number of countries have already undertaken significant steps in exploring how to set up functions that ensure financial stability. In 1998, the Regulatory authority in England was separated out from the Bank of England. The Financial Services Authority was thereby set up and signed memorandums of agreement with the Ministry of Finance (Her Majesty's Treasury) and the Bank of England. The new regulatory authority was given explicit duties and responsibilities. Despite the lack of a universally-accepted model of financial regulation, the situation as practiced in England may lend us considerable insight into our own situation.

The lack of financial stability is divided into two different categories in the international arena. One is called "financial crisis." The other is described as "financial worsening" or financial deterioration. The first is characterized by having depositors withdraw their savings from financial institutions in a precipitous way, which leads to inadequate liquidity of the institution. This can be aggravated when the market sells off the currency of the country at the same time, leading to depreciation in its value. The second is characterized by financial institutions that have high ratios of nonperforming loans as well as inadequate capital reserves.

The frequency with which financial crises occur is not in fact very high, although the rate at which crises occur is increasing over time. In the past decade, there have been 15 financial crises in the world, including three in Asia, three in Europe, and nine in Latin America. Financial deterioration, on the other hand, happens much more often. In a research report of 1996, the World Bank noted that there have been over 100 episodes of both financial crises and financial deterioration over the past 20 years, in 90 countries. All transitional economies were represented in these figures.

There can be many causes of financial instability. One is the issuing of credit that far outpaces the real growth in underlying output. This leads to a notable decline in the quality of the loans. Another is the issuing of large quantities of "bail-out" type loans to State-Owned Enterprises, knowing that the State will never pay that money back. Others include: loans tied to shareholdings and the fraudulent practices of insiders who conduct the business, real estate market bubbles that burst, leading to collapse of financial markets, severe imbalances in international receipts and expenditures, leading to distortions in the value of the currency. We should be on the alert at all times for any of these problems, so as to avoid them in a timely manner.

International experience tells us that financial crises are hard to predict. Almost none of the many crises were accurately foreseen by economists. Nevertheless, almost all economists agree that ongoing long-term financial deterioration is something that will necessarily lead to financial crisis. The international practice often uses two different measurements to gauge the cost to a given country of its financial instability. One is the cost in lowered social output, and the other is the financial cost in registered capital of banks. Some authorities calculate that, on an average basis, the cost of a financial crisis to any given country is between 8 and 10 percent of the country's GDP.

One thing should be emphasized here. Financial regulatory agencies should not have the dual responsibility of regulating the country's financial industry and, at the same time, managing the country's State-owned financial assets. Institutions that are being regulated (banks, insurance companies, securities firms) include not merely State-Owned Enterprises but also enterprises owned by different types of ownership. These include increasing numbers of foreign-invested financial enterprises as well as privately-operated enterprises. At the appropriate time, therefore, we should transfer the task of managing State-owned assets over to specialized institutions. For example, these might include a State-owned financial asset management commission. As an investor, this organization would participate in the internal governance of the financial organizations in which funds were being invested. As such a participant, it would provide another powerful layer of regulatory oversight in addition to or outside the bounds of the existing authorities in the regulatory agencies.

China's accomplishments in reform and opening up and economic growth have already astonished the world. China's economic responsibilities in the region, and also the world, have grown accordingly. In order to consolidate hard-won results of reform and opening up, and ensure ongoing stable growth, it is imperative that the country now implements effective mechanisms to ensure financial stability.

Right now, the most important element is to form a consensus among all relevant government departments about the objectives, framework, substance, and tasks that relate to financial stability. Departments involved will primarily be those handling macroeconomic affairs and financial regulation. Each must understand its own responsibilities and must be willing to take up the task.

## Note

1 This article was based on a speech made by the author when he addressed the "Financial Risks and the Chinese Approach" International Seminar jointly sponsored by the Development Research Center of the State Council and the World Bank in Beijing.

# 10  China's energy sector

Issues of government regulation,
and making the sector more
market-oriented[1]
(November 17, 2003)

The future development of energy resources is a highly strategic issue for China in
light of the country's goal to realize a moderately prosperous society for all.

Demand for energy is expected to grow dramatically in line with China's ongoing rapid economic growth and the improvement in people's standard of living.
To meet this demand, not only do we need to make use of a comprehensive range
of energy resources, including oil, natural gas, coal, hydropower, wind energy,
and nuclear power, but we need to encourage enterprises under a diverse range
of ownership systems to participate in energy development. We must use market-
oriented measures to improve supply and increase efficiencies, while also meeting
our goals for socio-economic development and environmental protection.

This requires that we formulate energy policies and development strategies that
are appropriate to China's level of economic development and the realities of its
energy production. We must take steps to set up and improve upon relevant laws,
regulations, and systems, and provide the country with policy support and reliable
institutional safeguards to ensure that our energy development is both sound and
sustainable.

The energy industry is a comprehensive sphere of activities that touches upon
and links up many industries. Energy production and consumption have unique
and highly complex technologies and economic features. Economic theory, as
well as the experience of all countries, indicates that the exploitation of coal, oil,
and natural gas resources is highly competitive, whereas transporting and installing such things as natural gas and electricity tends to be natural monopolies.
Hydropower and nuclear power, on the other hand, have their own issues in terms
of environmental safety and externalities. Different areas and links in the process
have led to different patterns of market competition around the world. Different
industrial forms also have determined various kinds of governmental administration and intervention.

Since networks that are involved in supplying and installing electric power and
natural gas are not fully competitive, incomplete information and externalities
often lead to imperfect markets. These require appropriate government intervention. Traditionally, most countries around the world have adopted systems that are
State-owned, State-operated, and vertically integrated to deal with these industries. This is one way to deal with imperfect markets. Another can be seen in the

way the United States and Canada have chosen to handle the industries. Together with a handful of other countries, they have allowed privately-operated firms to carry on monopoly operations under strict governmental regulation, so that the results approach a market-oriented model.

Over the past 20 or so years, advances in technology, globalization, and marketization have led to major changes in the ownership systems and enterprise types that make up the market structure of global energy production. On the one hand, oil exploration, refining, and marketing, has formed a pattern of national and even global oligopoly. On the other hand, the consensus among both developed and developing nations is that countries should also implement market-oriented reforms with respect to such monopolies as electric power and natural gas. Many have therefore broken out of traditional forms of State-owned and State-operated vertically integrated industries. Different countries are separating out different parts of the industrial chain into separate energy markets. They have enabled market entry into any area that allows for competition, and have introduced such competition. In areas that do not allow for competition, while still implementing State-ownership and State operations, they have strengthened governmental regulation and adopted "corporate-type operations" that employ market principles and accounting methods. The United States and England, among other developed countries, have been pioneers in reforming energy-industry structures, enterprise-ownership systems, and regulatory systems.

Starting in the early 1980s, China began a number of reforms in the various industries governed by the country's energy departments. These included adjustments in the industrial structure of the industries as well as reform of enterprise systems. Of particular note is the way China partially opened up investment in electric-power generation in the mid-1980s, when it implemented a policy that allowed for diversification of investors. China's implementation of this reform was even earlier than many market-economy countries in Europe, including England.

While pushing for ongoing reform of enterprises and industrial structures, the Chinese government also implemented synchronized reform of governmental institutions in the energy sphere. This was in line with the requirements of market-economy systems. In energy spheres that allowed for competition, China gradually, and with certain restrictions, opened up market entry into certain industries. The country created market entities via administrative procedures ("administrative guidance"), by restructuring the industries into forms that could allow for competition. The idea was to move quickly into a pattern that allowed for reasonable competition and to allocate resources via competitive markets as much as possible. In areas that were natural monopolies, such as natural gas supply, urban installation of natural gas systems, and the transmission and installation of electricity, China dismantled and separated out the industry depending on the technologies and economics of specific parts of the process. The aim was to explore how to introduce competition into any sphere that could allow for it, while at the same time strengthening specialized regulatory oversight of the non-competitive portion.

After more than 20 years of continuous market-oriented reform, China has gradually broken down the monopoly of the State-owned sector and introduced competition by enterprises that have a variety of ownership structures. It has realized a separation of government functions from enterprise management. It has gone from being a participant in market competition into being an entity that formulates and enforces the rules of the market.

A market structure composed of various interest groups and imperfect competition requires that the government be an independent and specialized market regulator. It must resolve problems when the market becomes ineffective, and must protect market fairness and particularly the rights of consumers. This calls for establishing a regulatory framework of industry laws and regulations, specialized regulatory agencies, transparent procedures, clear definition of authority, and high caliber personnel. Regulatory oversight must address issues of market entry rules, prices, market behavior, service quality, occupational safety considerations, and environmental protection, among others. We believe that the long-term development of China's energy sectors will be served by setting up institutional guarantees. These include government regulatory systems that are effective in regulating industrial sectors that demonstrate a certain degree of natural monopoly.

We are fully aware that China has a very long way to go in the process of setting up modern regulatory systems in the energy sphere. In overall terms, management of the country's energy sector has undergone substantial reform but this cannot be said of its modern regulatory system. From an institutional perspective, in the broadest sense, such a system should include a sound legal environment and professionalized regulatory agencies. It should provide wide latitude for "self-constraint" by the industry itself, while providing full protection for the rights and interests of consumers.

The core issue when it comes to modern regulation is the application of a rule of law to the process. Market competition and market order must be maintained through applying principles of fairness, transparency, professionalism, honesty, and checks on power via the medium of laws. At present, China's regulatory rules are highly incomplete. Regulatory agencies are not yet fully established and lack effective mechanisms for regulating the transmission and installation of natural gas in particular. This delays the formation of an effective pattern of competition in the market. It lowers the overall efficiency of the natural gas industry, allows prices for services to be unreasonable, constrains development of the industry, and hurts the rights of consumers.

In setting up a regulatory system, we feel that the following issues must be addressed.

First, market entry rules (rules governing market access) are unclear, while the "review and approval process" of administrative departments has not been reformed. The Chinese government has determined that it should gradually release some of the market-access restrictions that currently apply in the sphere of energy. We encourage all forms of social capital (capital owned by non-government structures) to invest in this sector, particularly domestic private capital. However, up to now we still lack the rules and procedures to enable such market entry in ways that are both open and transparent. The result is that not enough social capital is indeed coming into the sector, making it hard to create an adequately competitive sector.

Second, we lack the conceptual framework for modern regulation that operates according to laws. Administrative management departments (governmental authorities) are accustomed to being the "owners" of State-owned assets. They are comfortable with administrative measures as the way to govern the sector. Their mentality does not allow for modern regulatory concepts, or for transparent procedures that operate by the rules of fair and equal treatment under the law. There are no checks on authority in departments. Decision-making is opaque and arbitrary, due to numerous factors that allow for interference by individuals.

Third, we lack the legal foundation for regulation. Once many monopoly industries carried out market reforms, no set of laws and regulations was set in place to constrain the government departments that manage these industries or to define the rights and responsibilities of their enterprises and their consumers. Government departments have no set of rules by which to operate, or by which they are obliged to operate. Meanwhile, the standing of enterprises as the "primary entities" in the market is unclear and the rights and interests of consumers are not upheld.

Fourth, specialized regulatory agencies have yet to be established. In the area of electric power, China has undertaken reforms over many years yet still not set up specialized regulatory agencies to regulate the sector. This has led to the fact that a number of government departments simultaneously administer various management functions. Not only are functions dispersed across multiple departments, but the primary regulatory body is unclear and the resulting regulation is inefficient. Regulatory enforcement has not been separated out from departments that formulate policy. Without one body that holds primary responsibility, there is "an empty seat" when it comes to enforcement. In 2002, a State Electric Power Regulatory Commission was indeed established, but its responsibilities are still to be defined. In the natural gas sector, the situation is the same—there is still no specialized regulatory agency with clearly defined functions.

Fifth, price regulation fails to meet the requirements of a market-oriented economy. China's price regulation of such monopoly industries as electric power and natural gas has generally been determined by an equation that adds "a reasonable amount of profit" to costs. Since no rigorous standards apply to the cost structure of an actual enterprise, however, in fact, price regulation has no effective constraints on what an enterprise puts forth as "costs." Costs run rampant as a result. Prices are excessive. This affects the production costs of downstream industries as well as people's quality of life. In some cases, prices are kept intentionally low at certain industrial stages so that fictitious profits can be made in downstream industries. This then holds back the growth of these industrial stages, creating bottlenecks in the national economy.

Sixth, monopoly industries do not provide services on a universal basis to all people. Virtually all monopoly industries in China, including electricity and natural gas, lack rules and regulations about what they must provide in the way of services. This prevents the public at large from having fair, equal, and more efficient access to services. Practices that are universally available in other countries are hard to implement inside China as a result.

A modern regulatory apparatus represents a systemic guarantee of effective market regulation. It represents systemic arrangements by which a government regulates enterprise behavior within the context of a market economy. The Chinese government has explicitly stated that it is moving further in transforming government functions and reforming methods by which economic activity is managed. Reform objectives include creating administrative structures that are fair, transparent, clean, efficient, well coordinated, and that have clearly defined functions and behavior. At the same time, the government has emphasized that government functions and the limits to government authorities will be defined according to laws and regulations at both the central and local level. The government has a great deal to do to achieve all of the above objectives. The government must "put in proper order" (clean up) the vertical lines of authority between central and local governments. It must improve its administrative approval procedures in line with principles of simplifying, unifying, and making more efficient. It must coordinate policy-making, implementing, and regulating, and improve its functions relating to economic regulatory capacities, regulatory oversight of the market, social management and public service. It must clarify departmental functions in a more scientific way. It must create a more reasonable institutional structure, and improve its staffing structures.

In the context of an increasingly global economy and China's entry into the WTO, China will be pushing forward systemic reform of its energy sector as per the demands of developing a market economy. I believe that we should focus on the following guiding principles as we do this, and particularly as we set up specialized regulatory systems.

1   We must handle the relationship between "policy-making departments" and "regulatory departments" in the proper way. This means pushing forward a separation of the two functions. I recommend that at the appropriate time we set up a comprehensive State Energy Administration. Depending on the policy objectives for economic and social development in a given period of time, this body would formulate energy development policies, market entry policies, pricing policies, and such industrial policies as the development of clean energy. We must achieve a separation of policy making from policy implementation and regulation. Specialized regulatory agencies should implement specific regulations in the various spheres of economic regulation, occupational safety, environmental protection, and so on, in order to ensure the effective implementation of policies.

2   We must accelerate the establishment of regulatory agencies that are independent in terms of their organization, specialized in terms of operations, and well defined in terms of responsibilities. We should improve the regulatory systems that apply to energy, the environment, occupational safety and so on, as per principles and concepts of a modern regulatory system. China has set up a regulatory agency specifically addressed at the electric power industry,

but the organizations, institutions, and functions of this body are yet to be defined. In the area of natural gas, while the marketization process is rapidly moving forward, we must set up a natural gas regulatory commission as soon as possible. This will give all stakeholders, but consumers in particular, greater confidence that their rights and interests are being protected.

3　Using scientific approaches, we should clearly define the horizontal and vertical authorities of regulation. From the perspective of improving efficiency, we should make rational distinctions among the authorities of different regulatory agencies and departments. As soon as possible, we should set up a unified regulatory agency at the central level to handle long-distance transport of natural gas, so as to form a consolidated national market. According to general principles as established by the national government, we should encourage local governments to set up corresponding regulatory bodies to carry out regulatory oversight of the installation of natural gas facilities in cities.

4　We must strengthen coordination among the different functions of different regulatory agencies. We must pay particular attention to coordination at the downstream level which includes, for example, coordination of the natural gas and electric power regulatory activities. We must strengthen not only economic-type regulation, but also social-type regulation that relates to safety and environmental protection. We should create quantified standards that enable better regulation of such things as public health, safety, and environmental protection. The goal here is to internalize these "externalities" in order to make regulation more effective.

5　We should build up the organizational capacity of regulatory agencies. This means setting up clearly defined incentives as well as constraint mechanisms. It means having work procedures that are transparent and rigorously followed. It means having support systems that supply necessary information and that allow for effective communication with the public at large. We must raise the organizational capacities and training levels of regulatory personnel as well. We must pay particular attention to improving price regulation methods, measures, and technologies. We should use incentive-based procedures to ensure effective results of this kind of regulation.

In sum, we must speed up the construction of a modern regulatory system in the energy sector. This will help create a market environment that enjoys fair competition, but it will also help the energy sector itself by providing institutional safeguards for long-term sustainable growth.

## Note

1　This was a speech made by the author at the China Energy Forum.

# 11 On income inequality and being industrious[1]

[Being industrious improves people's livelihoods and provides ample supplies]

(February 2005)

Statistics in certain cities in China indicate that the gap in per capita disposable income between the highest and the lowest household incomes has been widening. It has gone from 3.1 to 1 in 2000 to 4.7 to 1 in 2003. This has aroused considerable debate.

Income distribution is an acutely sensitive topic. It has the ability to arouse extreme emotions among people and it is also highly disputed among economists. Reaching any kind of consensus on the subject is not an easy task, given the many aspects that are involved, but over-simplification has the effect of misguiding both policies and social understanding.

China's traditional system led to "universal poverty," which in turn led to Deng Xiaoping's statement about "Letting some people get rich first." This policy, dating from the early period of reform, stimulated an enormous response from the public at large. One of the key reasons China was then able to become the fastest growing economy on earth was that a series of guiding principles and policies soon followed that correctly provided incentives for creating wealth. The well-springs that enable social wealth began to bubble up, including sheer hard work, intelligence, technology, management skills, and capital. These were reinforced by a social atmosphere that encouraged industriousness and entrepreneurship.

Development has been "the necessary path" from the start of history itself. The ancients have many sayings that point in this direction and that condone and indeed celebrate wealth creation. The prosperity of the nation at large is made up of the wealth of its hundreds of millions of people. Meanwhile, the wealth of each household, and each individual, is inseparable from the industrious hard work that each performs. In its most concrete expression, the creation of wealth, the actual realization of making money, comes down to the decision by each individual to do all that he can. Chinese people have always had a great respect for the virtues of hard work, and have always had a feeling that one will be all right if one only works hard enough. This plain and simple truth is reflected in various ancient Chinese classics, including the *Zuo Zhuan*, written in the 22nd year of Xuan Gong.

The fundamental way to achieve common prosperity, that is, inclusive prosperity for everyone in the country, is "development" and economic growth. We cannot rely on distribution policies that call for egalitarianism. Only if we make the pie bigger will everyone's share increase. The question for economists is how to make that pie grow, and specifically, what kind of distribution policies will be most effective in growing the national economy.

The only sound distribution policies are those that lead to an absolute increase in the income of every individual in the country, so that standards of living will improve for even the lowest wage earners. To return to the statistics cited above— one cannot assume that this kind of income disparity automatically requires that we take immediate measures to resolve it.

In the past, China's egalitarianism, its "one big pot" approach, led to a lifeless economy. During the "ten years of domestic turmoil," egalitarianism developed to such a degree that things could not become any more egalitarian. Even the country's eight-tiered pay scale system was criticized as being a capitalist-class approach (evidence of bourgeois rights). People recognize the lunacy of such criticism today. Even under the traditional system, however, China did indeed have an income differential that was as much as 4.7 to 1 in the country's larger cities.

The problem is to determine how great a differential is reasonable and acceptable, if one, for example, feels that 4.7 to 1 is too great. Some economists in China were already saying that income disparities were too great ten years ago. I personally feel that this kind of simplistic judgment and deliberate exaggeration is divorced from the realities of China's economic development. The result can only be to fan the flames of public opinion and to call for a return to traditional egalitarianism. It will then be hard to counter the attack on a consensus that has developed since the start of reform and opening up. The results will be detrimental to any respect for property rights, and to the process of setting up the conceptual and legal basis for protecting property rights.

The idea that it is "better to have the same as everyone else than to allow for unequal distribution" is deeply rooted in the soil of China's small-scale farming traditions. At every step of the way, however, this old way of thinking is in conflict with the needs of modernization and a market economy. In the course of participating in economic globalization, of encouraging foreign investment as well as investment from private domestic capital, we can only look upon widening income gaps with certain tolerance if those gaps are caused by different levels of wages, technologies, and returns on capital. Indeed, without a certain degree of income disparity, we will not achieve capital accumulation and private-sector growth at all.

Fairness and efficiency can both be served by policies that allow for income disparities that arise from the causes noted above. We do not need to choose between "unfair" and "egalitarian" in our approach.

If income disparities are not caused by the above factors, however, then the situation is different. We know full well that what the public is upset about is income derived from corruption, kickbacks, and the siphoning off of State assets through illegal means. Our policy emphasis should therefore be put on attacking this kind of illicit income, while at the same time protecting the most vulnerable groups in our communities. Naturally, we also need to correct income disparities that are caused by systemic factors, given differences among departments and industries. It should be pointed out, however, that attacking illicit income is not at all the same as formulating "income distribution policies." Illicit income falls in the category of criminal behavior and criminal law. The two different things should not be talked about in the same terms.

Jobs are the primary means of livelihood for people. The government must do its best to promote economic growth and expand job opportunities. At the same time, the government must provide occupational training to build up skills so that people in need of social support can develop their own talents and make their own living. It needs to be said that China is experiencing the greatest economic growth period in its history. In 2004, the employment situation improved overall in cities. In rural areas, policies adopted by the government in support of farmers have led to a fairly rapid growth in incomes. There is only so much that government subsidies and reduction of taxes can do, however. If we are to realize any kind of high-level prosperity, we must recognize that individuals need to rely on their own hard work and entrepreneurial talents.

In sum, at a time when many developed countries in the world are finding it hard to sustain their welfare policies, we absolutely must avoid being infected with the disease of thinking we are already "affluent." Waving the banner of "compassion for the poor" as a way to argue for moderating income-distribution policies will not only hinder our economic development and economic efficiency, but it will not help the lives of the disadvantaged or contribute to greater social justice.

## Note

1  This article was first published in *Caijing Magazine*, 2005(3) (February 7), Vol. 126.

# 12 A look at the stock market from a new perspective[1]

(February 2005)

Tens of millions of Chinese shareholders passed the Spring Festival holiday of 2005 in trepidation. Although the market had closed out 2004 with a rise of over 2 percent, which lent a ray of hope, this did not change the feeling of gloom that accompanied the recent 68-month low. People's expectations now varied dramatically, buttressed by various reasoning, and it was highly uncertain whether the New Year would be one of celebration or despair.

People primarily focused on market prices (to the exclusion of fundamentals). Many felt that resolving the "split share structure" of listed companies would be essential to revive the market. It was the immediate "key link," whereas other issues were ultimate goals. Some articles even proclaimed that if this issue were resolved, it was not impossible to think that the market could go to 5,000. Articles in this vein stayed on the Internet for months.

Trading always blows hot and cold and a market goes up and down. Looking at a market purely from the perspective of government policies is not necessarily the right approach. At the 2005 *Caijing* Conference, I pointed out that problems with China's stock market are of a comprehensive nature. They need to be addressed from a number of different angles. The allocation of share rights is one thing that needs to be resolved, but it is not the most important nor is it susceptible to quick solutions. This idea aroused a certain amount of controversy.

It is interesting to note that there is a consensus on this issue of different classes of shares ("split-share structure") among people who previously held diametrically opposite views. There are, of course, some people who disagree. Some people feel that it is a kind of self-deception to think that the current system of a "split structure" will necessarily lead to different share valuations of the two different classes of shares, and who therefore argue that "A" shares should carry certain rights with them. This illusion was popular for over a decade and hoodwinked countless investors.

From what the media is telling us, the current market is being upheld by the idea that investors will be compensated when the split-share structure is changed. The problem with this idea is that the structure was created by many factors in China's recent history. Changing it over any short period of time, with simple solutions, is fundamentally impossible. Moreover, even if we allowed "complete liquidity of all shares" in explicit laws and regulations to that effect, in reality this would not change the split-share structure of shareholding rights. The reason is that allowing State-owned shares to become fully tradable would undermine the standing of the existing management of those enterprises, and would weaken the power of government departments in charge.

Therefore, if we attribute the root causes of China's ailing stock market to the split-share structure, it is very likely that this superficial problem will simply become an excuse for postponing more fundamental reforms. It will be the cause of even greater losses to shareholders as the opportune time for reforming real problems passes us by.

The majority of countries in the world may not have laws and regulations that allow for a listed company to have such a split-share structure. Nevertheless, share structures are indeed the product of local cultures and legal systems and, in fact, they differ greatly. "Common law" countries, such as the UK and the United States, practice so-called "individual capitalism." Traditional share rights in these countries are fairly dispersed, although nowadays various kinds of legal-person funds are the primary shareholders. "Continental law" countries, such as Japan and Germany, practice "legal-person capitalism." These countries have an interlocking equity ownership structure with legal persons and "primary bank systems" holding shares in each other. In Japan, traditionally, equity transactions among legal persons can only be done within a certain scope of participants.

Hong Kong's stock market basically follows the British practice. In order to enable State-Owned Enterprises to list on the Hong Kong market without any problems, and in order to avoid misunderstandings, in principle it was decided that State-owned shares would not be traded and that there would be different voting rights associated with different classes of shares. This was to protect the interests of those shareholders who had tradable shares. Later, a portion of State-Owned Enterprises that had been listed started to sell their "old shares." In this process, no investors criticized the "split-share system," nor did anyone raise demands for compensation.

The issue of how to compensate people who own circulating or tradable shares has been hotly debated for several years, but nobody has put forth any decent proposal as yet. In fact, this is not a matter of methodology but of principle. Without even talking about whether or not there should be compensation, how to compensate and who to compensate are highly unclear. People have calculated that China's stock market investors have lost something in the neighborhood of RMB one trillion over the past 15 years. As we all know, shares move from one hand to another all the time. Many who suffered losses have long since left the market. Some who are still in the market bought in at different prices. Given these complexities, what kind of compensation scheme could possibly be fair?

It is worth noting that certain interest groups may well have misled the media and this may well have interfered with the policy-making process. The fairytale that "A" shares come with associated rights has drained the last penny out of countless investors. We have reason to believe that an attempt to resolve the split-share issue and the compensation issue will provide another huge chance for illicit dealings. As a proposal is designed, its various considerations and the timing of its release may lead to another nightmare on the part of the millions of dispersed individual investors.

Anyone who is unbiased can recognize the root causes of the problems of China's stock market. Crimes committed by insiders in listed companies working together with securities companies are so serious that they endanger the very survival of the market. In comparison, issues of the split-share system are not only unrelated to such things but they are inconsequential.

For many years, large quantities of funds have entered the market through such channels as the interbank lending market and asset management companies. This has enabled insiders in securities companies to cover their tracks as they "convey" their interests. It also means that they are building an uncovered liability. When the market falls, the crisis of securities companies will be exposed on a massive scale.

Listed companies are the same (in terms of undertaking illicit behavior that will be exposed by a falling market). Only since the beginning of the New Year, ten listed companies have been investigated, and 11 senior officials have either been arrested or have fled abroad as a result. Scandals involving high officials may well become the hot topic this year in the stock market news.

We must address deep and fundamental causes if we aim to resolve the problem of "the broken capital chain" of securities companies, and if we aim to deal with asset stripping in listed companies. We must withstand the pressures of a temporary fall in the market, focus on the fundamentals and start by fixing loopholes in the system rather than by bailing out listed companies. We must not simply pour massive amounts of money into the system, or even pour money into just specific companies, cover for them and also for securities companies. In a steady and sure-footed way, we must carry on the working of building institutions. I believe that in a short time we can reverse the decline and restore confidence in the market. Only if we take this approach will we be able to change the market's hyper volatility. Only then can we have a market that fulfills its proper role as a way to allocate capital effectively, and that grows in a sound and relatively stable manner.

## Note

1 This article was originally published in *Caijing Magazine*, 2005(4) (February 21), Vol. 127.

# 13 Concepts that underlie market regulation[1]

## (May 2005)

Government regulation is a necessary process given that markets have the potential to malfunction. In essence, such regulation is a relationship between government and the market. It is unlike administrative behavior that has no constraints on it, however, and is not simply a matter of commands and control. A market regulatory system has the ability to stimulate market growth and social progress through a defined set of rules and procedures that have been put in place after discussions with all stakeholders have taken various points of view into account. Such regulation has developed within market economies in order to supplement and correct deficiencies in the market itself.

As defined by the field of "new institutional economics," government regulation is a kind of mechanism that allows a third party to apply enforceable measures to contractual exchanges. This plays a similar role to other types of third-party enforcement of contractual obligations, including the courts and self-regulatory organizations. It constitutes an organic part of a market economy system.

The establishment of modern regulatory systems is carried out according to legal requirements as well as the "three principles" that sustain a market economy, namely "fair, just, and open." The systems ensure that information disclosure is open, and that transactions are carried out in a highly efficient and fair environment. Regulatory agencies set up *a priori* sets of rules and regulations. Once these are established, the agencies carry out regular monitoring of the subjects under regulation to ensure that they are not breaking the rules. They do not in any way interfere in the normal operations of regulated entities and they absolutely must not participate in any market transactions of those entities. Regulatory agencies are therefore not responsible for the profitability of regulated entities, or for the ups and downs of their share prices on the market. It is only by making sure that specific rules and regulations are being followed that they can coordinate and protect the interests of all parties concerned.

The experience in other countries around the world has shown that any administrative actions that go beyond the bounds of normal regulation, and particularly any intervention in market prices, has a multiplier effect on adding to market risk. Not only does such interference not contribute to market stability but, on the contrary, it leads to loss of confidence in the market. Investors who take a mature approach to their investing do not expect regulatory agencies to come in and sustain or create market prices at levels that everyone likes to see. They do have every right to see regulatory agencies come in and ensure market order, so that everyone feels at ease.

Under a planned-economy system, administrative bodies were generally responsible for two different functions at the same time, that of "owning" the entity under their jurisdiction and that of "managing" or "regulating" that entity. Because of this, such administrative bodies have continued to feel a sense of "ownership" over these entities even during the period of transition. As we switch tracks, habitual behavior that was acceptable in the previous period has led to what is now considered an "overstepping of authority." Owning and regulating are still mixed in together.

For example, a particular regulatory agency encountered a situation in which a company was clearly transgressing rules and regulations, and perhaps even breaking the law. It therefore demanded that the company present all previous board meeting minutes to the agency, and it also sent representatives to attend the next board meeting. On the surface of it, this seemed a good idea. It appeared to strengthen regulatory oversight, guard against risk, and so on, but if one looks deeper into regulatory principles and consequences, questions begin to appear.

First, there is no guarantee that personnel in the regulatory agency are any more ethical than those in the entity under investigation. They also may not have any more ability to judge the merits of the matter in terms of managerial acumen. Prior to an actual incident of misconduct, therefore, they have no ability to ensure that improper behavior does not happen, nor do they have the ability to stop that behavior. Moreover, given that the regulatory agency itself participated in and knew about policy decisions, if there were to be an incident involving misconduct, how could the agency protect itself from the charge of complicity? How could it say its personnel were taking a selfless and fair approach?

Second, in the case of listed companies, any person who attends a board meeting must respect confidentiality agreements. If personnel from regulatory agencies attend board meetings, or are in possession of minutes from board meetings, they too must respect the confidentiality of any market information. If, for example, any insider trading were to occur, anyone who has had access to insider information is subject to being investigated. Regulatory agencies are precisely the ones doing the investigating, however. How can a regulatory agency stay clean enough to regulate itself?

Even more importantly, once an agency has entered deeply into a company's daily operations and decision-making processes, the agency tends to be "captured" by (bribed by) the very subject it is investigating. That is, at least, the experience in many other countries around the world.

In order to deal with these problems, we might consider doing what other countries have done. They require that companies, particularly financial institutions, set up a Compliance Office within the entity, and that they designate a Compliance Officer as the person specifically responsible for complying with rules and regulations of the regulatory agency. One problem in China right now is that some regulatory agencies are trying to deal with too many matters, or, one could also say, they are not taking care of what they should handle while trying to meddle in things they should not handle. The most outstanding example of this is the way that some administrative departments still intervene in highly specific matters despite having gone through years of reform. Indeed, administrative interference is wielding ever-greater power, not less.

In market economies, so long as a person, including a legal person, abides by the law, he is responsible for all profits and losses in the market. His affairs are his own and no other person, including the State, has anything to do with it. This is the most basic principle of market economies. Going against this principle can only harm the development of market mechanisms. If government departments take on responsibilities that rightfully must be borne by individuals or enterprises themselves, and impose too much protection or indeed too much pressure, even if it is done with all best intentions, it can lead to no good.

Agencies regulating the stock market always hanker for "good corporate results" and a rising market overall. Because of this, when the market is in the doldrums they take a somewhat more lenient approach to speculative behavior. They "look without really seeing," even when the behavior is very clearly illegal. Their intent is to stir up the market to better levels. In contrast, when the market is exploding, they tend to panic, instead of taking macroeconomic regulatory measures to treat the underlying problems. They come up with numerous measures to suppress the normal functioning of the market.

In recent times, there have been occasions when the stock market and the real estate market were performing at opposite ends of the spectrum—one was like sparks off a fire and the other like a calm ocean. To deal with the overheated market, some media declared that we should "attack" speculators in the market. This statement has a very confused idea about the rule of law.

## Note

1   The article was first published in *Caijing Magazine*, 2005(10) (May 16), Vol. 133.

# 14 Incentive mechanisms, moral hazard, and the basis for a market[1]

(May 2005)

We came together with members of the World Bank not long ago to look at the subject of how to stabilize financial markets and guard against risk. This was at our invitation and the talks included a number of experts from within China as well as from abroad. During the talks, the foreign guests raised some doubts about China's regulations on depositors' insurance, as put forth in the November 2004 *"Opinion"* called *"Opinion on purchasing the creditor's rights and securities settlement obligations of individual creditors."*

They felt that the compensation terms were too generous. The minimum payment (floor) of RMB 100,000 was 12 times the average per capita GDP in China. (In urban areas, it is seven times average per capita GDP.) Moreover, they felt that a ceiling that paid out 90 percent of losses was too high. Even though this kind of government insurance did not apply to the deposits of institutions, still they felt it was too high. In the European Union, for example, governments pay deposit insurance only up to the amount of 20,000 Euros, which is lower than the average income of a person in the European Union. (Italy is somewhat different in that it pays to a limit of 103,300 Euros per person.) In the United States, even the famous generosity of the Federal Deposit Insurance Corporation (FDIC) only pays up to USD 100,000, which is roughly 2.8 times average per capita GDP.

Chinese experts then explained the reasoning behind these levels of compensation. In overall terms, Chinese people are not wealthy and a considerable part of their savings and investments are put toward such things as old-age security, medical treatment, the education of children, and so on. Meanwhile, only very limited types of financial investment can be made in China, so there is little opportunity to spread risk over different investments. Moreover, in the past the government paid depositors 100 percent of any losses made by financial institutions. Accomplishing this particular reform was already difficult since it discounted the compensation by 10 percent. It could be considered a historic step in the right direction. One should not underestimate the contribution that this made to raising investors' awareness of risk.

This explanation silenced any further debate on the subject but it was clear that the western experts were not fully convinced.

Nevertheless, a consensus that was achieved at that meeting by both Chinese and foreign parties was the main thing. All believed that deposit insurance could only be extended to citizens' savings in financial institutions, such as savings in banks and the "guarantee funds" (or "margin") with securities firms. The government's responsibility absolutely could not extend to any losses incurred by citizens' trading on the stock market. The best way to disperse risk is to reveal the nature of risks before any unfortunate event takes place, and to strengthen prudent measures for guarding against crises. It is not to extend unwarranted protection to depositors and investors.

When stock markets fall, any "boosting" efforts undertaken by the government are of a universal nature. International experience shows that such universal measures not only cost an enormous amount in public spending but they can distort incentive mechanisms among investors who should be taking responsibility for their own risk. This leads to the longstanding negative side effect of moral hazard.

With respect to stock market volatility, in particular, the government should not simply attempt to suppress such volatility. Instead, it should look at the systemic defects that lie behind volatile stock prices. In Germany, the "new market comprehensive index" fell by 96 percent over the course of two-and-a-half years before the market was closed in 2002. Over the same period, the Nasdaq market in the United States fell by 80 percent. Neither government took steps to block what was happening in these markets.

The problem is that those who enjoy "the right to be heard" are often those who are most directly affected by a falling market. Since they have the power, they lobby the government for assistance. Meanwhile, "moral hazard" is also present within the regulatory authorities of some countries. Faced with the opposition and condemnation of institutions that might be forced to close down, the "failures" in the marketplace, they shift the ultimate costs onto the backs of taxpayers. In this way, they make up the losses to investors who otherwise would have to pay themselves. In this way, they disperse the pressures of the market by shifting them onto others. Except for in Asia, very few countries in the world have set up official "market-boosting funds." If any country does have such a thing, it is resorted to only under unusually strong pressure. Experience has indicated that it is impossible to rely on a government's buying and selling of shares in order to smooth out share prices. Meanwhile, in the process of trying to do so, every stage in the process allows for an increase in corrupt behavior, due to the collusion between officials and people in the business.

Hong Kong's monetary authority has indeed adopted policies to deal with international "manipulators" in its stock markets. Nevertheless, those policies are a last resort, set up to protect the Hong Kong dollar and Hong Kong itself. Taiwan, South Korea, and China's Taiwan province have all seen cases of "market boosting" in the 1990s. Subsequent analysis of these actions, however, has shown that its positive results are minimal in turning around the market while instead it often results in the bailout funds getting deeply stuck. Meanwhile, as regulatory authorities have focused their efforts on dealing with market interventions they have neglected ongoing reforms. In point of fact, although such reforms also have an indirect impact, they are even more effective in driving up stock prices.

Investment in any market has those who win and those who lose. If investors are unwilling to take the consequences of losing, one cannot hope that they will ever engage in rational market behavior, or that their behavior will be beneficial to society in the end. When severe moral hazard infects regulatory authorities, and incentive mechanisms are skewed as a result, a healthy market cannot in fact be resurrected.

No country in the world can completely avoid policy failures in the process of setting up markets. History has proven time and again, however, that when policies do fail, the government cannot promise compensation to failures so long as policies were implemented in an open and non-discriminatory way at the time. At the end of the day, the money a government promises to spend is money from taxpayers. What's more, promising to pay it out goes against the most fundamental principle of the market: responsibility for oneself. The problem is that any hypothetical compensation is, by nature, hard to quantify and standardize. Not only can investors' desires never be satisfied, but it is nearly impossible for compensation to be fair and just.

What's more, investors put major effort into negotiating with governments. Investment concepts that have been built up over years and standards for measuring "value" can disappear in an instant in the face of their desire for compensation. Given this, any effort on the part of a government to compensate for losses may be distorted, no matter how much it might stem from the best intentions to create a "bull market," or from highly ethical considerations. That distortion may well be further distorted, to the extent that the market faces an unending sequence of bad consequences.

Some points of view feel that "compensation" and market boosting is in fact a way to protect the most vulnerable groups in the country. It should be recognized, however, that "universal market boosting" is a highly expensive measure. Since large quantities of financial assets are, in fact, held by wealthy people, they are the primary beneficiaries. To help the disadvantage, we might need only a fraction of the total cost and we might target the recipients more effectively. Moreover, since universal market boosting has a "regressive" effect, it serves only to worsen income disparities. In the future, this may well intensify broad resentment among the masses. This should be taken carefully into account in the process of formulating policy.

## Note

1 This article was first published in *Caijing Magazine*, 2005(11) (May 30), Vol. 134.

# 15 Xue Muqiao

A great master who experienced
the vicissitudes of a century[1]

(September 10, 2005)

One of the great elder statesmen in the field of economics has passed away. Xue Muqiao was 101 years old. On the last day that he drew a breath, his heart still pumped with uncommon vigor, breaking all records and astonishing the medical personnel around him. It may be that his profound love for this land, and his concern for China's reform and modernization efforts, kept him fighting to the end.

The century in which our respected Xue lived was one of monumental change in China. Xue-*lao* (*lao* being an honorific) was born in the 30th year of the Guang Xu reign of the Qing dynasty (1904). He witnessed the three great revolutions in modern Chinese history: the Xinhai Revolution (1911), the founding of the People's Republic of China (1949), and the reform and opening up of the country. As one of the primary architects of and advocates for China's economic reform, Xue-*lao* must have been gratified to see and be a part of the rejuvenation of the country after a century of humiliation.

People regarded Xue-*lao* as a person of tremendous integrity. He lived a long and satisfying life and can be remembered as a venerable gentleman who embodied all that is good. Shortly after the celebration of his 100th birthday, he was honored with the very first award for "Outstanding Achievement in Economics in China." Economists gathered in Beijing for the awards ceremony and the media gave the event close attention. Xue-*lao* was fully worthy of the honor. Over the next few days, however, I noted some questions from younger people on the Internet: who is Xue Muqiao and what exactly were his contributions?

Indeed, contemporaries of Xue Muqiao have long since faded away and many of our younger generation of economists as well. Despite the information explosion on the Internet, in an age when few read books any more, somebody like Xue Muqiao is at a far remove from younger people. Starting in the 1990s, despite his tremendous influence on reform and opening up in China, Xue Muqiao began gradually to fade from the economic scene due to his age and poor health. Other than the occasional article summing up his own views on economic philosophy, there were only four occasions in which the media gave him focused attention.

The first of these was on October 25, 1994. At the time, Zhu Rongji was a member of the Standing Committee of the Central Committee's Politburo, of the Communist Party of China, as well as Vice Premier of the State Council. He presided over a forum in honor of Xue Muqiao's 60th anniversary of participating in economic work and economic theoretical research. This was jointly sponsored by the Development Research Center of the State Council and the State Planning Commission.

The second was in 1996, on the occasion of the publication of the book "*Memoirs of Xue Muqiao.*" This was completed with the help of assistants who had worked with him over the years as he was in increasingly poor health. The third was on January 25, 2004, when Politburo standing committee member Premier Wen Jiabao visited Xue-*lao* at the hospital and described the contributions he had made to economic reform and development in China. The fourth was on January 25, 2005, when Zeng Peiyan, Politburo standing committee member and Vice Premier attended a "Forum on Xue Muqiao economic thought." During the forum, he made a speech noting that economic theorists in China as well as practitioners should learn from Comrade Xue Muqiao. They should make sure that theory is firmly integrated with practice, they should carry out their work in accordance with the laws of economics, they should take a scientific approach to development and constantly improve the capacities of a socialist market economy.

In fact, it is quite hard for those who did not experience the years that Xue Muqiao lived through to understand the significance of what he did, and the way he changed our very social fabric. Change in China over these years has been too fast, and our economic progress has been too fast, for younger people to grasp what came before. Those who were brought up in a market economy simply cannot comprehend what was behind the writings of Xue Muqiao. They cannot understand how hard it was to criticize a planned economy and to espouse a market economy while using a vocabulary that was still steeped in an earlier age. They cannot understand how hard it was to argue for change while still operating within a "traditional" conceptual structure. They cannot comprehend the painstaking effort that was required, nor the mental courage and the extent of political risk.

Xue-*lao* was roughly half a century older than I. It is hard for people even in my generation to understand him completely. I was very fortunate to become his assistant in the early 1990s, to help him put his writings in order. For a period of time, therefore, I had the opportunity to listen respectfully to his wisdom and to study his works systematically. I have perhaps a greater familiarity with this member of a former generation than others who are my age. In what follows, therefore, I would like to put forth my own impressions and memories, as well as to express my profound respect.

## A pioneer in "liberating" one's mind

Xue-*lao* was self-taught. In the earliest period, he participated in both economic theoretical research as well as field trips to understand the realities of the country. In the 1930s, he was a key member of "China's rural economic research team," which was a leftwing group studying economics. This group was active in exploring a development path for China's rural areas and for China's society in general. During the anti-Japanese war period, he participated in economic work in the base area in Shandong province, where he became the head of financial work. After the country was founded (1949), he was appointed to a number of highly responsible positions in the economic sphere. He participated in drafting the very first Five-Year Plan, as well as the "Three Great Transformations." It could be said that he was one of those laying the earliest foundations for the planned economy and a publicly-owned system.

This personal history, as elevated as it was, did not however serve as an impediment to his thinking as time went on. During the Cultural Revolution, he began to have doubts about China's mode of economic development, the deadlocked systems of a command economy with their high costs and low efficiency. He not only had doubts but he quietly began to think long and hard about how things should change.

He began to present certain criticisms of the system both before and after the Third Plenary Session of the 11th Committee of the Communist Party of China. In 1979, he published a work entitled *"Research into issues concerning China's socialist economy,"* which systematically described the experience of China's economic development to date. It presented a serious reconsideration of the course of China's development. Some ten million copies of this book were printed and it became a source of enlightened thinking about economic reform for China's communist party cadres and the public at large.

Xue-*lao* was the earliest person to propose that reform should start, first and foremost, with the circulation system. He felt that this was more important than starting with the distribution system and he called for efforts to expedite price reform and circulation-system reform. He recommended releasing prices as fast as possible, under the premise that money supply must be strictly controlled. He saw this as the best way to enable the market to play a role in allocating resources.

In September of 1980, at a meeting convened by the Central Government, he represented the Office of the State Council for Structural Reform in making a key report. In this, he declared, "At the current stage, China's socialist economy is a 'commodity economy' in which public ownership of the means of production is absolutely dominant while diverse other economic elements [sectors] also coexist." In a very pioneering way, this recommended that China move in the direction of market-oriented reform. (*Translator's note: "commodity" in this sense means goods that are bought and sold as opposed to being "circulated" via a plan.*)

Xue-*lao* believed that socialism could not attempt to be "purer than pure," a publicly-owned system that championed the "largest" and "the most public." He repeatedly said that China should allow other forms of economic "elements" to coexist together with the publicly-owned sector. He felt that the public sector should withdraw from any operations that were better suited to private ownership. Existing small-scale State-Owned Enterprises could be sold at open auction. Some enterprises could be "leased" to private operators on a pilot-program basis. Competitive industries could employ share-holding systems on an experimental basis. He advocated opening up the market for trade in agricultural goods, actively encouraging families in rural areas to carry on sideline businesses, allowing farmers to carry on long-distance trade. He put forth numerous recommendations with the aim of accelerating the development of a private sector. He once said, "since we are doing our best to attract in foreign investment, why can't we put the same effort into developing a private sector on our own soil?"

Xue-*lao* transitioned from being one of the most important participants in and proponents of a planned economy to being a pioneer in criticizing the rigid economic system and promoting reform. This was a kind of paradigm shift that started from within his very bones. Given his unique standing and prestige in the former system, his advocating for a market-economy system was immeasurably important at the time.

## Stay firm like a big rock in the midstream of reform

Xue-*lao's* adherence to market-oriented reform stemmed from very deep reflection. Because of this, he never wavered in his belief in reform despite being subjected to unfair criticism on several occasions, and also despite having to go against his own conscience at times in accepting such criticisms. Over the past 20 or so years, we have had occasion to watch a number of people equivocate about reform, never truly embrace it. Sometimes they are "true believers" in a planned economy, and sometimes they are unconsciously protecting their own vested interests. They either "doubt" or "reject" any kind of reform or systemic change altogether. Sometimes, for form's sake, they give it lip service. At any opportune moment, though, they oppose it either obliquely or head on. In the meantime, they equivocate, saying what they do not believe in their hearts. At this very moment, indeed, some economists are placing the blame for our economic problems on market-oriented reform. This seems to be quite fashionable, and is a trend we should be highly concerned about.

As a person, Xue-*lao* was calm and composed. He was easy to get along with. On major issues of principle, however, he could be scathingly clear. At key times in the course of reform, he stood for what he believed in without regard for how this would affect himself. He did not "hide the sharpness of his blade" at these times, but instead declared his position loud and clear. After 1989, some people expressed doubts about the correct orientation of reform and even began to censure it. The tone of their argument was that we should reaffirm socialism, and to do that we must reinstitute a planned economy. What's more, we should criticize market-oriented reform as a form of "capitalist liberalization" that is "against the four basic principles." Articles in this general vein were published in various newspapers and journals. They blamed certain policy mistakes on a "deviation" that they defined as "excessive worship of market mechanisms." They resurrected the whole debate on the subject called "is reform capitalist or is it socialist," and they drew a direct line between the underlying social system and the "either–or" choice of a planned economy or a market economy. At this, Xue-*lao* was unable to stay seated in his chair. He declared in no uncertain terms, "The general orientation of our reform is correct. We are right to pursue the path of a socialist commodity economy with a plan."

On July 5, 1990, Xue-*lao* attended an economic forum hosted by the Standing Committee of the Politburo. At this forum, an intense debate broke out about whether economic-system reform should be "plan-oriented" or "market-oriented." Xue-*lao* expressed his owns views in a clear-cut way, but after the forum he still felt that his words had not hit the mark. Saying to himself, "If I don't speak out, who will," he took up his pen and composed a letter to comrade Jiang Zemin. It was written with tremendous fervor and agitation. In it, he said, "People are arguing about the political changes in Eastern Europe. I personally do not believe they can be attributed purely to the desire of capitalist countries to promote their 'peaceful evolution.' In my view, the primary reason for the difficulties in Eastern Europe is that they have not yet carried out sufficiently thorough reform. They cannot jump out of the circle of irrational prices, soft public finance, and soft loans. They keep trying to mend the traditional economy with a patch here and a stitch there. Or they apply reform in a very piecemeal way. All this can do is delay the eruption of the problems. It puts the economy in a state of chronic crisis. It cannot fundamentally improve the economic situation, nor can it achieve any kind of victory in a contest with capitalism. By the time the leaders of these countries realize they absolutely must institute reform, it will be too late. The people will have lost their confidence in the current leaders. They will doubt their ability to carry out reform in the context of a socialist system [and they will want to change that system]. They will refuse to give the leadership the slightest bit of support and soon it will be too late for leaders to repent."

This letter represented not only Xue-*lao's* selfless approach and political courage, but it was an expression of his highly acute understanding of the historic situation. In advance of Deng Xiaoping's "tour of the South," it set forth a distillation of the "call for reform" that Deng Xiaoping was soon to be making. Clearly, Xue-*lao* was not absolutely alone and without support in his views. At his side stood Liu Guoguang, Wu Jinglian, and a number of other younger and middle-aged economists. At a critical moment, however, a moment that could determine the fate of reform, Xue-*lao* played an undeniably crucial role. He stood firm like a rock in the middle of the stream.

## Doing the right thing

In July 1980, with authorization from the Financial and Economic Steering Group of the Central Committee of the Communist Party of China and from leaders in the State Council, Xue-*lao* took charge of establishing the State Council's Economic Research Center. Not long after this research center formally began work, he began to draw in various people he had known and worked with at various times in his life. These included former colleagues, associates, and outstanding intellectuals whom he had come to know well, particularly those who had been attacked and beaten during the several political movements after Liberation, including the Cultural Revolution.

These were people with tremendous knowledge, vision, and capability. He now gathered them together and began to put their talents to use. At the time, some of these cadres had still not been completely politically rehabilitated. Nevertheless,

Xue-*lao* made proper arrangements for them in the Center where they could have a safe "perch" and carry on with their work.

I have a particularly abiding memory of one of these people, a man named Xu Xuehan who indeed just passed away this year. He and Xue-*lao* had a very profound friendship. Xu-*lao* was younger, but was just 16-years-old when he was made head of the Hangzhou Communist Party organizing group. This was in 1927, at a time when Xue-*lao* had just joined the Party. During the war years, Xu-*lao* was engaged in underground work in "white areas" (Kuo Min Tang-controlled areas), and his personal experiences are legendary. After Liberation, he was imprisoned for a long time due to a particularly great political injustice. When Xue-*lao* invited him to join the Research Center, he had already stopped working for over 20 years. I was fortunate to have a certain amount of contact with Xu-*lao* and recognized in him a man with a powerful reform instinct and a strong sense of responsibility. When he was young, he engaged in underground work in Shanghai for a long time, then was in charge of economic work in liberated areas in the northern part of Jiangsu province. He was highly experienced in handling real economic issues but he also had a profound understanding of market economics. In his later years, he kept a close eye on the progress of reform, and was concerned as it moved forward with difficulty and in highly circuitous ways. He would always say to me, with a grave tone in his voice, "The heavy burden of China's reform is now on the shoulders of you all!" His concern for the nation and concern for the people move me to this day.

After the passage of so many years, it was quite extraordinary how Xue-*lao* managed to gather together this eminent group of elders and put them to work in the Center. This was particularly true since a number of them were still in unfortunate political positions and also living under tough living conditions. He reached out a confident hand to them, and offered a form of assistance that allowed the public to feel it had done the right thing, as well as he himself. It was the action of a true prince of a man.

## A leader in the mold of a scholar

After Liberation, Xue-*lao* spent the rest of his life in senior positions. The impression he gave people was quite the opposite, however, for he seemed to be much more of a scholar than a leader. In daily life, he appeared to be quite a bookworm. Comrade Zhu Rongji remembered this aspect of him when he spoke at the celebration of Xue Muqiao's 60 years of economic work. He said that Xue-*lao* was outstanding in all of his professional work, but rather less successful in handling matters of daily life. He recalled one story that harked back to the "May Seventh Cadre Schools" (note date). Xue-*lao* was being "labor reformed" at the time. Each person was supplied with a "mazha," a kind of folding stool that was to be used during meetings. Xue-*lao* was not familiar with this device, and so he stood it upside down and sat on its legs. This story continues to amuse people to this day.

When it came to researching economic issues, however, Xue-*lao* was a great master. He was tireless when tasked with looking into complex economic matters.

He wrote prodigiously and left a large body of written works. Nobody of his stature in economic circles has come close to him in terms of his output.

Xue-*lao* wrote all of his articles in his own hand. In later years, only after he began to suffer from Parkinson's and could no longer hold a pen, did he begin to use an assistant. Nevertheless, the assistant did not stand in for him as his "spearman." When I helped him, for example, he was absolutely lucid and used his mind to think through issues for himself. He dictated what he wanted to say and I wrote things down. We then would revise what was written and discuss it in depth, or he would ask for other opinions on the matter and we would think them through. No article was ever published that had not gone through his painstaking revisions.

For a period of time, Xue-*lao* was not well enough to keep working. Instead of submitting things to publishers, as they would have liked, however, he put them on the shelf for later review. He would not allow for anything to be published that he had not personally approved. Later, somebody asked Xue-*lao* to write a new book systematically setting forth his own experience of reform and opening up, and describing how new understandings have altered the process. He felt that his health did not allow for this, however. He also put aside his intent to write a book systematically laying out his own economic reform philosophy and instead concentrated his remaining energies on finishing his memoir.

Xue-*lao's* rigorous approach to scholarship should serve as a model for all of us in later generations.

## A gentleman

By the time I had the opportunity to be in close proximity with Xue-*lao*, he was no longer in any leadership position. To me, he seemed a very approachable and amiable older gentleman, smiling, sometimes even a kind of Buddha. According to people who worked under him in earlier days, however, he had the same demeanor then as well, gentle and gracious. Nobody could seem to remember having seen him angry. Nowadays, this seems to be the exception rather than the rule. Those in leadership positions have to show their temper or they can't be regarded as maintaining real authority. Moreover, a hot temper often gets hotter the more senior a person becomes. Xue-*lao* was different. He never put on airs. He gave the impression of being a man of real substance, whom people could simply respect.

In talking to those of us in a younger generation, Xue-*lao* was always conscientious and deliberate. He would not send for any of us on the spur of the moment but first had to be prepared. Later, as he had less and less energy, our talks became shorter. Once, after he became ill, his daughter said to me that her father would be anxious prior to a meeting on economic issues, and would stay focused, but then be completely exhausted afterwards.

Xue-*lao* demanded perfection of himself but did not insist on it in others. This may have been related to the fact that he was born into an enlightened gentry family in the south (south of the river). His parents were both highly literate and open-minded. Due to our work relationship, I maintained close contact with members of his family. His wife, Comrade Luo Qiong, was a senior revolutionary with impeccable credentials, starting with being sent as a representative to the Party's Seventh Congress in Yan'an. She served in a senior position in the All-China Women's Federation after Liberation. She too was kind and gentle in demeanor. Xue-*lao*'s sons and daughters are all thriving in their various jobs. They are carrying on a tradition of generosity and uprightness and are highly regarded by all.

A great master has peacefully taken his leave. His spirit and his way of being will remain an inspiration to us forever.

## Note

1 This article was published in *Economics Research* 2005(9), and was later included in *One-Hundred-Year Vicissitudes and A Great Master*, a collection of articles in memory of the first anniversary of Xue Muqiao's death, published by China Development Press in 2006.

# 16 What exactly do we want to learn?[1]

## (November 4, 2005)

Today's forum has been extremely informative. Both the speakers and the commentators were superb. The organizers asked me to give a summary of today's discussions, and specifically to address the subject, "What is it that we have learned?"

I reflected on this subject for a while, and it occurred to me that it is indeed important to "learn" things, but it is even more important to ask the question, "What do we want to learn?" Only if you aim to learn will you be able to learn. If you are not so interested, then you won't learn anything.

I have a reason for mentioning this. We in China were only able to come to the correct line of thinking about reform after we had broken out of the mentality that bound us before. Only after we bravely "emancipated our minds" were we able to see the world in a new light and learn new things. Before then, by the fixed patterns of our traditional thinking, any kind of reform and opening up was heretical. It not only deviated from the line, but could be considered traitorous. This whole question of whether a market economy was "socialist" or "capitalist" was, after all, not resolved for a long time after 1978. It remained a theoretical issue. The debate did not end until after Deng Xiaoping took his "southern tour" in 1992. That finally set the tune with a "decisive hit on the gong."

Now, the most serious schism since 1992 has appeared in China's economic circles. We are now hearing opinions that have not been heard in ages. Some of these reject the whole idea of China's economic structural reform. The voices against reform seem to slander and attack the whole process. Some seem to be aimed at certain problems with reform, and attack only one specific point. In doing this, however, they achieve the underlying aim, which is to attack reform altogether. Some of the criticism appears to be aimed at the so-called "mainstream school of economics." Nevertheless, the real target is reform.

I believe that these voices are powerless to change the orientation of China's reform. They cannot shake our determination to take the path of "socialism with Chinese characteristics," but the power of these things to do damage should not be underestimated. They come wrapped in the guise of "traditional theory" and of righteous indignation. It can be said that China's economic circles are facing the greatest threat they have seen since the 1990s. When I suggest that we address this question of "What do we want to learn?" therefore, this is not an idle exercise. It truly is something that needs to be taken seriously.

This morning, David Dollar, as Country Director for China and Mongolia for the World Bank, spoke on behalf of that institution's Vice President. Among other things, he said, "China's economic growth over the past twenty-some years has been outstanding. That is, as an economy containing more than one billion people, China has managed to have an average annual GDP growth rate of over 9%. The per capita GDP has risen over this period by eight times. Roughly one-quarter of the labor force has moved from low-efficiency agricultural production to higher-efficiency industrial and service sectors. Four hundred million people have emerged from what officials define as a state of poverty. This is the most successful poverty alleviation plan in the history of mankind." I believe this statement can serve to represent the views of most international organizations, and that it is the mainstream view of some of our foreign friends. All generally give high marks to China's economic success.

Why is it, then, that voices are now being raised against reform, and indeed that they are currently becoming ever more strident? I personally think we need to look at this question very seriously. The tendency right now is to attribute a host of negative things to reform. These include those aspects that reform has not perfected in the past 20 years, as well as things that became negative side effects of reform over these years. Some people even attribute problems that existed under the old system to the process of reform. This is a fairly dangerous trend. In addition to attributing problems to reform, blame is laid at the feet of mainstream economics and also mainstream economists. This term "mainstream" is not clearly defined, but the criticism nevertheless triggers a certain emotional response in people, even widespread acclaim. For this reason, economists in China are feeling a bit of pressure during this period.

This morning, Professor Qian Yingyi said, "It is impossible to avoid bringing up certain problems if you talk about China. First, we have to address the conflicts that have come up when inadequate institutional structures, full of loopholes, try to deal with twenty-seven years of fast-paced economic growth. Second, from the perspective of regulation, we need to propose policy recommendations that are realistic and feasible and that are, at the same time, acceptable to people. The current state of China's institutions can accommodate a per capita income level of USD 6,000. However, we may well reach this level fairly soon given the speed at which the economy is growing. We will quickly go beyond the ability of our systems to cope. We therefore need to accelerate institutional reform and raise the quality of our institutions."

At the end of the day, the challenges that face us today as the result of economic growth must be addressed through better systems or institutions, systems that can deal with high-speed growth as well as economic globalization. Because of this, reform is facing tremendous challenges now and in the future.

Looking back over the process now, we can see that our reform was really a matter of checks and balances on systems and choices among systems. No system in the world is perfect. All we can do is choose those that have greater strengths and fewer shortcomings. The market economy is just such a system. As we go along, we therefore must reform the problems that come up, some of which are the necessary cost of reform and some of which are the result of not yet being thorough enough in reform. With the correct mentality, we must resolutely push forward what we confirmed, in the early 1990s, to be the proper choice of market-oriented reform. We absolutely cannot move toward the old path of a deadlocked and rigid planned-economy system. It has been proven, through actual practice on a global scale, that this is a system that is doomed to fail.

## "Fairness" and "efficiency"

A considerable amount of discussion among our economic circles has lately been addressing this question of fairness versus efficiency. We certainly must focus on the living conditions of low-income people. We must go further in raising the income levels of farmers as well as low-income earners in cities. These critical issues have been the focus of policy makers and economic circles from the start. The question has been how to do that. What kinds of systems will be helpful in raising the income levels of all people in the country? Should we use methods like "leveling out rich and poor," or "draining the pond to catch all the fish?" Should we use methods that constrain economic growth, methods that enable the government to have full control over the economy, in order to reach this illusory goal of "fairness?" Do we seek fairness in opportunity, or fairness in the final results?

A great deal of theoretical research and also international experience has already addressed this question and concluded that the design of systems is of ultimate importance. To what extent we can actually improve the living standards of low-income people is not in fact something that can be determined by our hopes and desires alone. It depends on our capabilities and the (economic) stage in which we currently find ourselves. In a country like China, in particular, aiming for "fairness" in ways that are overly abstract can easily call forth a return to the demand for egalitarianism. We should remember that our egalitarian past is not all that far behind us, or that egalitarianism leads to a socialist form of universal poverty. China's economic circles must be very conscientious now in looking at these questions, and they should use both quantitative and qualitative forms of analysis to evaluate what should be done.

It turns out that the most fundamental and important economic principles can provide a foundation for our further discussion of these issues. These include understanding that only by following the laws of the market can an economy grow, and only through economic growth can the fundamental right to work of the great majority of people be satisfied. Government controls over the labor market should only be of a targeted nature, while excessive intervention will only hurt the fundamental long-term rights and interests of workers.

I was in Hainan a few days ago attending an international conference, and at this conference a person asked me a question. He said, "You all keep focusing on this issue of low-income earners, and that is the right thing to do. However, have you considered the 'carrying capacity' of enterprises in the process?

Have you considered China's international competitiveness in the process?" I have to say that is something we should consider. As we raise wages, have we considered at what level foreign enterprises will begin to move their factories elsewhere, to Vietnam, for example, or Cambodia. Naturally, we would like to see higher wages for people, but we must keep in mind that working in a factory earns a much higher wage than working as a farmer on the land. If factories shift to other countries and workers are left without factory wages, they will have no alternative but to return to farming. Not only will this obstruct and delay China's process of industrialization, but it will keep the great mass of our rural population from shaking off poverty and moving toward a more prosperous life.

Naturally, some employment groups in the country are in a more vulnerable position and the government should adopt policies to protect them. Nevertheless, we have to be extremely cautious in how we do this. International experience shows that any excessive "protection" is detrimental to expanding employment. That then is unfair to people who cannot even access this kind of employment opportunity. The best of intentions will then not get the intended results.

## How to sum up China's reform

How can we sum up 27 years of reform? Any summation has to be inclusive, so we naturally need to include the failures as well as successes, the criticism as well as the praise. That makes sense, but in addition our standpoint is extremely important. That reform must be market-oriented is incontrovertible. As noted above, this is something we know in our bones, from what each of us experienced in the planned-economy period, the painful lessons of the actual process of conducting a planned economy. Some people are now saying that this or that specific part of reform has been a failure, and they say it is the fault of "marketization." I feel this is an oversimplification and also an unjust criticism. The reason is that moving from a planned economy to a market economy is something that mankind has never done before. Reform is a matter of "feeling for the stones as you cross the river." It calls for constant improvements. Despite the various detours we have taken in the past, the great majority of these "explorations" were necessary. They were the result of our inexperience, but now we can continue moving forward. It may well be that we cannot achieve success in the latter stages without setbacks in the former stages. All that has come before serves to establish the foundation on which we carry out reform in the future.

Medical reforms can serve as one example. Recently, I have been discussing this subject with David Dollar (Du Daiwei) and various foreign experts from the World Bank project. Debate has been going on for some time now as to what kind of medical system China should set up. The conclusions of academic circles and government policy makers have already been written into several Decisions of the Party (Congress) with specific regard to principles of social insurance systems in particular. One can see the importance of the subject. Discussions have been carried out in China's domestic media and the whole thing has become a "hot topic."

During the last administration, I worked in the State Council's Reform Office as the coordinator of efforts among State Council officials to push forward medical system reforms on a nationwide basis. Many problems that currently exist were precisely those that we hoped to address through reforms. I am intimately acquainted with how difficult this reform is. I can cite some figures to indicate the scale of the problem. In 2004, medical costs in the United States came to USD 1.8 trillion. In that same year, China's entire GDP was only USD 1.6 trillion. The United States has over 200 million people while China has over 1.3 billion. If we used a standard of medical care that was just one-tenth that in the United States, China's entire GDP would still not be able to cover the costs.

Right now, we need roughly RMB 2,000 per person to ensure the medical insurance levels of people employed in cities. Some people have suggested that the government itself cover all costs of insuring people in the country, in both urban and rural areas. Naturally this idea is attractive to people. The "support rate" is extremely high as measured by Internet surveys. Has anybody actually figured up the bill? At a per person cost of RMB 2,000, this would come to the entire spending budget of both central and local governments in 2004. Our fiscal revenues, in their entirety, come to roughly RMB 2,000 per capita.

Meanwhile, let's look at other countries. The United States spent USD 1.8 trillion on medical costs in 2004, but it still had 40 million people who were completely uninsured. Hong Kong has a population of six million people. Of Hong Kong government expenditures (and this does not include money paid out by individuals and enterprises on healthcare), some HKD 40 billion were spent on medical care (in 2004). Government departments involved spend roughly HKD 100 million per day to support medical insurance for six million people, but budgets are already stretched to the breaking point. This level is going to be hard to keep up in the future.

In my opinion, the question about what kind of medical insurance China should adopt is not one that should be fought out in the media. We also should not rely purely on hopes and wishes, or best intentions. We need to seek truth from the facts. We must respect the lessons of history and take China's real capacities into consideration before we decide on this issue. If we were to comply with the emotional desires of the public at large, would the solution be in the interests of all? Could the nation actually bear the burden of the costs? We must think seriously about these things.

## "Government" versus "the market"—revisiting the same questions yet again

We just heard Professor Wei Shangjin and Professor Bai Chong'en talk about China's enterprise reform and the financial markets, and I commend them for their remarks. The commentary by Professor Tong Daochi then touched on the way China's financial markets operated in the past, namely that we applied a quota system to the issuing of new shares. That is, according to administrative region, we granted a specific quota or number of new initial public offerings (IPOs) that could be undertaken by each government department and each local government. Doing things in this way was, indeed, the product of an utterly planned-economy mentality at the time. It used new share issues as a kind of "benefit" or "subsidy" to the entities involved. In order to take advantage of the quota, a given province might not in fact have any "listable" company, or indeed it might not be in such a hurry to put its most profitable enterprises on the market.

What happened, therefore, was that provinces put forth companies that could not pay their wages to employees and listed these instead. They used the money derived from the public listing to pay employee wages. Listing on the market thereby became a "benefits measure." Naturally, companies like this quickly became known as "ST" in China, that is, "special treatment" companies. Some departments and governments really could not come up with any company at all to list, so instead they sold their quota to others. The money was simply regarded as a subsidy from the central government. Clearly, capital markets that operate under such mechanisms are bound to be stillborn.

Objectively speaking, China's capital markets have made progress over these years. Nevertheless, we should also recognize that progress made over a dozen or so years can also begin to turn in the wrong direction and retrogress. For example, the question has been raised about the responsibility of the government when it comes to the stock market index. If the index is falling, should the government spend money to try to prop it up? Once a company is listed on the market, its shares begin to be traded and at each trade some investors make money and some investors lose money. Given the poor quality of our capital markets overall, it may well be that there are more losers than winners. Nevertheless, the prevailing mood of the public right now is resentful because quite a few people have lost money in the market. Is the government now responsible for putting up money to pay these people? If so, who exactly does it pay? How does it manage the process in a way that is "fair," "reasonable," and "legal?" I believe these things need to be looked into. If we do not handle the issues of "saving the market" and "providing subsidies" correctly, it may well be that a dozen or more years of progress in our capital markets will come to nothing. The lessons we have derived from all the stormy weather over these years, the tiny bit of correct understanding we have been able to garner about how a stock market works, will flow like water out to the ocean.

I repeat now, at the end of the day, what is it that we want to learn? With respect to the stock market, I personally feel that our understanding is highly immature. The "management levels" in the government that handle the markets would like for markets to go up, and never down. Investors would like for the markets to deliver only profits, never losses. There is no stock market on the globe that can deliver that promise. Perhaps there is one on another planet?! I'm not so sure. I do know that if our understanding of these things stops at this level, China's stock markets will have a very long and arduous road ahead of them.

Just now, John Sutton talked about industrial policy, and I very much appreciated his remarks. He noted that the results of industrial policy may not become apparent for several decades. It seems to me that the results of an industrial policy depend on whether or not there is a mature market foundation and industrial foundation for that policy. It also depends on whether or not government functions as applied are truly appropriate to the laws of a market economy.

It also seems to me, however, that the results of China's industrial policies may not in fact require decades before becoming apparent. We may be able to see that they are indeed ineffective and failing after only a few years. Now departed, the economist Gui Shiyong was my superior for a time; he spent the second half of his life working mainly in the State Planning Commission. While he was still alive, it was probably in 1997, he expressed the following thoughts to me with some emotion in his voice. "Having worked in the State Planning Commission for so many years now, some things have made a very strong impression on me. For example, in the past people said that Chinese would never be able to have air conditioning at home. They also would never develop 'pop-top' cans. They certainly would never have their own private cars. These things were almost set in stone. They were almost carved into the plaque at the door of the Planning Commission. They were an iron law that people who came after us would have to abide by. Written in stone, cast in iron, there simply was no discussion. Looking back on it now, it seems simply ludicrous."

Throughout the time that he was talking about, a very thick volume would come out every year on "industrial policy." In addition, we would send out countless "red-titled documents." I remember very clearly that we even put out one that forbad the development of pop-top cans. We forbad the development of windows made of a certain tin alloy. We forbad the development of air conditioning, the development of family cars, and quite a few other things. Looking back on it, these documents clearly had no effect.

If you are an official sitting in an office and doing calculations, it is quite true that you might have the impression these things should not be developed. Let's take pop-top cans. Back then, China had only a few billion US dollars in foreign-exchange reserves. The thinking went as follows: if China developed pop-top cans, we would have to import thin-sheet aluminum for the purpose (this was in the early days), and depending on how many cans people used, we would then have to spend a considerable amount of our reserves. Air conditioning was similar. Sitting in an office, you might be inclined to think that if everyone used air conditioning, we would consume a prodigious amount of electricity. Where was the money going to come from to build power plants? How could we possibly mine enough coal to fuel the power plants? Where would we find the money to build the mines to mine the coal? Having built the mines, how many railroads would we need to get the coal to the power plants? Then how much would we put into transmission lines to get electricity to consumers? At that time, we had to import compressors in order to produce air conditioners, and where was the foreign exchange going to come from for that? Then there was the question of people's income—when would people ever be able to purchase air conditioners? Once we had built all the plants to produce air conditioners, who were we going to sell them to?

Even if people sitting in offices at the time had tremendous imaginations, they could not have dreamed of what has happened between then and now. They could not have known that air conditioning would bc ubiquitous in urban homes, or that everyone drinks liquids out of tin cans. Meanwhile, private cars are not uncommon among urban families.

Once we have a fairly well-established market, and once the government has management concepts that are fairly mature, then and only then will industrial policies begin to play even the tiniest role in supplementing the inadequacies of the market. Before these conditions are met, it is a mistake to elevate the role of industrial policy to an unreasonable level and think that it can be all-encompassing. It will not be many years before we find out how much of a mistake, and how large a price we have had to pay.

## Note

1 This speech was delivered by the author at "The International Forum on China's Economic Development," jointly held by the School of Economics and Management of Tsinghua University, the World Bank, the School of Economics of the University of California, Berkeley and the School of Economics of the London School of Economics. It was published in Vol. 22 of *Comparison* by China CITIC Press with some changes.

# 17 A letter on income distribution[1]

(December 23, 2005)

Dear Comrade XX,

Right now, the public is engaged in a major debate about reform. Indeed, we are seeing the most intense disputes on the subject since 1992. Given differences of opinion, any consensus on reform has become a problem. Voices that criticize reform are getting louder, and most of the criticism is aimed at the gap between rich and poor. The whole subject of income disparity has turned into the Achilles' heel of reform, since a groundswell of opinion feels that reform has actually widened income disparities. Everyone has a take on this, from the public at large to cadres, from economists to sociologists. I personally think this is something we need to consider seriously. To that end, I have put some rough ideas of my own down on paper. I respectfully submit them to you as below.

## How should we evaluate the current degree of income disparity?

In the early period of reform, Deng Xiaoping proposed the policy of "letting some people get rich first." Highly strategic in its approach, this was aimed at the extreme egalitarianism as practiced under a planned-economy system. It was absolutely correct, and was profoundly significant in breaking up the "one big pot of rice" egalitarian mentality. However, many people at the time lacked a very acute understanding of this strategic way of thinking. Due to inadequate "thought preparation," they did not realize that income disparities are a necessary part of a market economy. Moreover, it was unclear exactly how much income disparity was necessary and must be tolerated during the primary stage of socialism. Such things were not given adequate attention at the time.

Now, some people who were firm in their resolve to carry through with reform in its early stages have begun to express doubts. They may have felt that reform would raise everyone's level of wealth uniformly, given that productive forces were developing and society's wealth overall was increasing. In fact, people's wealth has grown at different levels. This has been due to market competition, differences in people's naturally endowed capacities, their different degrees of effort, and so on, but people have not been mentally prepared for this. Their faith in market-economy reforms is wavering as a result, which is quite understandable.

Many people are naturally upset about income disparities and about a pervasive atmosphere of corruption. Unfortunately, these two things are being mixed together and discussed as one thing. Resentments and anger are festering about this combination of factors, making clear solutions hard to come up with. Corruption is not the result of primary distribution, nor the result of secondary distribution. Distribution policies are fundamentally not at fault here. These things must be addressed by strict adherence to laws and severe punishments for breaking the law. Meanwhile, the excessive incomes of monopoly industries can only be and indeed will be dealt with through reform. Most people have long since accepted the normal income differences that come along with competition. In mixing together income disparities, unfair distribution, and the practice of corruption, we only confuse people and arouse social tensions.

When we talk about income disparities, therefore, we must separate out normal disparities from those caused by corruption and monopoly industries. In discussing these things, we must remember that we have consistently supported getting rich through working hard and having initiative. From what I see, I believe that we have not reached the limits of allowable income disparities via hard work and initiative. This certainly has not become an explosive social issue. We need, therefore, to have a correct understanding of what we are talking about.

## What exactly are our levels of income disparity right now?

First, let us explore the question of what "common prosperity" means. In the process of reform, the great majority of people in our society have living standards that are higher than they were before, in absolute terms. This in itself has achieved a degree of "common prosperity." One fundamental fact, commonly accepted, is that living standards are higher for all levels of society than they were 20 years ago, including those vulnerable groups that include some tens of millions of impoverished people. This is simply undeniable.

A few years ago, Nobel laureate Joseph Stiglitz, Senior Vice President of the World Bank at the time and its Chief Economist, drew a comparison between China's "transition" and that of Russia. During the first few years of Russia's "switching tracks," the economy went into a deep recession and the standard of living of the great majority of people suffered a notable decline. Life expectancy in Russia also became distinctly shorter. Stiglitz had high praise for China's reform as he made this comparison. He noted that China's economy maintained fast-paced growth once reform and opening up began. People's standards of living improved on a universal basis and life expectancy also improved. China and Russia presented a clear-cut contrast to the world. The evaluation of Stiglitz was in line with the opinions of most international organizations and most international economists.

As reform has proceeded, it is as though the entire body of people in the country has been sitting aboard a fast-moving train, and not a single class of people has been cast off that train. A host of problems remain to be addressed in terms of caring for vulnerable populations, and we must deal with these. Due to the inertia of the old system, our distribution of social guarantees is irrational in many respects, and this must be improved through further reforms. However, in my view, so long as we do not try to see China's reform through rosy-tinted glasses, we have to admit that reform has indeed improved the lives of the Chinese people to a very great extent. It is not an exaggeration to say that these past 27 years have seen faster improvement in people's lives than at any other time in the last few thousand years.

Last year, the World Bank convened a conference in Shanghai on global poverty alleviation. Representatives from countries attending the conference gave China high marks for its enormous accomplishments in this area. Since the start of reform and opening up, China has reduced the numbers of "impoverished" by 400 million people, and that was at a time when the number of impoverished people around the globe was growing. That is, the number of impoverished populations outside China grew by even more than 400 million. It is internationally recognized, therefore, that China has made a contribution to reducing global poverty overall. We should be comforted by this thought.

If we view China's reform efforts with rational and objective eyes, we have to agree that "common prosperity" has been handled appropriately, overall. The process has not been utterly without redeeming factors, as argued by some. Yes, regional disparities have increased and the gap between urban and rural areas has increased. Moreover, both of these trends will continue. Nevertheless, in specific terms, we should note a number of statistical problems that lead to errors in judgment and mistakes in analysis. For example, a per capita income disparity that looks only at household statistics does not take the "migratory labor" component into sufficient consideration. Second, it is inaccurate to use retail commodity sales in urban areas versus those in rural areas to estimate the difference in purchasing power between urban and rural people. The reason is that the purchasing power of many rural people is only made evident by buying goods in urban areas. The inaccurate use of such statistical data makes people who live in less developed areas (rural areas) feel that they have been left out in the process of reform. Meanwhile, people who live in urban areas may well feel that they are not as rich as the statistics make them out to be, and so they too feel resentful.

The Gini coefficient is an analytical standard by which income disparities are measured. Further work should be done on understanding how we should apply this standard to China, given the country's massive historical, regional, and geographical differences. Any over-simplified application of the indicator will necessarily lead to a bias in results. Research reports to date have pointed out that urban–rural income disparities are exaggerated by the way the cost of living index between urban and rural areas is ignored.

## The potential consequences of a resurgence of egalitarianism

China is a nation in which egalitarian traditions run very deep. People are less worried about being uniformly poor than they are about getting less than anyone else. This fact reflects the small-farmer mentality of a time when productive forces were very low. Through the ages, "peasant uprisings" in China were fought under the banner of "equalizing rich and poor." No ruling authority that came about as the result of such an uprising was able to actually "equalize" rich and poor, however. The reason is that it is not in fact possible. Despite this, there will always be those who believe that we should be living in an ideal society in which there are no distinctions among people. People's mentality gets off-balance the moment someone has more than someone else.

Because of this, we run the very serious risk of having the success of all our reforms be repudiated by using "income disparity" as the sole yardstick by which to measure progress. We have consistently felt that improvement in productive forces should be the measure of success, and this has in fact led to general improvement in the standard of living of the entire body of people. If we overlook that now, and focus on whether or not income disparities are growing, this gives people an excuse. They can repudiate reform in its entirety.

For example, our rural reforms are universally recognized and indeed are something that we all take pride in. Rural reforms broke through egalitarianism to the extent that they increased income disparities among rural households as well as individuals. This was a result that people wanted at the beginning, namely, "the more you work, the more you get." It was also a predictable result. Some people, however, could also use this result to repudiate rural reforms. Using the same logic, they could repudiate reforms in all other areas.

Right now, from the tenor of the media, anyone who speaks most loudly about income inequality, or even exaggerates it, is able to take the high moral ground. This goes for economists, sociologists, and even government officials. As a result, there is a kind of competition going on among all levels of cadres to see who can be the most "shrill" in this regard. I find this extremely dangerous. Some people in the country right now, who are rather influential, are even brazenly saying that our society is a "man eat man society" (quoting Lu Xun). Articles calling for another "Cultural Revolution" have begun to appear on the Internet. These have the potential to induce social chaos. It is extremely urgent, therefore, that we guide public opinion in the direction of rational analysis when it comes to the issue of income disparities.

Exaggerating this issue can lead to serious political, social, and economic consequences overall. As a former head of state of an Asian country has said to us, a government must take income distribution policies very seriously, but it absolutely must not exaggerate income disparities and certainly must not make any promises about eliminating disparities. No country in the world has absolutely equal income among its people and no government is capable of eliminating differences. If a government makes any commitment to do so, it is essentially putting a noose around its neck.

Recently I read an article by a sociologist in China who said that we should move in the direction of northern Europe in terms of welfare policies that lead to greater social equality. He noted that the governing concept in northern Europe is that it is better to support a lazy person than it is to have society allow for a poor person. I have not verified this in other articles to see if the reference is correct, but I do believe that this way of doing things is simply not feasible in China.

We should support individuals and families who are facing hardship due to one reason or another, those who cannot work because they are old or infirm, but we have no responsibility, nor do we have the authority, to use taxpayer money to take care of those who are lazy. If China returns to egalitarianism, Chinese people will again face starvation. The lessons of the Great Leap Forward and the People's Communes have taught us that. The day we eat for free is not far removed from the day we have nothing to eat. We must not forget this.

What we seek to establish is a well-functioning market economy, but we also know that reform is a matter of choosing the right options and balancing power. Any system is going to have its advantages and its defects. Indeed, at the outset of reform we knew that a market economy was not perfect. The reason we chose it is that we had been through the experience of a planned economy for long enough to know that it was not able to resolve the problems of shortages and poverty. The development of all other countries in the world has also shown that a planned economy has no future. So we chose a market economy and, since competition is the fundamental nature of a market economy, no matter how good it is, it is not going to make pennies fall from heaven.

A well-functioning market economy can motivate people to create wealth through their own endeavors. It absolutely cannot guarantee that everyone gets the same amount no matter what their contribution is or how well they perform. That is not the definition of a well-functioning market economy. When a market economy is just being set up, its deficiencies may be more obvious, and may be used by people to say that a market economy overall is not going to work. If that were the case, China would have no way out at all. It is absolutely beyond doubt that the reform goal we have set for ourselves, that of a socialist market economy, is one that we must firmly stick to. Returning to a planned economy is a dead end.

## How to resolve this problem of a disparity between rich and poor

It is unacceptable to deny that income disparities have appeared since the start of reform, and to deny the ongoing trend. We have to let people know the true situation. Nevertheless, we absolutely must not exaggerate it. The reason is that it is essentially impossible to come to any consensus about what degree of income disparity we should accommodate in the primary stage of socialism.

Instead, we must publicize the progress we have made since the start of reform in raising the overall standard of living of the Chinese people. We must point out steps taken to address income disparities over the past few years, and the enormous results we have achieved. If we do not stick to this fundamental judgment, the "moral image" of our reform will suffer, and the legality of the ruling authority of our Party will be undermined.

Second, we must state clearly that while income disparities are a necessary consequence of a market economy, the government is using all kinds of measures to moderate those disparities. Right now, egalitarianism still exists in China.

For example, pay scales are too equal among different levels of staff within government, universities, and research institutes. Moreover, given that we want to encourage the development of the private sector, and hope that it will "stride forth with strength and vigor," we must accommodate a certain degree of wealth accumulation. Naturally, at the same time we must promote the idea of having those who "get rich first" help out those who come later. We must actively promote the practice of contributing to social endeavors. In sum, we want to build consensus via positive explanations, and build social cohesion and a mental tolerance for income disparities.

Third, we must take certain specific actions that display the determination of the Party and the government to resolve issues. The term "fair" (*gong ping*), for example, embodies both meanings of "just" (*gong zheng*) and "equal" (*ping deng*). In terms of achieving a more *just* society, we must combat corruption and break down monopolies. We do this through reform and through improving our institutions. In achieving a more *equal* society, we must emphasize equality of opportunity and not equality of income. We aim for an equal process, not equal results. Right now, we are instituting nine years of compulsory education in rural areas. This is to ensure that the children of rural families have equal educational opportunities and so can have an equal chance at employment. The government is already focusing on other initiatives, such as the guarantee of a minimum standard of living, basic medical care insurance for employees in cities, the "new cooperative medical care" in rural areas, student loans, and so on. All of these have already achieved results. Naturally, we must continue to improve them as time goes on.

Finally, we must correct any bias that has been caused by misapplication of statistical measures. Our economists and statistical departments are in fact already well aware of statistical bias. Given the current atmosphere, however, nobody dares to stand up and point to the problem. If senior levels of government demonstrate the right attitude on this, the problems can be cleared up quite easily.

Right now, public opinion is quite strident on what we call the "three major issues," namely education, medical care, and housing. All these things are unusually hard to tackle. I recommend that we organize specific teams to study and then deal with them properly. If we simply make promises lightly, or deal with them in a simplistic way, we will pile up a legacy of even worse problems.

My views as described above are a heartfelt response to certain tendencies that I have seen in the media. It is hard for me not to focus on one side of the matter as a result. I will welcome all comments and criticism.

May you govern in peace!
Respectfully,
Li Jiange
December 23, 2005

# Note

1 This is a letter to a leader by the author.

# 18 Why are medical costs so high?[1]

## (February 2006)

Blaming our high medical costs solely on hospitals and doctors is unfair. Since the second half of last year, the issue of rising medical costs has become a hypersensitive topic in the country. Some of this is exacerbated by media coverage that triggers even greater resentment among people. Resolving the whole issue is going to require rational discourse and specialized research.

The problem of an exceedingly fast rise in medical costs is being criticized not only in China but throughout the world. Many countries are complaining about the high prices and wastefulness of their medical systems. The problem in China is similar to that in other countries in some ways, but it also has its own unique causes.

First, the amount of money that each person is willing to spend on medical costs is a function of how much value he puts on his own life. Once people have enough to eat and drink, they are more willing to spend money on health. Meanwhile, the rate at which they are willing to spend more on health generally goes up faster than the rate at which their income increases. Similarly, the rate at which healthcare budgets of a given nation go up exceeds the rate at which its GDP goes up. In the 1960s, spending on healthcare in the United States came to 5.3 percent of GDP. By the 1980s, that had gone up to 8.9 percent, by 1990 to 12.2 percent, and by 2000 to 13.5 percent. In 1992, people in the United States spent more on medical and healthcare costs than any other item, and for the first time more than food and tobacco. By 1997, 17.4 percent of the average American salary was being spent on medical insurance, 15.1 percent on food and tobacco, and another 15.1 percent on housing. In China, this trend is similar and is unavoidable, as people get beyond mere subsistence and move into a period of "moderate prosperity."

Second, the percentage of GDP that is spent on medical costs also increases rapidly once a population starts aging and its life expectancy goes up. Meanwhile, an increase in average life expectancy is also the result of spending more on medical costs. China uses 2 percent of the world's medical and healthcare resources, but this goes to caring for the health of 22 percent of the world's people. The average life expectancy in China has reached 72 years, surpassing that of many moderately-developed countries, which is of some pride to our healthcare endeavors. Statistics indicate that the medical expenses of a person after the age of 65 will be roughly one-half the medical expenses of his entire lifetime up to then.

Meanwhile, medical expenditures in the last year of life may come to a full half of that second half. As a society ages, therefore, its medical expenses will unavoidably rise.

According to statistics and forecasts of the United States Census Bureau, it has taken 68 years for the over-65 cohort of the population to go from 7 percent of the total population to 14 percent in the United States. In France, this has taken 115 years, in Sweden 85 years, in England 45 years, and in Japan 26 years. In China, the figure is only 27 years. China is transitioning to an "aging population" in a much shorter time. For this reason, medical costs are expected to rise dramatically in the next few decades.

Third, everyone would like to use the most technologically advanced and effective medical treatment available. This presents a problem for China, which ranks below #100 in GDP per capita in the world. By the end of 2005, China's GDP per capita was not even USD 2,000—we are still a developing country with a middle-to-low level of income. At the same time, life sciences are advancing extremely rapidly and medical costs are soaring, facts that we have to accept. In an age when economies are globalizing, we in China can receive medical treatment that represents the latest technological advances worldwide. Twenty years ago, China's hospitals were helpless in the face of severe cases of cardiovascular disease. Nowadays, for a few tens of thousands of RMB, one can have bypass surgery or have a stent put in. The cost has gone up substantially, but a patient might gain health and a life in return.

Fourth, our traditional way of thinking, and traditional ethics, required that the government do all it could to keep a person alive. This was an unconditional responsibility of the government. Even in the most prosperous countries, however, a government is unable to meet the demands of every single person who needs an organ transplant or other major procedure. In the end, considering a government's spending capacity and society's ability to bear the burden limit, what can be done? Any government should provide medical relief to its most vulnerable populations, but it must also be prudent in the scientific methods it uses. In the United States, emergency rooms are often full of people hoping to receive treatment for what are chronic diseases. Treatment is provided for free to the poorest segment of the population, which keeps real emergencies from getting the attention they require. Hong Kong has some of the best medical care in the world, but it is said that some people take an ambulance to the hospital just because they get a stomach-ache. Economics tells us that demand is elastic when it comes to the pricing of medical services. When the price that a person himself has to pay approaches zero, demand will be distorted. It will grow beyond reason. At the same time, the system will incur moral risk (moral hazard). Exaggerated promises by any government, therefore, will necessarily become unrealizable as well as unsustainable and the end result will only be greater resentment.

It should be pointed out that skyrocketing costs of medical care in China are not altogether reasonable. Indeed, there are many unreasonable aspects to this problem. If we were to improve hospital management and standardize doctors' behavior, we would find that we are left with a great deal of margin to lower costs.

To do this, however, we cannot rely exclusively on administrative commands. We must also make sure there is adequate competition among medical services.

To do that, we must break down the current situation in which State-owned hospitals are uniformly governed in a centralized way. While retaining certain State-owned not-for-profit hospitals, and increasing government spending on these, we should enable the greater majority of State-owned hospitals to take in private investment and become profit-making, multi-service, institutions. While competing with one another, hospitals can also then satisfy the needs of multi-tiered medical services. In order to reduce the burden on patients themselves, we must also set up a medical insurance system that balances medical supply and demand and that is paid into by the public at large. We must rectify and regulate current practices that govern both the production and circulation of pharmaceuticals. All of these are tasks for our reform as we move forward.

Pushing forward such medical reforms will call for the active participation of people in the profession. We have complex historical reasons for misguided incentive mechanisms that encourage doctors to prescribe medicines as a way to make money. There are profound reasons for this and it is a mistake to attribute the entire problem to hospitals and doctors in an overly simplified way. The result of this mistaken understanding has been to pit doctors against patients. In the future, such attributions may contribute to massive conflicts between the medical profession and what we refer to as a "harmonious society." The media should be very clear about this particular issue.

## Note

1 The article was originally published in *Caijing Magazine*, 2006(3) (February 6), Vol. 152.

# 19 How to pull medical resources together and distribute them in a reasonable way[1]

(February 20, 2006)

In the face of soaring medical costs, some media reports have been suggesting that we reevaluate the medical system we had during the planned-economy period, and that we give it high marks. As a result, this has triggered a kind of nostalgia among people for the old days. The idea is that if we went back to a system of publicly funded medicine, with universal coverage (including labor-protection medical care), we would get rid of the problems people currently face—namely, that they can't get in to see a doctor unless they pay dearly for the privilege. The situation is not as simple as it seems.

A variety of models exist around the world for gathering together medical resources and making them available to people. Two opposite ends of the spectrum can describe their main characteristic. One is that the market determines everything in entirety. The other is that the State is responsible for everything in entirety. Right now, fewer and fewer countries around the world adopt either one of these extremes. The majority of countries employ systems that integrate the two and that enable one model to supplement the other.

Given that the medical sector has strong externalities, relying exclusively on market operations has obvious drawbacks. Any government in the world feels a responsibility for controlling contagious disease, and for putting money into basic life sciences. Without adequate government inputs, for example, and unified, high-efficiency deployment of resources, the world would not have been able to eradicate such infectious diseases as smallpox and polio, or to improve community defenses against such non-contagious diseases as cardiovascular disease, diabetes. We could not have contained the severe acute respiratory syndrome (SARS) outbreak that China confronted in 2003. There is no doubt whatsoever that such things as infectious disease control and basic scientific research require funding from governments. In addition, most countries in the world have insurance mechanisms that, to varying degrees, prevent low-income earners from falling into abject poverty when they get sick and that provide relief to households and individuals who cannot afford to pay for medical costs themselves.

The past few years have seen the greatest advances in history for China's healthcare endeavors. Right now, everyone is complaining about not being able to see a doctor, but this can be attributed to the parallel trend of inadequate medical resources and a surfeit of such resources. The problems are institutional and structural. In 2003, China's total health expenditures came to RMB 658.4 billion, which was 5.6 percent of that year's GDP. This was slightly less than the average level of 6 percent spent on healthcare by middle-income countries. Taking into consideration statistical adjustments that had to be made for China's census figures, China's total expenditures on healthcare actually came to higher than quite a few middle-income countries.

Within this figure of total expenditures, spending by the government came to 17 percent, and represented 5.14 percent of the country's entire spending budget. As economic growth continues, this figure will rise. We cannot, however, expect it to rise by too much, since China's total budget for all expenditures came to only 18.5 percent of GDP in 2005. This was very considerably lower than any welfare state in the world.

Expenditures on healthcare that were paid for by individuals themselves came to 55.8 percent of the total. This was higher than the world average of 43 percent, but as a percentage of personal income the figure is not all that high. On a nationwide basis, China's citizens spent roughly 7.35 percent of their income on medical care in 2004. This is less than what they spent on clothing, which was 9.56 percent, or on transportation and communication, which was 11.75 percent. It was even lower than what many people spent on eating out. In 15 provinces, people spent less on healthcare than they did on outside meals.

Statistics from a number of countries indicate that the elasticity coefficient of an increase in healthcare prices with respect to increases in personal income is greater than 1. However, the percentage of an individual's healthcare expenses to his total expenses depends on the system in which that person lives, and these things are hard to compare. The rule seems to be that when government and enterprise health guarantees are high, personal expenditure is less. Personal expenditure is more when the opposite is true. It is therefore quite natural for people to yearn for the old days, based on this instinctive understanding. People would rather have the government take on the entire responsibility for funding healthcare. Such a wholly-funded system is, in theory, a way to ensure that every citizen gets equal treatment while social solidarity is enhanced. Naturally, the demand for medical services these days is almost limitless, making it hard for any country's medical insurance system to do it all. Most countries cannot do more than provide a basic level of service, although that depends on the economic resources of the country.

In fact, a system under which the government funds everything is not unrelated to how much its citizens can bear the burden. The reason is that the ultimate source of funding is tax revenue from individuals. The higher the level of government guarantees, the more people have agreed to hand over money to the government to spend on their behalf. A government that "bears the costs" is not the same as a beneficent government that somehow showers welfare benefits on people.

The problem is that, generally, government-funded systems face the "tragedy of the commons" and the "third-party payment syndrome." It is hard to avoid a massive amount of moral hazard as resources are wasted. During the planned-economy period, we have plenty of examples of doctors "prescribing" such things as pressure cookers, sheets, bedding, and other daily needs and "health supplements." Not until cost-sharing systems were implemented did this kind of thing come under control, and then only to a degree.

Right now, countries in which universal healthcare is practiced still require cost sharing to one degree or another. For example, they set up a payment threshold, a certain amount of cost that must be borne by the individual. After that, individuals also cover certain medical costs depending on percentage. Even though countries have strengthened "third-party" regulation, such a non-price-based distribution system cannot ensure that demand and supply of medical services is fully balanced. The result is "waiting in the queue." This form of distribution system is not in any way different from lining up to buy scarce items during China's planned-economy period. As a result, "going through the back door," and "jumping the queue" become impossible to hold down. Special rights and privileges insist on intervening. Some countries, exhausted by trying to deal with such problems, are currently considering their own reforms.

China's previous system only covered a portion of people, and only those in cities. Why did it need to be reformed? Because it too had serious defects, to the extent that it was impossible to sustain. Given our history, and the "dual-economy system" that separates cities from rural areas, all we can hope to achieve at this point is a low-level medical insurance system that we know we will have the capacity to fulfill.

In the future, the percentage of medical costs that the government might fund will depend on economic balancing as well as political factors. Whatever that percentage is, however, we must abide by certain principles. That is, we must provide better medical services to the population while not sacrificing the reasonable interests of doctors and not obstructing the development of the healthcare endeavor. Only by observing the realities of our national situation, by correctly choosing the orientation of our reforms, and by speeding up the process of reform, can China grasp historic opportunities and develop its life sciences and medical technologies in order to improve the wellbeing of its people.

## Note

1 This article was originally published in *Caijing Magazine*, 2006(4) (February 20), Vol. 153.

# 20 China's evolving industrial policy[1]

## (May 2006)

It is hard to know exactly when the concept of "industrial policy" entered China. We can say with some certainty, however, that it had become an officially used term by the late 1980s. At that time, a report from an investigation trip made to Japan got the attention of senior leaders, who affirmed its conclusions. From that time on, "industrial policy" was something to "formulate" and to "implement" and became part of the daily work of macroeconomic departments.

Because of this background, there should be no question that Japan was the source of this whole approach. At the time, Japan's economy was like hot oil cooking over a blazing fire. Japanese capital was making major moves into the American markets, buying up assets, shocking the public in the US and raising eyebrows around the world. We in China instantly took in industrial policy as a kind of holy script, which was only natural at the time.

It is said that Japan's industrial policy, in turn, can be traced back to the protectionist policies of Germany prior to that country's development. Since Meiji times, Japan already had a tradition of fostering industrial development through dedicated government policies. It was therefore easy for industrial policy to evolve into an all-encompassing policy structure in Japan.

At the end of the 1980s, China was taking initial steps to transition from a planned to a market economy. Direct intervention by the government in economic affairs was the "habitual" condition. Those who supported reform believed that industrial policy could serve as a transitional step, gradually enabling a "guided plan" to replace a "command-type plan." Those who supported adherence to the planned economy thought that industrial policy could serve as a shield for them as it preserved, to the greatest degree possible, the lifelines of the traditional economic structure. Because of these two forms of support, industrial policy was brought into China essentially without any reservations whatsoever.

Not long after industrial policy was reborn in China, the academic community began to look into it more closely and think about it with a more discerning frame of mind. Researchers looked at its substance as well as form, at the means by which it was implemented and at its results. In early 1991, I pointed out, "The term 'industrial policy,' which began to be popular in China from 1987 onwards, together with the much revered phrase, 'firmly control upstream products with the plan, while allowing prices of downstream products to be liberalized,' deserves discussion and further research if industrial policy is being seen as a way to integrate the plan and the market" (*Reform* magazine, Volume 1, 1991).

By now, industrial policy has been practiced for close to 20 years. The effectiveness of its results can be properly evaluated. It can be said that when we first started studying and adopting Japan's industrial policy we did not go deeply into all aspects, and our approach was defective from the very beginning.

First, we relied mainly on impressions and conclusions drawn from very brief meetings with Japanese government economists. These were rather one-sided and superficial. Nevertheless, even those Japanese officials believed that industrial policy must be realized through market mechanisms. Such policy must have full respect for the independent standing of private market forces (the "civil sector"), and should attempt to mobilize the initiative of private enterprises. That is, they felt that the actual results of industrial policy depended mainly on whether or not there was a mature market foundation that was based on solid property rights. Moreover, they felt that the government's functions had to be truly suited to the laws of a market economy. Only on the basis of market allocation of resources could government put into effect concepts that respected the market, and only then could industrial policy play its intended role of filling in when the market was inadequate. Without the above conditions, society would pay a very heavy price for overestimating the benefits that industrial policy might bring.

Second, we were oblivious to the fact that many Japanese enterprises themselves had a negative reaction to industrial policies. In fact, their criticism and obstruction of such policies has never really stopped from the beginning. Some world-renowned automobile companies that we all know today were, at the time, suppressed and repudiated by officials in the Japanese government. Many companies therefore feel that they were made strong and mighty by their constant battling with the Ministry of International Trade and Industry (MITI). Japan's industrial policy looked down upon small companies. The feeling was that they were inefficient and also created too much competition. They argued for relaxing the anti-monopoly law, and for consolidating companies through mergers and acquisitions. This kind of "blind belief in scale" naturally did damage to the ability of a small company to survive. Countless examples prove, nevertheless, that Japan's small companies had superior talent when it came to innovations and technology, and they had a much greater ability to open up new markets. In Japan, therefore, the general pattern was for large companies to purchase small companies just for the technology transfer. Technology exports of small companies, meanwhile, were far livelier than those of large companies.

Third, we did not put sufficient weight on the opinions of Japanese scholars who were critical of the government's industrial policy. Mainstream economists in Japan confirmed the positive role that such policy made in transmitting information. In overall terms, however, the negative opinions of such economists, repudiating industrial policy, outnumbered the positive opinions. Economists felt that although Japan's industries were under government pressure, the reason they could rise up and do anything at all was because the vitality of the private (civil) sector had not been totally squelched. Except for a short period after the war, the rapid growth of the Japanese economy was due mainly to competitive market mechanisms and a strong sense of entrepreneurship. Empirical studies of some economists now show that the industrial policy that excited such admiration in the 1950s and 1960s was, in fact, often dismantled by the force of private-sector innovations. In fact, it did not play all that much of a role.

The homegrown (local) theoretical foundation of Japan's industrial policy can be summed up as "a bias toward production methods." This concept has a common thread with our own traditional theory as practiced in the planned economy. One could define industrial policy as follows: the government selects certain key industries, and uses all kinds of measures to support them. At the same time, the government selects certain industries that are to be restricted and it either outright forbids them or holds back their growth. If this is indeed the way one defines "industrial policy," then it is not anything new to China. A number of slogans used in China's past echo the same theme: "put emphasis on agriculture and light industry," "take steel as the key link," "take grain and the key link," and so on. All of this was a kind of "bias toward developing specially designated industries." It was, in fact, a kind of "industrial policy."

The reason that we opted for a market economy as our reform objective was that we knew people's ability to grasp and use information was extremely limited. It was insufficient if one wanted to "weave a basket" that was all-encompassing, a plan that could handle the resource allocation of a myriad things. This was already apparent at a time when things were put into such simplified categories as "agriculture and light industry." Nowadays, with globalization upon us, it is even more obvious.

Now, some Japanese scholars are pointing to the cause and effect relationship between the last century's industrial policy and the country's economic decline. That is, they point to long-term interference by the government in the economy. They also think that one of the reasons Japan's economy is beginning to revive is that industrial policy is gradually being replaced with pro-competition policies.

At this point, it would behoove us to take a moment to look back over our own industrial policy of the past 20 years, and reflect upon the experience and the lessons we have learned.

## Note

1 This article was originally published in *Caijing Magazine*, 2006(9) (May 1), Vol. 158.

# 21 Striking a balance among wages, employment, and efficiency[1]

(May 2006)

Government intervention in job markets is generally carried out with the best intentions, whether the aim is to protect workers or expand employment. This is true of any country. Modern economies are extremely complex, however, and the cause and effect relationship of policies may not be in line with intuition and common sense. Although it may be imperative that we take certain actions, we must proceed with great care so as not to end up with results that are counterproductive.

The government is the protector of workers' rights. That is not to say, however, that the more a government intervenes, the more those rights will be protected. Indeed, undue intervention may well harm the long-term rights and fundamental interests of workers. A classic case relates to India where, in 1947, the country passed a law that attempted to give workers in large manufacturing industries greater rights (*The Labor and Capital Disputes Act*).

We now know, through copious amounts of documentation, that this actually prevented workers from getting jobs in these industries. It placed stringent controls over job markets and excessive protections on the rights of existing employees. Over the past half century, the Act held back growth in India's manufacturing industries and intensified the poverty at the lowest levels of society. In addition, it created a kind of "workers aristocracy." Service industries were not subject to this Act and were, as a result, able to draw in a larger labor force. India's service industries therefore seem to hold a higher percentage of the economy than such industries do in China, making that country seem more "industrialized," but in fact this is the result of an under-developed manufacturing sector.

Employment is the basis of people's livelihood. To expand employment, a government must not only develop its economy but it must also reform its institutions (system, structure). In this regard, one particularly unfortunate example comes from France. Demonstrations erupted there recently in opposition to the "First-time employment contract law." France's original labor law had stipulated that enterprises had to present legally binding documentation when they fired a person that listed the reasons for dismissal. Without this, the employee could take his employer to court. The result of this previous law had been that enterprises were very careful not to hire young people without experience, and this led to an unemployment rate among young people of up to 25 percent. The new law stipulated that a company could fire an employee at any time within the first two years of employment, if the company had over 20 employees and if the person being employed was under the age of 26. The employment had to be done through a contract, but this contract could be terminated in the first two years without any further documentation. Clearly, this law was intended to raise employment but young people in France did not see it that way. They saw it as a form of discrimination against them and an erosion of their labor rights. Demonstrations erupted in 80 cities and towns in France as a result.

Once ideas become fixed, and markets become accustomed to certain practices, whether those are enshrined in laws and regulations, understood as promises by the government, or simply confirmed by the traditional patterns, the situation is extremely hard to change. A survey recently questioned newly hired staff in the "Department of Society, Economy, and Markets" of a financial group in Japan. This discovered that roughly 40 percent of young people longed for the old days of a "lifelong employment" system. Research is increasingly showing, however, that breaking out of this system has been a key reason why Japan has begun to emerge from the shadows of a decade-long recession.

While the government's responsibility is to expand employment, the goal of an enterprise is to seek profit. At this stage in China's development, we should institute reasonable policies that promote the growth of labor-intensive industries. We should encourage the development of small, privately-held enterprises that can absorb quantities of labor in particular. We must protect the fundamental employment rights of the public, but at the same time we should not apply rigid standards to wage levels. Wages and employment levels must be the result of market competition. Only when efficiency improves across the entire spectrum of society will wage and employment levels improve as well.

Right now, our attentions are all focused on the countryside and rural issues. All sides are working hard to raise farmers' incomes and improve the lives of those living in rural areas. International experience shows that the only real way to do this is to shift labor from agricultural to non-agricultural industries, that is, to move the great majority of "farmers" to other types of occupation.

Such a shift is both the cause of economic growth, and its result. In a fundamental sense, realizing such a shift is not determined by our own objective desires but is subject to all kinds of objective constraints. Nevertheless, our policies and our underlying concepts can indeed influence the speed and scale of the process.

A shift of rural labor from agricultural to non-agricultural industries is acutely related to the marginal growth rate of the national economy. When the economy grows at a fast pace, the shift will be faster. When it slows down, the shift slows down. Due to the multiplier effect of investment and the "accelerator" principle, the process of having farmers move into non-farming occupations can also turn in the other direction. Because of this, the entire process is often determined by the scale of investment being undertaken by the entire economy. Right now, the percentage of government investment is already rather modest. Because of that, investment by other sectors of the economy is going to play a decisive role.

Only if there is an expectation of profit will enterprises be encouraged to invest. Investment must necessarily be in pursuit of profit. Without constraints on such behavior, employers will always attempt to keep wages low. The nation must therefore formulate laws and regulations that ensure a sound and healthy work environment and that provide for a basic pension and medical care. At the same time, the market itself provides powerful constraints on employers. So long as labor can move about freely, and information on wages is made public, those hiring cannot hold wages below average market levels for any length of time. In the southern part of China, we are already seeing a "labor desert," a severe shortage of labor that is already putting pressure on wages to rise.

When farmers first move into cities, they generally can only take work at the low end of the spectrum. As they become more experienced and gain skills, their income will gradually improve. This reality is something that everyone simply has to face over time. It should be noted, however, that average wages in any kind of non-agricultural industry are vastly higher than what they were in farming. This is the fundamental reason we will continue to see ongoing movement of labor from the countryside into cities.

In the primary stage of socialism, the primary goal of our economic policies must be to expand employment and accelerate the shift of rural people into non-agricultural sectors. The most urgent task before us right now is to formulate policies that ensure occupational safety and that require compulsory implementation of social security systems. We must have firm guarantees for the life and safety of workers, including basic pension and healthcare coverage. As for increases in the personal income of people, we must avoid making any proposals that are divorced from the demands of our current stage of development. If we cannot turn our promises into reality, we will find that people turn even more resentful in the end.

**Note**

1 This article was originally published in *Caijing Magazine*, 2006(10) (May 15), Vol. 159.

# 22 A new approach to the old problem of "empty accounts" in pension funds[1]

(May 2006)

While we in China are madly searching for a solution to our "empty accounts" problem, to make up for shortfalls in our pensions, some countries have already been experimenting for years with something called "non-financial defined contributions" (NDC). This approach began in Sweden. It was recommended for China as well, one year ago, when a study group composed of both Chinese and foreign experts looked at the possibility. This group felt that adopting an NDC approach was a realistic and effective solution to the problem of empty accounts currently plaguing China's pension system.

NDC works as follows. Participants contribute to their individual accounts according to a fixed percentage of their earnings. Authorities in charge of the system then record interest income for each account that accrues at the legally-defined interest rate. The money in the accounts does not actually remain there, however, but is paid out directly to pensioners at the same time. When participants retire, they are allowed to receive the accumulated sum as calculated in their own pension account. The experiences of other countries has shown that an NDC approach has the advantage of maintaining responsibility for specific individual accounts and it can avoid the drawbacks of excessive risk in the way funds are accumulated. It has incentive mechanisms (to keep people paying in), and it also lowers the costs of transition.

Pension systems involve systems that are both cross-disciplinary and span long periods of time. The establishment of such systems is therefore highly complex and difficult. It is hard not to expect the process to require years of exploration and a certain amount of "back and forth." Right now, all systems practiced in all countries have their problems and most countries are therefore either in the process of or are considering their own reforms.

After the Second World War, most of the public pension systems set up in developed countries were of a kind that established the retirement benefits in advance (the so-called "defined-benefit system"). They were also "pay-as-you-go" systems, in that current payments into the system were used for making current payments out of the system. By the mid-1970s, the economic growth rates of many countries were slowing down, and their populations were aging. Countries therefore raised their required contributions amounts while lowering the benefits, in order to avoid a shortfall in pension funds. This kind of simple remedy not only did not resolve problems, however, but it led to a crisis of confidence in the system on the part of both enterprises and young people. Because of this, a number of experts around the world are now saying that "pay-as-you-go" systems should be changed into individual contribution systems, with each individual having his own accumulated amount. (This is known as the "defined contributions" (DC) system featuring accumulated contributions.) Only this new approach can get at the root of the problem of an aging population (that uses up the money) and few incentives for younger people to pay into the system. With support from the World Bank, a number of countries have therefore abandoned their "defined benefits" (DB) systems and instead are adopting DC systems featuring accumulated contributions. This experimental approach started in Chile and is now being extended to certain other countries in South America, the Middle East, and Eastern Europe.

This new approach has also run into a whole series of other problems, however, including the massive cost of switching systems and the risk involved in investing in capital markets. In its early period, the system worked well in Chile. When the first group of contributors began to draw out their retirement funds, however, they discovered that the results were not what they had expected. Some pension funds, together with their staff, have run into problems. After 25 years of this experiment, people are now conceding that the accumulated contributions system can only address the funding requirements of the immediate period. It cannot, of its own nature, resolve future needs. The future level of pension funds depends not only on savings rates, but also on the return on investment of pension funds.

The Chile example shows up the enormous cost of managing pension funds in a country where capital markets are not well developed. Moreover, it shows that such an approach contributes to criminal activity by making pension funds the "prey" of criminals. Indeed, even in countries that have well-functioning capital markets, the management of pension funds can run into serious problems. The United States has 33,000 pension-fund plans, which hold the pensions of some 44 million employees. In late 2003, these plans were showing a deficit of USD 300 billion. The Pension Benefits Guarantee Corporation in the United States is responsible for paying out funds that fund management companies themselves are unable to pay. At present, this corporation is responsible for paying out benefits to roughly one million former employees. In 2001, this corporation had a surplus of USD 7.7 billion, but by the end of 2003, it had a loss of USD 11.2 billion. At the end of 2003, the Dow Jones index fell by 34 percent from its highest point, causing pension funds in America to shrink by USD 500 billion.

In the last two decades of the twentieth century, the World Bank began to require any developing country to which it was extending loans to institute certain reforms of its public pension system. Such reforms included establishing "three pillars," or three different approaches to handling pension funds. The first was a publicly managed, unfunded, defined-benefit pillar. The second was a privately managed, funded, defined-contribution pillar. The third was a voluntary private pillar. By now, the World Bank no longer requires strict adherence to these three pillars, since it determined they are not universally applicable as a way to resolve problems.

China is in the midst of economic transition and is also a country with a rapidly aging population. It cannot accomplish the task of setting up an entire pension system in one go. As one component of overall reforms, China successfully initiated social security reforms over this past dozen years, so the embryonic form of a social security system is in place. The basic framework for this system is in line with the requirements of developing a market economy, and is in accord with the global trends in developing pension systems.

Nevertheless, there is undoubtedly room for improvement. Right now, China's pensions are managed by local governments in a fragmented way. Their coverage is narrow. They need to use individual-account contributions to help cover deficits in the pooled funds of the public. This has led to what we call the "empty accounts" syndrome in individual accounts. As time goes on, these problems will necessarily impact the willingness of individuals and companies to pay into the system. That will add to the difficulty of expanding coverage, which will put ever-greater pressure on public finance.

Under our existing system, we either need to increase the rate of individual contributions to make up for the empty accounts problem, or we need to increase subsidies from central government coffers. Both of these will, however, add to the burden on individuals, enterprises, and the government alike. Moreover, ensuring that accounts are not empty has the potential to lead to moral hazard among those entities managing the funds.

Accounts under an NDC system do not need to actually be in place (so we do not have an empty accounts problem). Using them also allows us to avoid having younger people pay a double burden. It allows us not to require an income shift from one generation to the next that is unreasonable. This system can be guaranteed by the credit of the government. It can be operated by public agencies. It can get around the constraints and inadequacies of private-sector financial capacity and management capability. It can avoid the risk of short-term volatility in capital markets, which is extremely important at this stage when China's capital markets are not yet mature.

To improve our social security system and set up job markets that encourage mobility (by allowing social security accounts to move along with the person), we also need to formulate mandatory pension regulations that are nationwide in scope and legally defined. We need to set up a nationwide unified system for pension-fund management. What's more, we need to extend retirement ages. When the relevant laws were set up with respect to these, the life expectancy of Chinese people was shorter than it is now. As life expectancy gets longer, early retirement is not a luxury that the Chinese people can afford. We should therefore curb any measures that either encourage or mandate early retirement, and we should gradually increase the age at which people retire. This will not undermine the creation of new jobs. In a market economy, an increase in the supply of labor itself will keep wages from rising, which will help in the creation of even more jobs.

## Note

1  This article was carried by the 160th issue of *Caijing Magazine*, the 11th issue in 2006, which was published on May 29, 2006.

# 23 NDC

## A pension-fund reform model that is worth considering

## (June 2006)

We have held a number of conferences on the subject of social security, with particular focus on our pension fund system. In addition, we've convened a number of joint forums on this with the World Bank, but opinions have been divided enough that it has been hard to come up with policy proposals or action plans.

As we all know, pension systems involve systems that are both cross-disciplinary and span long periods of time. Many economists who are not actually engaged in this particularly field might therefore put out an opinion or two, but one opinion generally contributes little to the whole subject. It might seem reasonable from one perspective but then is not workable in terms of other reforms or creates unintended consequences. Creating a pension system is therefore an extremely complex and difficult task. It requires years of exploration and a certain amount of going "back and forth." Right now, all systems practiced in all countries have their problems and most countries are therefore either in the process of or are considering their own reforms.

China is in the midst of economic transition and it is a developing nation with a rapidly aging population. Setting up a pension system under such circumstances is not something that can be accomplished in one "go," and indeed it is not certain that we can formulate correct policies at all if we do it in a hurry. As one part of overall reforms, China successfully initiated social security reforms over this past dozen years, so the embryonic form of a social security system is in place. The basic framework for this system is in line with the requirements of developing a market economy, and is in accord with the global trends in developing pension systems.

Nevertheless, there is undoubtedly room for improvement. Right now, China's pensions are managed by local governments in a fragmented way. Their coverage is narrow. They need to use individual-account contributions to help cover deficits in the pooled funds of the public. This has led to what we call the "empty accounts" syndrome in individual accounts. As time goes on, these problems will necessarily impact the willingness of individuals and companies to pay into the system. That will add to the difficulty of expanding coverage, which will put ever-greater pressure on public finance.

Even as we in China have been madly searching for a solution to our "empty accounts" problem, some other countries, starting with Sweden, have been experimenting with "non-financial defined contributions." One year ago, a study group composed of both Chinese and foreign experts looked at the possibility of applying this to China and they came away with fresh ideas. Even though we all take note of the very intense difference of opinion on this subject from many different sides, it may be that this method is actually a feasible and effective route to solving our empty accounts problem. Adopting an NDC system may help China improve its pension system. We feel that this system can take advantage of clearly-defined responsibilities in the individual account system, while also avoiding the drawbacks of excessive risk in the accumulated funds system. That is, it preserves incentives while also lowering the costs of transitioning to a new system.

Several years ago, we made an attempt to reform our public pension system by applying the "three-pillar model" in China. Those three pillars included a "publicly-pooled system," a "private accounts system," and "a voluntary private system." With respect to individual accounts, we were getting ready to manage and operate accumulated funds. However, once we had carried things out for a period of time, we discovered the following problems.

First, under our existing system, we must either increase the contribution rate or increase central government subsidies if we intend to fund the empty accounts. Either of these means a heavier burden on individuals, enterprises, and the government. The original intent in switching from a pay-as-you-go system to an individual contribution system, with each individual having his own accumulated amount was to address the problem of an aging population on the one side and inadequate incentives to pay into the system on the other side. Starting with Chile, this was tried and implemented for a number of years, but to this day it has failed to accomplish the result of people having faith in the system. Chile's system performed well in the early stage, and quite a few fund managers turned in good results. Since then, however, quite a few companies were closed down or merged with others, and only a very few have managed to stay alive. When the first group of contributors began to draw out their retirement funds, they discovered that the results were not what they had expected. After 20 years of this experiment, certain staff in Chile have been put in jail.

Second, there is an enormous degree of risk in putting accumulated individual retirement funds into capital markets that are not yet mature. In addition, those managing the funds are susceptible to moral hazard. Adopting a funded type of pension system can be highly costly in a country with insufficiently-developed capital markets. Such a system may also fall prey to criminal elements. Looking back on it now, even countries with well-developed capital markets have seen their share of problems—funded pension systems have not been all that successful. The United States has 33,000 pension-fund plans, which hold the pensions of some 44 million employees. In late 2003, these plans were showing a deficit of USD 300 billion. The Pension Benefits Guarantee Corporation in the United States is responsible for paying out funds that fund management companies themselves are unable to pay. At present, this corporation is responsible for paying out benefits to roughly one million former employees. In 2001, this corporation had a surplus of USD 7.7 billion, but by the end of 2003, it had a loss of USD 11.2 billion. At the end of 2003, the Dow Jones index fell by 34 percent from its highest point, causing pension funds in America to shrink by USD 500 billion.

Third, China's savings rate is already over 40 percent. This country does not need a mandatory system to ensure that its people save enough money. Whether or not a society has the capacity to cope with an aging crisis depends on its ability to produce sufficient output to meet demand, including the consumption demand of employees and retirees, and the investment demand of business. The output of a society depends on three factors: (1) quantity and quality of capital, including human capital; (2) the number of people in the workforce; and (3) most especially, the ability to take in and make use of better technology.

People have come to realize that an "accumulation"-type pension system can only resolve near-term needs but not those in the future. By itself, it cannot ensure the actual supply of funds in the future. Over the long term, if the savings rate remains too high, that may in fact lead to severe waste of capital since too much capital will depreciate its value and its price. In this sense, China's problems in terms of its future pensions will not be because savings rates are too low and public spending is too high, or because of the "hidden debt" of future pension liabilities, but rather because the overall return on investment and the efficiency of the financial system are both too low.

Fourth, in order to fund the empty accounts, we lowered contributions as a percentage of the total, and we eliminated the employers' contributions as originally planned for, making all "contributions" the responsibility of the individual. In addition, we promised the funding of 3 percent of the total in pilot programs, then lowered that to an insignificant 1 percent, which made any kind of "funding" purely a matter of form as opposed to substance. Not only did this heighten a sense of distrust on the part of the public, but it also dampened the desire of individuals to contribute. What's more, given that this tiny drop of money was not worth too much attention, the funds that were injected into pension funds were supervised in a very lax manner. At present, cases of corruption are being discovered in all parts of the country, with the remaining pension funds siphoned off to essentially nothing. What this says is that our implementation of the "individual accounts system" is by now simply an illusion.

A non-financial defined contribution system of accounts (NDC) is not only completely different from a system of individual accounts with "empty accounts," but its accounts do not need to be funded. The very term "empty accounts" signifies that a previously designed plan has not been effective, which affects the confidence of participating enterprises and individuals. With "defined accounts," participants contribute to their individual accounts according to a fixed percentage of their earnings. Authorities in charge of the system then record interest income for each account that accrues at a legally-defined interest rate. The money in the accounts does not actually remain there, however, but is paid out directly to pensioners at the same time. When participants retire, they are allowed to receive the accumulated sum as calculated in their own pension account. This allows us to avoid having younger people pay a double burden. It allows us not to require an income shift from one generation to the next that is unreasonable. The system can be guaranteed by the credit of the government. It can be operated by public agencies. It can get around the constraints and inadequacies of private-sector financial capacity and management capability. It can avoid the risk of short-term volatility in capital markets, which is extremely important at this stage when China's capital markets are not yet mature.

Implementing a "defined-accounts system" of individual accounts requires that government agencies be able to meet the following four conditions: (1) The government must indeed have access to and control over relevant work data of individual workers. (2) The government must be able to keep track of migrant workers and maintain a record of what work they are doing. (3) The government must have meticulous records on the accumulated sums in the account of each worker. (4) The government can be able to allow each worker himself to easily retrieve the information that has been put into his account. All of these tasks require massive amounts of time and money if they are to be properly accomplished.

To this end, through legislation, we should formulate mandatory pension rules that are applicable nationwide and then go on to implement a nationwide, unified pension management system. In order to ensure the voluntary nature of participation by both individuals and enterprises, the government should strengthen both legislation and regulatory supervision. A single, dedicated, regulatory agency and a clearly-defined system of laws and regulations should be put in place that govern all individuals, employers, and local government organizations that are in the voluntary pension-fund system. Tax revenue authorities should take on the responsibility of expanding coverage. At the same time, we should raise regulatory supervision over insurance companies that offer annuity types of pension plans.

Given that, mandatory pension rules applicable to the whole country should be introduced through legislation and a nationwide pension management system should be put in place. The government should improve legislation and regulation to protect the voluntary pension plans of individuals and businesses. A dedicated regulatory authority and a clear legal framework should be put in place to manage all voluntary contributions including the voluntary pension plans made by individuals, employers, or local governments. Tax authorities should take on the responsibility of increasing the coverage of pension contributions. In addition, the regulation of insurance companies offering annuities should be tightened.

When rules on retirement were implemented years ago, China's life expectancy was shorter than it is now. In 1949, the average life expectancy of a person was 35 years. This has increased to a life expectancy of over 72 years today. It is inappropriate to continue to use the retirement age set back in the 1950s for any of our planning. In Europe, retirement ages are already over 65, while in Japan, the retirement age is approaching 70. Because of this, China should put an end to any measures that encourage early retirement or that require mandatory retirement. The age at which people retire and draw a pension should gradually increase.

Naturally, there are many questions about China's pension systems that need to be addressed in addition to the above. This article deals only with the feasibility and applicability of using "defined individual accounts." We can speak to other issues at a separate time.

# 24 Prudent handling of the three main relationships[1]

(December 2006)

"Harmony" is a universally valued social objective. In China, many fine people have put enormous effort into trying to achieve social harmony over this past century. The process has not been an easy one and the Chinese people took a major detour in the wrong direction. In order to achieve social harmony, the country has already paid a heavy price.

After the Third Plenary Session of the 11th Central Committee of the Communist Party of China, the Party resolutely cast off the mistaken political line that called for "class struggle as the guiding principle." It shifted the center of gravity of Party work toward economic affairs. It called for "promoting reform and opening up" and "building modernization," and put unremitting effort into achieving social harmony. By now, the Chinese people have made enormous progress in this direction as measured by such things as ample food and clothing and lives that are pursued in a country that is at peace.

Since the 16th National Congress of the Communist Party of China, the Party explicitly defined the position of "building a harmonious society" within the overall scope of the endeavor to create "socialism with Chinese characteristics." It made a series of resource deployments which were able to achieve new results by creating advantageous underlying conditions. The Sixth Plenary Session of the 16th Central Committee of the Communist Party of China confirmed the objective of building a harmonious society, and brought forth the *"Decision of the Central Committee of the Communist Party of China on major issues regarding the building of a harmonious socialist society"* (referred to as the *Decision* below). The grand objective, as specified by this Plenary Session, was in line with the tide of history and in accordance with the people's desires. Because of this, it is an entirely achievable goal.

Naturally, "building a harmonious society" is not remotely an easy task. We cannot expect to achieve it in one fell swoop. We must remain clear-minded about the requirements of this particular stage of China's development and must use a scientific approach to analyze the causes of contradictions within society that influence "harmony." We have a long-term historical mission as well as the massive task of facing immediate reality and we must know how to handle the relationship between the two. We need to handle the relationship between our needs and our abilities, and the relationship between the most prominent issues and those that can be dealt with in due course. These three things are crucial if we are to accomplish the tasks as set forth by the Sixth Plenary Session.

The year 2007 marks the start of our process of bringing the *Decision* to fruition, so our correct handling of the three relationships as noted above should also begin in 2007.

First, we must correctly handle the relationship between our historic mission and the tasks that confront our immediate reality. Building a harmonious society runs through both the long-term historic mission of building socialism with Chinese characteristics and the major need right now to create a moderately prosperous society that is inclusive. We have to have our feet firmly planted in the here and now, while also looking out to the longer term. We must integrate these two things, the immediate and the future, and consider the process from an overall and unified perspective.

Making constant improvements in the living standards of people is both an immediate task and a long-term mission. Given rapid increases in the GNP in recent years, and improvements in both corporate profits and the State's tax revenues, there are indeed many reasons for asking the State to improve wage levels and welfare benefits. The State has already put major effort into doing so and our work in this regard is moving forward at a steady pace.

However, it should be recognized that a country's level of welfare benefits depends upon that country's level of economic development, while wage levels are fundamentally a factor of market supply and demand. They are not determined by the subjective will or hopes of people. Given changes in the regional and structural nature of supply and demand in China, wages are already showing a rising trend, and in some parts of the country the increase has been extremely fast. We should be alert to this new development. Given China's situation, any artificial attempt to suppress wages, or to push them higher, will impact economic development.

In this regard, it would be useful to research certain questions. These include, "what are reasonable labor costs at our current stage of economic development, what costs are economically feasible, and what wage levels are beneficial to long-term growth for the nation and ongoing improvement in people's lives?"

We must not forget that China's GNP per capita in 2005 was only around USD 1,700, which put it among middle-income developing countries. We should also recognize that we are not carrying out our process of "building up the nation" behind closed doors. We are living in an era of globalization, and in an economic context of intense international competition. If wage costs exceed our ability to bear those costs, the results will lead to China losing its international competitiveness and prematurely losing its comparative advantage.

In the short run, rising wages may appear to improve the living standards of people. In the long run, they will lead to capital flowing elsewhere and industries moving out, with a consequent loss of job opportunities. In the end, this will not help our goal of raising people's standard of living.

Second, we must correctly handle the relationship between our needs and our capabilities. China is currently still in the primary stage of socialism, so the basic contradiction that we face remains a problem of "constantly increasing need on the part of people for material culture, as set against a relatively backward state of the forces of production." Needs are fully able to expand beyond a given stage of development, whereas capabilities are not. In the course of thinking about long-term development, we must therefore face this contradiction squarely and handle it properly.

The primary stage of socialism is a very long stage in history that will require the efforts of generations upon generations of people. Preserving social harmony in the primary stage means, first and foremost, enabling ongoing economic growth. To do that, we must adhere to growth and reform as the ways to address problems that come up as we move forward. We must put major effort into developing the forces of production, in order to build a strong material basis for social harmony.

As the *Decision* points out, we must proceed with a correct measurement of our own capacities and then exert those to the fullest degree. As I understand it, this means that Party and government cadres must put their hearts and minds into working on behalf of the people, they must "put everything into it" when thinking of this work. When thinking of formulating policy, they must "seek truth from the facts," and proceed with a correct measurement of strength. If we do not emancipate our minds and work on behalf of the people with all our might, we will not gain the support of the people. However, if we set our goals too high and make unrealistic and unrealizable promises, we will only gain people's resentment.

The country must be prudent in how it handles social security systems and other social policies at this particular stage of development and under current economic conditions.

The social development goals that any nation sets for itself must match the actual economic power of that nation, as well as its ability to mobilize resources. In making arrangements for welfare systems, it is always better to provide a man with the tools by which he can catch fish himself than to give him a fish. It is better to provide a person with the means and abilities to survive and grow than to provide him with daily bread. We must therefore combine an understanding of the need for emergency relief with the need for people's self-reliance. The key to this lies in expanding job opportunities and encouraging individual initiative.

We recognize from the examples of other countries that it is possible to slow down economic growth and employment by the excessive use of transfer payments, derived from tax revenues, as the means to address social problems. This ultimately leads to a country's economic stagnation. Some Latin American countries are even facing economic collapse as the result of accommodating the excessive welfare demands of the people.

We must be on guard against any unhealthy attitudes that think social harmony is something we do not have to put much effort into, or that believe welfare can simply be dispensed from on high and therefore all we have to do is wait and reap the rewards.

As a famous western politician once said, "Ask not what your country can do for you. Ask what you can do for your country." Should we not also reflect upon this with respect to our own situation? "What can I personally do on behalf of building a harmonious society?" Each and every one of us has the responsibility for enabling "harmony," and only if each of us does his part will we create a society that is vital and enjoyed by all.

Third, we must correctly handle the relationship between the most outstanding issues and those that can be given due consideration. Right now, the country has innumerable problems to deal with, while people are concerned about innumerable problems and urgent issues as well. The country's economic capacities go only so far, however, while the government has control over a limited number of resources. Time itself is limited, that is, the time that history has allowed us to accomplish our objectives. The government must focus on the essentials while taking the nonessentials into due consideration. This was what was meant by the phrase in the *Decision* about addressing problems in a sequential way and setting priorities that define what is most important.

The Sixth Plenary Session determined that the initial goal of building a harmonious society should be accomplished by the year 2020. The entire nation therefore has roughly a decade or more in which to work hard towards this objective. This policy determination is in line with "seeking the truth from facts," and also in line with our actual situation. It avoids the overly hasty impulse to "try to make the plant grow faster by pulling on it." As such, the policy guidance nature of the goal is quite powerful.

The standard by which we measure the correctness of all our policies should be whether or not the policies satisfy the people. This is beyond doubt. At the same time, however, circumstances can be highly varied and can also change in the process of actually formulating and implementing policies. The beneficiaries of any given policy may well be a majority of the people, or even a minority of the people, but not necessarily all of the people. Those who are not beneficiaries may actually be harmed. People who are formulating policies must evaluate them from the starting point of whether they benefit social harmony and social justice. In addition, however, policy makers must also correctly gauge the orientation and intensity of the policies.

At the same time, we must explain and communicate our policies to the public so that the great majority of people both understand and support them. We must ensure that the majority of our population is satisfied.

The principle we must follow, therefore, as we formulate policy is one of sequential handling of key issues. After handling the most prominent issues before us, and while handling them, we also must give "due consideration" to subsidiary issues and all the many interests that are involved. When issues relating to the great majority of the public become the major problem, our focus must be on resolving problems that affect the majority. During the process, the interests of a minority of people are given "due consideration." When issues of a minority of the people become the outstanding problem, we address those as our major issue while giving "due consideration" to the interests of the majority.

The imbalance in rural and urban economic development in China, and the disparity in rural and urban institutions are the deciding factors in the massive challenges before us as we formulate policy at this current stage. We are not starting with a blank sheet of paper. We can only proceed on the basis of highly complex "initial conditions" as we implement reforms. We must be frank in recognizing the different starting points that apply to different groups of people. We cannot ask those who already enjoy certain levels of social security to give them up. Nor, given our current finances, can we bring everyone in both urban and rural areas up to the same level all at once. The overall goal must be universal and equal treatment with respect to our public spending policies and public services, but this is not something we can achieve right away.

It should also be seen that not every policy or every occasion can address the needs of the majority. One of our current public finance policy objectives right now is to alleviate poverty. In most places, the impoverished constitute a minority. Addressing poverty is most definitely a matter of using public funds and resources that belong to the entire body of people to help out one portion of the people. Nevertheless, this is the universal ethical standard of humanity and is also in accord with the wishes of the majority. It therefore has broadly based support. Since government resources are limited, however, the goals of public spending must also be limited. We do not have the ability to bring the income of the majority up to the level of the highest income earners and thereby achieve universal income equality. All we can do is focus limited resources on the key areas that are affecting key groups of people. We must resolve the most pressing questions first. Those include providing a safety net for the poorest in our midst, who have no ability to provide for themselves. Only in this way will we ensure social stability and social harmony.

## Note

1 This article was originally published in the 2007 Annual of *Caijing Magazine*.

# 25 On transforming China's mode of economic growth and speeding up economic restructuring[1]

(January 4, 2007)

We have focused on this issue of economic restructuring and mode of growth for some years now, and have a certain amount of data as a result of international and domestic conferences and a great deal of research. Based on this already existing research, in what follows I bring together information as it relates specifically to our main policy line of transforming China's mode of economic growth. I do this with respect to the most salient contradictions in what we are calling our "new stage of development."

With regard to restructuring our economy, I mainly emphasize the coordinated development of urban and rural areas and different regions of the country as seen from an overall perspective. I look at how to upgrade and optimize industrial structure, as tied in to research that has been done on transforming our mode of economic growth. In looking at how to restructure the economy and transform the mode of growth in our new stage of development, I focus particularly on the unification of issues, on new connotations and new ways of thinking, and on defining our most important tasks.

In what follows, I report on two key aspects in particular.

In the new stage of development, there are new "connotations" to consider with respect to the urgent imperative of transforming our mode of economic growth and restructuring our economy.

The subject of transforming the mode of economic growth and restructuring the economy has been discussed for many years already. The Fifth Plenary Session of the 14th Central Committee of the Communist Party of China proposed that the 9th Five-Year Plan realize two fundamental transformations with respect to our economic structure and mode of growth. (Translator's note: the Chinese term used for "structure" can also be defined as "system" or "apparatus," and the more accurate term would be "apparatus." In most cases, western readers think of the term "system" as applied to an economy, but the Chinese term relates back to the Soviet model of a structured apparatus (hence *apparatchik*). "Restructuring" then makes more sense.)

Over the past ten years, we have made important progress in these two transformations and we now stand at a new starting point in furthering the transformation of our mode of economic growth. Meanwhile, China's economy and society are undergoing major changes as the result of economic globalization. We are at a "new stage of development" in wanting to build a moderately prosperous society. Among the changes, I would like to address four specific things that I feel need particular attention:

1 Demographic changes in China are leading to an unusually fast aging of the population and to the prospect that such aging will prevent China from achieving its wealth objectives. Our previous pattern of an over-supply of manpower has not fundamentally changed, but within this overall pattern we now see increasingly pronounced structural shortages. Within five years, the burden of caring for the elderly will reach its highest point in the country's history. Within 20 years, the percentage of China's aging population will be what Japan's was in 1995 (a year in which Japan's economy hit the bottom of its 1990s slump.) By that time, our savings rate will show a clear decline and our speed of economic growth will moderate to a notable degree. We must therefore grab the opportunities as presented by the "population dividend" in this immediate period. (This refers to the economic contribution made by the relatively high percentage of people in the population who are of working age. This population dividend will gradually disappear as our population ages.) As we complete China's industrialization, we will only be able to address the various problems brought on by an aging population if we rapidly increase productivity and return on capital, and raise the percentage of value-added or "processing" industries in the economy.
Major changes are currently taking place in the pattern of labor supply and demand in the country, on a nationwide basis. The supply of skilled labor in cities is becoming inadequate. Labor shortages are beginning to show up in certain areas. Meanwhile, as able-bodied youth leave the countryside to work in cities, we will see labor shortages in rural areas if we cannot change the traditional manual methods by which we carry out agricultural production. Transforming our mode of economic growth therefore relates not only to the secondary and tertiary industries, but also to the traditional primary sector, namely agriculture. Agriculture too must be revamped through the use of modern applied technology.

2 Changes in China's overall amount of capital have meant the country has gone from an absolute shortage to a relative degree of surplus. Ongoing increases in the balance of trade and foreign-exchange reserves, plus a savings rate that approaches 50 percent and comes to RMB 10 trillion in savings deposits are evidence of this. Our economic growth strategy must therefore switch from proactive efforts to import more foreign exchange to efforts to use domestic investment more effectively and efforts to improve our returns on foreign capital.
Given the context of globalization, our efforts to restructure the economy and change our mode of growth are ever more tightly linked to international markets. The constant increase in our trade surplus will necessarily lead to more trade disputes. Roughly one-quarter of China's enterprises are currently affected by trade barriers of one kind or another, leading to an annual loss of

USD 30 billion. Meanwhile, being the recipient of a shift of international production may also have the effect of increasing pressures on our own domestic resources. We must, therefore, shift from being an export-oriented economy to being one that has a better balance between internal and external considerations. We should gradually raise our standing in the international division of labor and enable full use of our comparative advantage. We can do this by having a more global perspective and participating in a broader market space, by developing more open-style economies that are of a win-win nature, by allowing capital to come in and also go out of the country, by forming mechanisms that allow for an orderly and open process of industrial restructuring, and by promoting innovation that is self-generated and that allows for private entrepreneurship.

3   China's dual urban–rural structure and its inherent regional disparities are "initial conditions" that have to be taken into consideration as we reform and develop our economy. These will be constraining factors for a long time to come. For the past 30 years of reform and opening up, we have made enormous progress in industrializing, urbanizing, and developing our rural areas. Two things have not been coordinated and therefore continue to be held back, however. First, we lack coordination among industrialization, urbanization, and rural development, which has held back rural modernization. Second, our cities have been expanding in size but without any concurrent improvement in their functions. Meanwhile, we have an increasing number of cities but they remain fairly small on average (according to 2000 statistics, on a global basis, 35 percent of people living in cities with populations over 100,000 live in cities that hold over 3 million people. In China, the figure is only 20 percent.) China's cities also have inadequate basic infrastructure given investment that does not correspond to their expansion, which holds back their ability to function as real cities.

As urban economies keep growing, we are actually seeing an increasingly large gap between urban and rural and among different regions of the country, given the mobility of production factors. Free movement of things like labor and capital is therefore increasing economic disparities. We have adopted numerous policies in recent years to try to "enrich farmers and strengthen the rural economy," and to revitalize underdeveloped parts of the country, but the disparities between urban and rural and among regions will be with us for a relatively long time.

4   The contradiction between our policy objectives of "accelerating the building of the country" and "improving the living environment" is growing more pronounced by the day. Consumption patterns in China are being upgraded very quickly as we move into a "moderately prosperous" era, as reflected in improvements in living conditions and means of getting about. Meanwhile, demands for improved quality of life are intensifying, including improved housing conditions for both urban and rural citizens. As industrialization accelerates, and as urbanization takes place at an increasing speed as well, our manufacturing industries, heavy industries, and chemical industries are expanding in scale. Although we can moderate our consumption of resources

and discharge of pollutants to a certain degree, on an overall basis, these will continue to rise for some time to come. As modern living standards become more universal, the consumption of such things as private cars, among other types of consumer goods, increases. The discharge of pollutants that all these things involve is rising dramatically as a result. As an example, China's sulfur dioxide emissions are already two times higher than levels that can accommodate sustainable growth. We want to satisfy people's desire for a higher quality of life and an improved living environment, but we also want to push forward industrialization and urbanization. (In 2005, China's level of urbanization was 43 percent. According to World Bank statistics, the average level worldwide was 49 percent in 2003, with middle- and lower-income countries at 50 percent.) Achieving both these things will present a major challenge during this stage of creating a moderately prosperous society in China.

Based on the above analysis, we propose "four transformations" with respect to the directions that restructuring China's economy and transforming its mode of economic growth should take. Those are as follows.

First, by 2020, when we intend to have completed the process of creating a moderately prosperous society, we want to transform our current urban–rural pattern. We want to change it from being a dual structure that does not interact smoothly to being a unified structure with fairly well-coordinated development. Second, we want to transform our current regional pattern with respect to the distribution of production forces. From the current irrational situation, with too large a gap in development and widely differing levels of public service, we want to have each region taking advantage of its own unique features, having a fairly strong ability to develop itself, and having a uniform level of public services.

Third, with respect to industrial structure, we want to move away from the severe problem of redundant capacity in all areas, and production capacity that remains at a low level of technology. We want to move away from backward service industries and poor ability to compete in high-end industries. We want to transform that into a situation of industrial capacity that has higher technological content, more developed services, and stronger competitiveness on an overall basis. Fourth, with respect to our mode of economic development, we want to go from a low-efficiency extensive mode of growth, which pays too high a price in terms of resources and the environment, to a high-efficiency intensive type of growth. Factors are integrated to their best advantage so that the conservation of resources in all processes contributes to sustainability. The aim is to make tremendous progress in creating a resource-conserving, environmentally-friendly society.

## A new mentality and new policies are imperative as we face our new situation

In our economic work, we must now put structural changes and the transforming of our mode of growth in a much more prominent position than before. We must not waver in this resolve simply because of short-term economic fluctuations. We must keep our eye on the long-term task ahead of us, whether the economy is in the ascending or descending part of an economic cycle.

In the past, our thinking and policies were aimed at a situation of overall surplus of labor and an intense shortage of capital. We are now seeing the beginnings of a structural shortage of labor and a relative over-supply of capital. Since these things may well be a long-term trend, as opposed to a mere cyclical change, we should gradually rethink and readjust our previous policies and mental approaches.

In our previous stage of economic development, as we were attempting to resolve people's most basic needs, we had to deal with an overall scarcity of production resources and an extreme scarcity of the means to support daily life. The development strategy for that period was, in a certain sense, both unbalanced and guided by GDP. Such a strategy was both rational and in line with historical imperatives. Now, however, as we are entering a stage of overall moderate prosperity, we must pay more attention to environmental quality and a more balanced approach to growth. We must focus on humanitarian concerns and on social harmony. The "scientific view of development" as put forth by the central government is the strategic compass by which we must now realize our new goals.

In our Report, therefore, we have made recommendations that may have new significance. These are incorporated in the following eight subjects:

1   We should focus on "institutional innovation" as a way to achieve structural change and the transformation of China's mode of economic growth. In this regard, we should enable the market to play a much greater fundamental role in allocating resources and improving economic efficiency. This applies to our ongoing efforts to further coordinated reforms in the critical areas of government administration, finance and taxation, banking, land, and investing. With respect to the functions of government in the economic sphere, we should define those in a scientific way and thereby reduce administrative interference. Any industrial policy that has a bias toward developing the industries that are under the authority of specific departmental jurisdiction should be changed. Such policies should be transformed into comprehensive, universal, and function-oriented policies that relate to energy, environmental protection, technology, and competition. With respect to rules and regulations in the public sphere, we should speed up the formulation and strict enforcement of mandatory standards as they apply to technology, quality controls, energy consumption, environmental protection, and safety.

    In the corporate sphere, we should encourage and support enterprises to improve their innovative capacities by setting up win–win alliances in ways that complement mutual strengths. We should encourage multinationals to set up all kinds of research and development institutions within China. We should guide foreign-invested enterprises to invest in technological innovations and structural upgrading and take full advantage of the role such enterprises can play. We should form our own large body of outstanding enterprises that have their own intellectual property. We should cultivate a group of industrial "groups" that are internationally competitive, have their own branding, and their own comprehensive R&D capacity.

2   With farsighted anticipation, we should recognize the shifts that are occurring in our comparative advantage, and should therefore move to increase the contribution of human capital to economic growth. On the one hand, we should continue to develop labor-intensive industries, create more jobs, and promote the shift of labor away from agriculture. On the other hand, we must also develop capital-intensive industries as appropriate. We should improve the marginal returns on capital in order to enable domestic capital to find better ways to be invested. We should be an active participant in the international division of labor and continue to employ the comparative advantage of low-cost labor, but at the same time we must develop new comparative advantages. We should take the initiative in implementing a much more proactive "opening up" strategy. This includes taking full advantage of foreign markets and resources in order to upgrade our own industrial structure.

We should support the growth of knowledge-intensive industries by actively taking in the outsourcing opportunities of international services. This can serve to advance our own industrial technology. We should put major effort into developing service industries of our own, including financial, logistics, R&D, legal, accounting and others that relate to production, but also medical, community, and cultural and leisure services that relate to the consumer sector.

In coping with the accelerated aging of our population and the burden that places on social security, and also in consideration of the longer life expectancies and longer time spent in getting an education, we recommend following the practice in Europe and the United States. At the appropriate time, we should start to delay the retirement age.

3   We propose that a unified national market and uniform provision of public services be regarded as the two fundamental "pillars" that support coordinated development of all parts of the country. We recommend focusing on the idea that the market and the government must each play a role in achieving an integration of urban and rural and different regions of the country. An overall approach to coordinated development must drive the situation. This means improving the ability of urban–rural policies and regional policies to conform to one another.

The primary functions of different regions vary, depending on situations. We propose that we improve the ability of "economic development zones" to push forward transformation of our economic growth model. In "key" economic development zones, we recommend a concentration of industry. In restricted development zones and areas that restrict development altogether, we must ensure that the carrying capacity of natural resources is protected and that humankind's own social and economic activities are protected as well.

We further propose that, in order to realize a more successful deployment of regional industries and greater utilization of the primary functions of a given region, we should set out plans for population distribution and industrial distribution from a holistic perspective. We should set up a nationwide resource development and ecosystem protection system in order for inhabitants in restricted development areas and areas that prohibit development to have an equal opportunity to develop. This is done on the premise of first clarifying the ownership of mineral resources as being State-owned, and confirming that ecological systems are a resource of a "public nature."

4   We should emphasize that things such as energy conservation, lower energy consumption, lower emissions, and greater efficiency are at the leading edge of how we transform our mode of economic growth. This relates particularly to the fields of construction, transportation, public utilities, government institutions, and people's daily life. Our aim is to develop a "resource-conserving" society.

To ensure the State's ownership rights to such things as mineral resources, water, forests and other natural resources, we must set up a sound system that requires payment for the use of resources. At the same time, we should create conditions that allow for competition in such important areas as electricity, petroleum, natural gas, and water, or into certain links in the process (of producing and transporting these). With respect to products on which we cannot fully release price controls, these should be subject to stronger cost regulation by the government. Prices should be adjusted to reflect changes in international prices in a timely manner. Depending on the type of customer and the time of use, prices for water, electricity, and natural gas should be set at different levels in order to guide the entire system toward behavior that is conservation oriented.

The conservation of resources and environmental protection involve engineering technologies but they also have to do with considerations of administrative management and social ethics. They are also extremely complex economic issues. We recommend that China strengthen its economic measures in this regard. China should implement a "green accounting system" for public finance and tax revenues. It should promote the "clean development mechanisms" (CDM), in pushing for a system that grants permits on pollution emissions and then the trading of those permits (trading of the emission credits). We should gradually apply higher taxes to production, circulation, and consumption processes that involve the highest waste and highest degree of emissions. In relative terms, we should reduce the tax on turnover.

5   By recognizing the way in which consumers can have a "pull" effect, we should guide the use of resources from the outset through guiding what people choose to consume. This raises the quality of economic growth and helps us optimize industrial structure. Uninformed and unsound consumption not only leads directly to massive waste by consumers, but it leads indirectly to an "extensive" form of operations in both production and circulation. To a degree, this guides the upgrading of consumption in the wrong direction, as well as the ways by which we adjust industrial structure. Because of this, we recommend that we go further in improving our income distribution policies and consumption policies. The aim is to guide more rational consumption, improve the environment for consumption. It is to stimulate better modes of consumption that both increase consumption and create healthier and more enlightened kinds of consumption.

6   We should create modern agricultural systems that are more competitive and that focus on comprehensive agricultural production, sustainable development, and environmental protection. To this end, concentrate on standardized production, modernized facilities, regionalized deployment, products that are "safe," and products that have diverse functions. We should make use of the results of applied engineering technologies to reform our traditional agricultural production methods in order to raise our agricultural productivity and levels of development. We must promote the sound development of biologically-based energy production and thereby increase the uses to which agriculture can be put and the efficiency of using agricultural resources. We should move further in implementing rural reforms, and help transform rural agricultural production through the use of innovative systems and organizations.

7   In keeping our focus on the broader issues of restructuring the economy and transforming our mode of economic growth, we should encourage more overseas investment in an effective and sequential (or staged) way. We should take advantage of the favorable condition China is in right now in terms of plentiful domestic production capacity and plentiful capital. We should match that with the advantages that can be found overseas, including resources, R&D, services, human capital, and production groups. We should expand our overseas investment in both industries and finance, as a way to drive the restructuring and upgrading of our own domestic industries.

We should actively participate in the liberalization process of multilateral trade systems, as well as expand bilateral and regional economic cooperation. We should constantly try to expand the market space for China's industries as a way to upgrade industries and improve the quality of our economic growth.

8   We propose the idea of a "new model of urban development." This model features compact arrangements, concentrations of industry, optimized urban functions, and resource conservation. It aims at urban development that is "open and harmonious." The idea is to increase the way in which large- and medium-sized cities in particular can serve as a model for others and can have a "radial influence" on the surrounding countryside. This is done by upgrading urban, industrial structures, and consumption structures, and by bringing together a concentration of technological innovations.

Finally, with respect to land use, we must improve the efficiency with which we "allocate" land-use rights, improve the price-formation mechanisms for land, and handle the expansion of cities in more appropriate ways. We should explore new avenues for financing the construction of basic urban infrastructure. We should get rid of the way municipal governments rely excessively on the sale (transfer) of land-use rights as a way to finance construction.

## Note

1   This is the outline of a report by the author.

# 26 Economic development and environmental protection[1]

## (February 15, 2007)

As many scholars and economists have long since recognized, environmental problems are in fact an economic issue. In the theoretical framework of traditional economics, they are, moreover, a particular kind of economic issue. They involve what are known as "externalities" in economics, as well as income distribution across generations. They also involve discounting issues, cost-benefit issues, and other economic considerations.

Years of actual experience in China have shown us that environmental issues cannot be regarded as purely engineering matters, or government administration matters, or matters of social ethics. The returns are very modest if we deal with them in that way. Environmental pollution only gets worse by the day. In order to study the relationship between China's economic growth and its environment, we therefore set up a research program under the auspices of the China Council for International Cooperation on the Environment and Development. I served as Director on the China side, and Professor Peter Bartelmus of Columbia University in New York served as the Director on the international side. This group was set up in 2005 with the aim of analyzing environmental pollution trends in light of China's future economic growth, and coming up with forecasting systems, early warning systems, and measures to deal with problems in a systematic way.

Professor Qi Jianguo served as the overall coordinator of the effort and the person responsible for implementation. He is Chair of the Research Center on Environmental Evaluation and Forecasting and Circulation Economics at the China Academy of Social Sciences (CASS), as well as Deputy Director of the Institute for Quantitative and Technical Economics at CASS. The research team was composed of over 20 experts from various countries, including China, the United States, Canada, Hungary, and others. Through their hard work, the team completed a research report in October 2006. This report was presented to the China Council for International Cooperation on the Environment and Development at its annual meeting in November 2006. This book is composed of selections from the series of reports that came out of the entire effort.

As we all know, China's economic growth and social progress since the start of reform and opening up in 1978 has been astonishing. Over the past 28 years, China's economic growth rate has averaged 9.67 percent. Using comparable prices, China's total GDP has doubled three times, and is 13.27 times what it was in 1978. In looking at these results, however, we must also recognize that such sustained high-speed economic growth has come at an enormous cost. Conflicts and problems have been accumulating as a result. These manifest themselves mainly in a great number of unfortunate issues in such areas as medical care, education, housing, environmental pollution, supply and demand for resources, social security, and interest allocations. In order to address these things and realize the kind of growth that is stable and sustainable, the Chinese government has brought forth a new strategy called a "scientific outlook on development," and "building a harmonious society." It has called for concerted efforts to address the problems and bring about solutions.

The problems that we now face are different from those we confronted at the end of the 1970s, when reform and opening up first began. At that time, China's social and economic development mainly faced the problem of "shortages," while now we face social problems across a range of issues. The common thread that unites all of these is that, to one degree or another, they all have to do with "the public" and "society" overall. Two primary causes are behind these conflicts and problems.

First, as seen from a development perspective, people's demand for public goods has risen across the board in concert with a rise in living standards. The demand for medical care, education, housing, and a clean environment has increased among the entire population. While market-oriented reform has led to improved efficiency, it has also led to drawbacks that become more apparent by the day. Under market-economy conditions, the benefits of economic growth do not automatically extend to the entire body of citizens. Fair allocation of "interests" is not something that happens on its own. In corresponding fashion, the market itself cannot automatically resolve problems that involve "externalities." The costs of development are not distributed to the beneficiaries of development in equal measure. Some groups enjoy the benefits of economic growth, while not bearing the costs of, for example, environmental pollution. This has led to a general increase in pollution and deterioration of our ecological environment.

Second, in this past period of reform, we focused more on market efficiency and not enough on reforming the government itself. This has held back the transformation of government functions in that functions that apply to the supply of public goods have not developed as they should have. Goods that have certain public attributes, such as medical care, education, housing, and the environment, are areas in which the market can easily fail to be effective. These are areas that require the actions of the kind of government that is appropriate to the functioning of a market-economy system. The government should adjust and regulate areas that the market fails to deal with properly, in order to satisfy the constantly increasing demand for public goods of urban and rural residents.

Environmental pollution and damage to the ecosystem are among those areas in which a market is ineffective, and these have become the most severe problems facing China today. The year 2006 was the inaugural year of the country's 10th Five-Year Plan. In 2006, economic growth reached 10.7 percent, lowering employment pressures. Prices were stable and our trade surplus reached more than USD 177 billion. We came in over the plan on most indicators, but we did not meet the requirements on two indicators that are of a "limiting type," that serve to hold back the economy. Those were energy consumption per unit of GDP, and the total amount of pollutants that were discharged and emitted. Instead of going down, these two indicators went up. In 2007, therefore, one of the major tasks for our macroeconomic regulation is to make sure these two numbers go down in aggregate terms.

In looking at the history of developed countries it can be seen that environmental problems began to appear as GDP per capita reached around USD 8,000. In China, GDP per capita was a mere USD 2,000 per capita in 2006, so one might wonder why we should place such policy emphasis on limiting energy consumption per unit of GDP and lowering pollution. The answer is determined by China's unique situation.

First, not only is China's population huge, but it is concentrated along the eastern seaboard and central parts of the country due to reasons relating to history and economic geography. The density of populations in these areas and the degree to which they are more developed means that pollution is more intense here (both discharge and emissions).

Second, China is not only in the midst of high-speed urbanization and development, but its industrialization has been compressed into a much shorter period of time. If China, as intended, achieves "industrialization and "informatization" by the year 2030, this means that it will have accomplished within 50 years what developed nations took nearly 200 years to achieve. Given that China's economy is characterized by its desire to "catch up with and surpass" the economies of other countries during this period in history, it has seen the ferocious development of industries that are highly polluting. Such high-tech industries as electronics have grown at a fast pace, but others that are major polluters have too. These include such resource-intensive industries as heavy and chemical industries, and also chemical fertilizer industries (given agricultural practices that feature the massive use of chemical fertilizers and pesticides). Problems that other countries were able to discover and deal with in a sequential fashion, such as pollution from traditional industries, pollution that comes off agricultural fields, pollution caused by high-tech electronics, are things that overlap in China and have to be dealt with all at once. On an overall basis, pollution in China has surpassed the ability of the environment to deal with it, or the "carrying capacity" of the environment. This in turn is leading to a very swift increase in all kinds of environmental pressures.

Third, with respect to the western parts of the country, China instituted a policy to "undertake major development of the West." In recent years, this has led to a dramatic deterioration of environmental quality given that the ecosystems in the western part of the country were quite fragile to begin with. With poor natural conditions and backward economies, resource exploitation and densely concentrated heavy and chemical industry development have led to a dramatic increase in pollution of all kinds. Given that the western part of the country is "upstream" from the rest of China, in terms of both water and air flows, destroying and polluting the ecosystem of this region has a direct impact on the central and eastern parts of the country.

Fourth, for both historical and institutional reasons, China's heavy industries and chemical industries feature decentralized and small-scale production. They use outmoded technology and require a high per-unit consumption of energy. Already existing well-established methods to deal with pollution are not widely used, so there are also technical reasons behind the speed with which China's various forms of pollution have grown into formidable problems.

Fifth, the speed with which China's economy went from being agricultural to being industrial was too fast for China's population to understand the fundamental connection between economic growth and environmental pollution. Awareness of the need for environmental protection is universally low. This means that any legal or policy measures do not have the understanding and support of the public behind them. Some local governments take no regard of environmental protection at all in their pursuit of the "accomplishments" of economic growth, more jobs, and "social stability." They team up with polluting-type enterprises, and pretend to comply with central government policies in public but then disregard these in private. The result is that efforts put into environmental protection by the central government cannot in fact be realized when it comes to implementation.

Sixth, and most importantly, China's economic and political institutions as they currently exist have strong incentives that work against resolving environmental issues. In terms of economic systems, the financial and institutional authorities of the central government and local governments are often in conflict. The public finance system of the country is often described as "each eats at his own hearth," which means that each local government is responsible for getting its own food. This motivates the local government to pursue industrial development as a way to provide public-finance income for social development and job creation. Such industrial development is seen as the vehicle by which to increase employment. In terms of political systems, each higher level of government evaluates the job performance of the main officials in the level below it in terms of economic performance. There are no institutions or lobbying groups that can put political pressure on the government to achieve environmental goals. China has already formulated a whole series of laws and regulations on environmental protection, but few have been fully implemented. The root of the problem is that the government has not in fact carried out its responsibilities in dealing with environmental issues.

Naturally, each level of government confronts its own problems in doing this. China's current system allows for each to be an "interest group" (or stakeholder) within the overall workings of the market economy. "Government" is necessarily in the position of trying to pursue conflicting goals as a result. One of these goals is generating income for government staff. In the face of conflicting interests, the government often "oversteps" its authority when it comes to goals that serve the interests of the government itself. It is often simply "absent," that is, takes no responsibility when it comes to areas that do not serve the government's interests at all.

China does not lack the technology required to deal with environmental protection issues. That is, in technical terms it can address the "supply of public goods that have a strong degree of externality." What China lacks is institutional change. A large number of polluting industries have fitted out their factories with pollution-control equipment, but they do not put this into operation. A large number of facilities are in place to treat garbage, but these are not in fact being used. These things point to the importance of carrying out institutional reform.

One of our major tasks in the next period of reform will be to reform the government itself. One of the core issues that we must address is this dual problem of "overstepping authority" and "being absent." The goal must be to set up government administration and government services that are in line with the needs of a market-economy system. As I understand it, this is the essential point that was conveyed by the recent Sixth Plenary Session of the 16th Central Committee of the Communist Party of China.

During the planned-economy period, China's social organizations operated by a fundamental principle, and one could even say it was a unique principle. That was the so-called "unit-based system." The core feature of this system was that all functions were unified in one body, including administrative functions, enterprise functions, and the functions of public institutions. This unavoidably led to the pervasive expansion of the powers of unit-based administration. That is, enterprise units and public institutions took on functions that should have been handled by a "government." Although this vastly lowered the numbers of people required to run the country, it also unavoidably led to a situation in which "enterprise" and "government" were one and the same.

The defects of this system were not apparent under planned-economy conditions. The reason was that these combined "units" were not independent or stakeholders in their own right. Once the basic role of a market economy came into play in allocating resources, however, not only did State-Owned Enterprises and public institutions turn into independent interest groups in their own right but local governments did the same. They came to be players in economic development on their own behalf. This brought with it a host of problems. The most concentrated expression of all of these problems, however, could be seen in the coexisting practice of "overstepping administrative authority," and "evading (or being absent from) any administrative authority."

The coexistence of these two things evolved in new ways as the principle of "material benefit from a market economy" took hold. Both of these things became intertwined with the pursuit of "interests." Government departments became highly interested in those areas in which one could derive interests (financial benefit) through administrative means. In contrast, they avoided any area that might require investment. Such things included investment in public goods and services. They evaded responsibility from anything that hurt their interests to the extent that they adopted an attitude of, "not my problem," putting off on the public any issue that the government should, by all rights, have been responsible for handling.

To government departments, administrative authority now became the means by which they could, in fact, "derive rents." Once started, the combined practice of evading responsibility and overstepping authority then intensified. The classic example of "overstepping authority" is the charging of all kinds of fees. Fees for traveling on regular public roads (not freeways) are a case in point. As the name implies, public roads should be built for the public. Under the excuse of paying off loans to build roads, however, many local governments set up tollgates to extract tolls. Any sphere in which a fee might remotely be possible is a sphere in which local governments are now charging fees and overstepping their authority in doing so. Any sphere in which the government might have to pay out money is a sphere in which the government claims it is not responsible. Such things include regulating polluting enterprises, picking up garbage, and ensuring public safety.

The Sixth Plenary Session of the 16th Central Committee of the Party explicitly brought forth proposals for reforming the government. These included building a service-oriented government (government that operates as a provider of services), strengthening the government's functions in both public services and social administration, performing "administration" through the provision of services" and "making the conduct of administration become apparent (be exhibited through) the provision of services." As I understand it, these are the "guiding principle" behind our next steps in reform.

A guiding principle is like the head rope of a fishing net. Once you have grasped it, all the rest falls into place. Only if we grasp this guiding principle will we be able to resolve all of the above conflicts and problems. Neither adherence to a "scientific outlook on development" nor the desire to set up a "harmonious society" can be divorced from excellent service as provided by the government. Not only must such service be in line with the needs of the market, but it must be regulated and administered when the market is not effective. Through coordinating the functions of the government and the market, we should be able to ensure both economic and social sustainable development.

The three issues of economics, the environment, and a moderately prosperous society are closely interrelated. This book deals with the relationships among all three, that is, economic growth, environmental protection, and building a harmonious and moderately prosperous society. It is not a work of systematic scholarship but it reflects the systematic way of thinking of foreign and Chinese experts as applied to the conflicts between economic growth and environmental protection. Based on a series of research reports, it presents policy recommendations that aim at creating a "harmonious and moderately prosperous society" that can achieve sustainable growth.

The reports made use of highly complex economic models to apply quantitative analysis and forecasting to economic growth, structural change, and pollution emissions during the period of China's 11th Five-Year Plan. In addition, it analyzed the roles and tasks of the government, enterprises, and the public from the perspective of "green accounting" of the national economy, systems analysis, and social theory. It studied the performance criteria by which local governments are evaluated. It explored the relationships among concepts put forth by the Party since the 16th National Congress of the Communist Party of China, including "a moderately prosperous society, "a harmonious society," a "new path for industrialization," a "resource-conserving and environmentally-friendly society," and a "circular (or recycling) economy." On the basis of both quantitative and qualitative analysis, it carried out early-warning forecasts for both economic growth and environmental problems during the period of China's 11th Five-Year Plan. It recommended a number of concrete and operable policies.

I believe that this book will help readers understand the relationship between economic growth and environmental protection. It will provide inspiration to government officials at all levels who seek to resolve the conflicts between economic growth and the environment, and who are exploring ways to speed up the establishment of a "harmonious and moderately prosperous society."

## Note

1 This is the preface the author wrote for *Economic Growth and Environment: Early Warning Mechanism and Policy Analysis* (China Environmental Science Press, 2007).

# 27 Resolving fairness issues must rely on "reform"[1]

(December 24, 2007)

Professor Qian Yingyi's observations on China's current stage of reform are extremely insightful and sound. It is indeed true that China is in the midst of unprecedented prosperity. As he has noted, in terms of market valuation alone, PetroChina is the largest oil company in the world, China Mobile is the largest telecom company, ICBC is the largest bank, and China Life is the largest insurance company. We should not pay too much attention to this, perhaps, since things may change in the blink of an eye. We certainly do not want to be complacent. The thing that is really worth getting excited about, however, is the fact that this year our fiscal revenues may increase by RMB 1.2 trillion, while our foreign exchange reserves have now reached USD 1.5 trillion. What's more, it looks as though both of these will continue to grow at a fast pace for some time to come.

For many years, we were all upset about a shortage of money. It seems we are now trying to find ways to spend it. We did not prepare ourselves for this mentally, nor are our institutions ready to deal with it.

Professor Qian believes that crises can expedite reform. He is worried that prosperity may whittle down our resolve as well as our courage to keep undertaking reform. As we all know, the prosperity we are experiencing, as symbolized by "plenty of money," is due fundamentally to China's current "population dividend." Many economists and scholars are predicting that this population dividend will only continue for another decade or so, as based on their statistics and modeling projections. If we do not keep a clear head as we move ahead with reforms, but instead get "drunk" on glorious prospects of prosperity, we may be led to commit two different kinds of mistake.

The first is to artificially depreciate the value of capital. This leads to wanton use and waste of capital. It delays our industrial upgrading and the transformation of our mode of economic growth. The second is to expand subsidies and welfare benefits too quickly and too broadly. This suppresses the role of the market itself, and it lowers the efficiency by which the market allocates resources. Both of these mistakes can lead to general inflation. We should see our relative abundance of financial strength right now as an opportune time to undertake reforms, to cover the necessary costs of reforms that we could not push forward for many years. We absolutely must guard against any kind of yielding to interest groups. We must not reinforce and solidify vested interests. We must not "poke out" a hole in our budget that involves rigid spending requirements and that makes us shoulder the burden of new spending. By doing so, we would actually damage mechanisms and put obstacles in the way of our next reforms.

Right now, two very important factors of production are in the midst of change. That is, capital is going from absolute scarcity to relative abundance. Labor is going from adequate supply to structural scarcity. Statistics indicate that the unlimited supply of labor in China kept down wage levels in the past. Those are now rising at an unprecedented pace. Manpower shortages are quite apparent along the eastern seaboard and even in the middle of the country. Even in rural areas, manpower shortages and the aging of existing labor is becoming quite serious. The measures that the government took for years to increase wages were generally ineffective. In a fundamental sense, the market has now become the decisive factor in determining labor supply and demand.

When labor was over-abundant, workers had the opportunity to participate in the results of reform only by increased job opportunities. When labor begins to become scarce, workers will be able to participate in the results of reform through higher wages. Looking at current patterns, there is still some room for wages to rise higher. Nevertheless, we should remember that any sustained improvement in incomes and welfare benefits can only come about through upgraded industries, technological advances, and higher productivity. If those do not support wage increases, then higher incomes and benefits are like water without any source and a tree without any roots.

At the end of the day, therefore, it will be detrimental to both job growth and improved wages and benefits if we do not apply appropriate administrative interference in job markets. I therefore agree with Professor Qian's point of view. Issues of fairness should make use of reform and the concepts underlying reform if we are to come up with solutions.

## Note

1 This article was originally published in *Caijing Magazine*, Vol. 201, with a title proposed by the editor. The title has been revised for this compendium.

# 28 Strategies and goals for a water-conserving society

## New conceptual approaches for handling water issues

## (March 2008)

Water is the source of life. It has been sought after and cherished since time immemorial. A number of the world's great water systems enabled the rise of four outstanding civilizations. China's own waterways have supported and nurtured generation after generation of people, including the Yellow River and the Yangtze River, among others. China is fortunate in that it has the third largest water system in the world, the Yangtze River, but also a number of other rivers that have in the past had ample runoff, the Songhuajiang, the Heilongjiang, the Haihe, and the Xin'anjiang.

Despite such rivers, however, China's per capita water resources are relatively scarce due to the country's large population. According to data from the Ministry of Water Resources, total water resources on the mainland come to roughly 2.7 million cubic meters per year. This accounts for 6 percent of the globe's total, which ranks China sixth in the world in water resources. Right now, however, China has one-fifth of the world's population and its per capita water resources come to only around 2,100 cubic meters, which is one-quarter of the average per capita amount in the world. As our population grows, this figure will continue to go down.

These scarce water resources are, meanwhile, highly uneven in terms of spatial and temporal distribution, which exacerbates structural shortages. Rainfall in the country is concentrated in the south and is highly seasonal. The monsoon season often brings floods in its wake. In contrast, the north is arid, with only 700 cubic meters of water resources per capita, and droughts often bring meager harvests as a result. The Haihe River Basin in the north, which includes the city of Beijing, encompasses a population of 120 million people but provides only 300 cubic meters of water per capita. This is a mere one-seventh of the average per capita amount of water in the country. The region has so few water resources that it is equivalent to the most water-deprived parts of the world.

In order to resolve the uneven spatial and temporal distribution of water resources, China must construct necessary water conservancy projects for storage and water control, but the country faces multiple problems in this regard. Inadequate facilities are among them, but also problems of irrational distribution and allocation. Urgent tasks that we need to address include turning the frequent incidence of flooding in the south into water that can be used efficiently, and taking a more holistic approach to limited water in the north, so that it can be used more effectively.

One very serious problem relates to China's ongoing industrialization which has increasingly concentrated on the country's eastern seaboard and along its major rivers. This has led to structural changes in the demand for water, low efficiency in the use of water, and lax controls on pollution discharge, all of which have intensified problems. In the past 30 years in particular, investments into water considerations have been inadequate. Pollution has spread across wide areas, making water unsafe to drink and unable to be used in many regions. Emergency incidents that relate to water pollution are now occurring with increasing frequency. Some water bodies that are severely polluted are affecting the lives of residents in the area and even leading to social unrest.

All of the above problems exist simultaneously and serve to amplify one another. Their resource issues and structural, engineering, and water-quality issues are now affecting China's sustainable development. The Chinese government regards this as a major issue and relevant departments are undertaking research into better models for dealing with the problems. Naturally, water conservancy issues have always been a major national concern through thousands of years of Chinese history. The country's agricultural heritage included a wealth of experience in how to handle water and created a unique kind of "water-conservancy culture." As China transitions from being an agricultural society to a modern industrial society, however, its production methods and social structures are undergoing change. The country's water-conservancy concepts and models must change as well. Indeed, they must now undergo fundamental change.

Given the low efficiency with which water was being used, the Chinese government adopted an "administrative-command type" approach over the past ten years. Measures included the use of economic incentives and technology subsidies as well, and results were quite notable. Calculated at 2000 prices, between 1997 and 2006, the amount of water used per RMB 10,000 of GNP fell from 705 cubic meters to 329 cubic meters. During the same period, the amount of water used per RMB 10,000 of industrial value-added fell from 363 cubic meters to 178 cubic meters. Naturally, the efficiency with which China uses water is still quite a bit below that of more advanced international levels. What's more, despite the efforts that the country has put into controlling water pollution and protecting the ecosystem of drainage basins, the results have been less than satisfactory.

As a result, the country is now incorporating water-resource issues into its medium-term and long-term strategic development plans. This comes about because of a full awareness of the impact that water resources have on China's future sustainable development. Important aspects that will be included are better water treatment, but also building "a water-conserving type of society," a "water-economizing society," and an "environmentally friendly society." In 2007, relevant departments in the government formulated an "11th Five-Year Plan with respect to building a water-conserving society" that was tied in to the country's overall 11th Five-Year Plan. This specified goals to be accomplished during the period, as well as priority tasks and measures. The Chinese government is currently engaged in implementing this process. It is setting up systems to achieve a 20 percent reduction in water use per unit of GDP and a 30 percent reduction in water use per unit of industrial value-added by the year 2010 as compared to 2005. By 2010, the goal is also to achieve a reusable water rate of 20 percent of treated sewage water in water-scarce cities in the north. Systems that are being implemented to accomplish these goals include a system of social norms and behavior that consciously conserves water, a system of engineering technology that allows for more efficient use of water, and a system of economic structures that are better coordinated with the carrying capacity of the water resources in any given area.

Among those doing research on policy formulation for China, there has long been a consensus on the fact that resource scarcity impacts the country's long-term sustainable growth. As noted above, this awareness is gradually being put into action in the form of policies. In the final analysis, though, we need to make the entire body of people realize how critical water resources are to China's economic and social progress. People need to understand the economic, social, political, and environmental factors that affect our use of water resources and they need to understand their complex interactions. We must come to a consensus on new mechanisms for dealing with water issues. This will require new concepts, a better legal framework, sounder institutions and systems, better technology, and improved government capacities. If we are to address this problem of water scarcity, we will need the efforts of the entire nation.

Among the above tasks, the first is to set up a new conceptual framework for approaching water issues. This includes new concepts with respect to resources in general, resource rights, water rights, the market, and a holistic approach.

Water is an important renewable resource that has a critical economic value. That realization must be what drives us to take the necessary steps in finding the institutional arrangements and technical means to allocate water resources in rational ways—to industry, to people, across different areas, and through time. The aim is to maximize the greatest long-term benefit for society.

- *Concept of resource rights.* Water is one of the most fundamental requirements for human life. All of the nation's people should have the right to enjoy the water necessary to their survival. This is the legal and moral basis for ensuring that people in rural areas have potable drinking water, and that poor people in urban areas have adequate water for daily use. This is a basic right that applies to every person in the country.
- *Concept of water rights.* Our current age of urbanization and industrialization requires that we specifically define the ownership of water rights, that is, the property rights that apply to water. Moreover, the allocation of such water rights must be differentiated according to whether the owner is the State, the community, an economic entity, or an individual. Rights and responsibilities must be defined with respect to ownership but also as they relate to the protection and transfer or sale of water rights. As a rule-of-law society, we must protect and ensure legitimate ownership rights, but we must also take full advantage of our native experience as rooted in our history and culture. We

must use all means to clarify the starting point or initial definition of water rights in China.

- *Concept of the market.* Given that a market is the most efficient way to allocate resources, we must make full use of market mechanisms to improve the efficiency with which we handle our water resources. We should draw upon the experiences of other countries in this regard as we develop our own market for water rights. We should set up mechanisms that include not only trade in water rights but also the trade in pollution credits. As the market develops, we should explore new means, including financial tools, to enable water resources to create the greatest social value.

- *Comprehensive or holistic approach.* Given that water resources embody highly complex economic and social features, we must think of them in the combined light of politics, economics, society, and the environment. We must encourage the public at large to participate in decision-making with respect to water. While using the market to raise the efficiency by which water is allocated, we must also guarantee that every citizen has the basic right to clean drinking water. We must ensure adequate water and sewage treatment in order to make sure we all continue to have "clear water and blue skies" in which to live. This requires a comprehensive approach to water issues that is strategic, long-range, and all-inclusive.

Within the objectives as defined above, we must now improve upon our legal system as it relates to water and clarify the rights and responsibilities of all different interest groups. We must accelerate the process of setting up market mechanisms for both water use and pollution prevention. As soon as possible, it is imperative that we straighten out (or rectify) the organizations responsible for handling water issues. We must constantly improve our water infrastructure and technical processes. We must improve government capacities even as we enable the market to carry out its fundamental role.

China's efforts to cope with its water scarcity are an important aspect of China's own long-term sustainable development but also that of the entire globe. Because of this recognition, China has received support from the World Bank and various other international institutions. Ten years ago, the World Bank published a volume called "*Clean Water and Blue Sky: The Chinese Environment in the New Century,*" which discussed China's water resources and environmental problems. Since that time, the World Bank has maintained a strong interest in China's water-scarcity issues. In 2005, it initiated a project called "Addressing the scarcity of water resources in China—from research to action." This brought scholars and experts from international institutions together with those from China to carry out systematic research on such subjects as water pricing, water pollution control, measures to prevent pollution emergencies, water management, and water treatment.

This project resulted in a number of research reports that were presented to various government departments, together with policy proposals for how to improve water-resource management. The reports and recommendations served as important reference materials as policy makers deliberated on the next steps. This book reflects only one part of the important results of the whole process.

I must emphasize that these results are an excellent beginning but only the beginning. They represent an important foundation on which to carry out further research into China's strategies for handling water resources. China must now mobilize much greater resources if it is to push forward modernization and sustainable development. The country must have a strategic, long-term, and comprehensive approach. We must be much more systematic in how we formulate policies to deal with the problem of water scarcity. This is not only a highly urgent and immediate task, but one that will be with us long into the future.

# Major works by Li Jiange

1 *Standing in the Forefront of Market-Oriented Reform*, Shanghai Yuandong Press (Shanghai), 2000.
2 *Major Issues in China's Medium-Term and Long-Term Development (2006–2020)*, China Development Press (Beijing), 2005.
3 *Historic Opportunities,* Peace Book Co., Ltd. (Hong Kong), 2005.
4 *The Emergence of the Central Part Of China: Strategies and Countermeasures*, Economic Science Press (Beijing), 2006.
5 *Reform of China's Pension Systems* (Editor-in-Chief), Shanghai Yuandong Press (Shanghai), 2006.
6 *Reform of China's Housing: The Current Situation and Prospects for the Future* (Editor-in-Chief), China Development Press (Beijing), 2007.
7 *Research into Management Policies that Address the Formation Mechanisms and Ways to Categorize "Priority Development Zones,"* China Development Press (Beijing), 2008.

# Index

For Product Safety Concerns and Information please contact our EU
representative  GPSR@taylorandfrancis.com
Taylor & Francis Verlag GmbH, Kaufingerstraße 24, 80331 München, Germany